W9-ADN-762

Гис. Фрукова

Peint par Argoun

Императоръ Павелъ I   L'Empereur Paul I

Russia and the Mediterranean, 1797-1807

RUSSIA AND THE
MEDITERRANEAN
1797-1807

Norman E. Saul

The University of Chicago Press · Chicago and London

Standard Book Number: 226–73540–0
Library of Congress Catalog Card Number: 72–96755

The University of Chicago Press, Chicago 60637
The University of Chicago Press, Ltd., London

Contents

Contents

MAPS

Preface

Russia entered actively into the affairs of the Mediterranean during the decade 1797–1807. The tsars of Russia, Paul I and Alexander I, joined two formidable coalitions that aimed at reversing the tide of French advances in continental Europe and the Mediterranean. In these wars between France and the coalitions, Napoleon Bonaparte rose from commander in chief of a French army in Italy to emperor of France, and the Russian Empire gained in relative military and diplomatic prestige. At the end of the decade only two real powers were left on the continent, France and Russia. The events in the Mediterranean region played a major role both in the rise of Napoleon and in the formation of Russian foreign policy for war or peace.

In this period Russian warships sailed through the Bosporus and the Dardanelles for the first time, a joint Russo-Turkish expedition liberated the Ionian Islands from the French, Tsar Paul accepted the title of Grand Master of the Order of Malta, and Russian squadrons patrolled the Italian and Balkan coasts while the army of Suvorov occupied northern Italy. Between the signing of the Treaty of Campoformio in 1797 and the conclusion of the Treaty of Tilsit in 1807, Russian diplomacy was actively involved in the affairs of the small Italian states, the Ionian Republic, the Ottoman Empire, and Malta. The extent and continuity of Russian participation in Mediterranean affairs set these ten years apart from preceding and succeeding periods of Russian history, when Russian appearances in the Mediterranean were relatively infrequent and inconsequential. Why did Russia suddenly enter the Mediterranean in 1798? What were the effects of the Russian presence there? Why was the Russian withdrawal so complete in 1807? These are some of the questions to be answered in this book.

After a brief discussion of the background to Russia's Mediterranean interests, the diplomatic and military involvements of Russia in the Mediterranean during this period will be examined in detail. Special attention will be paid to Russian motivations and goals, to the reaction of other governments, and to the role of individuals in the making of policy. Although the focus will be on foreign relations, the internal history of Russia will not be ignored, especially when it is concerned with the character and personality of the men involved in decision making.

My research on this subject was supported by the Ford Foundation, the William Bayard Cutting Traveling Fellowship of Columbia University, and the Inter-University Committee on Travel Grants. The latter sponsorship enabled me to study at the Leningrad State University, utilizing library resources not readily available in the West. The New York Public Library, the British Museum Reading Room, and the University of Helsinki Library were especially valuable for their collections as well as affording excellent places to work. Original materials were collected, not only from the famous repositories such as the Public Record Office in London and the Austrian State Archives, but also from lesser-known ones in Dubrovnik, Corfu, Naples, and the Sovereign Military Order of Malta. The author is indebted to the staffs of these and other archives and libraries for their aid.

In spelling Russian family names the most common English form has been used in the text. Some first names are in English form—Michael, Alexander—and others have been transliterated from the Russian—Andrei, Vasili, Fedor. Where modern Russian usage differs from the older spelling, the former has been used—Tomara, Fedor, rather than Tamara, Feodor. The common English form of place names current at the time has been used—Ragusa, not Dubrovnik. All dates, unless otherwise indicated, are according to the Western Gregorian calendar (new style).

The problems encountered in conducting research on Russia's Mediterranean affairs during this period proved to be greater and more complex than expected. Many secondary accounts I found to be biased, sensational, or simply handicapped by limited source materials or points of view. The published documentary sources, especially the Soviet and Imperial Russian collections, have been edited from national or personal points of view, and in many cases it was impossible or impracticable to verify the texts in the archives. Where I was able to find relevant documents in the archives, sometimes many more than expected, I encountered difficulties in legibility due to the poor condition of the papers.

But even in the instances when perfect archival records are available, the documents tell only a portion of the story. This problem is aggravated by the distance involved in communications and the rapid changes of the military situation at the time. The original document usually cannot be taken at face value. Much more must be known: Who was the writer? Who was the receiver? What was the time lag between sending and receiving? What were the circumstances under which the letter was written? To what extent did diplomats understand or misunderstand each others' foibles and prejudices and act and write accordingly?

After considering the many difficulties concerned with distant communications, one wonders how nations managed to conduct diplomatic relations at all. But many of the ministers and diplomats of the period under discussion knew how to use communication problems as part of their diplomatic tactics, calculating time for return, counting on interceptions, manipulating the local news.

Where one would expect the record to be more complete, the reverse is often the case. In the capitals of the great powers, policies were formulated and decisions were made. But how? The prime minister and the foreign minister would get together for tea, or an ambassador would call on the head of state, or the tsar would confer with his chancellor. Seldom were verbatim records of conversations kept, especially in Russia. Letters between chancellor and tsar refer to their private conversations without always disclosing their substance. When the key persons were easily accessible to one another, there was a .tendency to save ink and paper, and it appears that the more important the position a person held, the less likely he was to keep a diary or write memoirs, probably because he was too busy.

In approaching this subject, I have tried to be guided by the words of Sir George Macartney, a British envoy to the court of Catherine the Great, who wrote in 1768:

> To be free from prejudice is seldom the lot of humanity, and if ever we attain to such perfection, it is usually when we are too far advanced in life to exert it with vigour, or insure its success. . . .
>
> Hence in describing the manners of a foreign people we must proceed with delicacy, and avoid extremes. Perplexity occurs in every step; endeavoring to elude danger, we fall into error; aiming at eloquence, we lose precision; and disgusted by vulgar opinions, are seduced by ingenious hypotheses: even candor is not sufficient here; vigilance must guard, and prudence direct us, to the end of our career.

Professors Michael Florinsky and Oscar Halecki of Columbia University inspired my initial interest in this subject. To them I owe a humble debt of gratitude. Professor Alexander Shapiro of Leningrad State University rendered very helpful advice during the research phase. In all stages I have benefited from the criticism and encouragement of Professor Alexander Dallin of the Russian Institute, Columbia University, and Professor Henry L. Roberts of Dartmouth.

Russia and the Mediterranean, 1797-1807

List of Abbreviations used in Notes

ASN   State Archives, Naples

BM, Add. MSS.   British Museum, Additional Manuscripts

Dropmore   Historical Manuscripts Commission, *Report on the Manuscripts of J. B. Fortescue, Esq., preserved at Dropmore.*

HHSA   Haus-, Hof-, und Staatsarchiv, Vienna

PRO, FO   Public Record Office, Foreign Office Papers

SIRIO   *Sbornik Imperatorskago Russkago Istoricheskago Obshchestva*

VPR   *Vneshniaia Politika Rossii XIX i nachala XX veka*

SS, DAE   Senate of the Ionian Republic, Department of Foreign Affairs

1

Introduction: Russia and the Mediterranean, 1769–96

Portsmouth harbor was the scene of an unusual burst of activity in the winter of 1769–70. The storm-battered ships commanding the attention of carpenters and hawkers, as well as of the seamen and officers of the Royal Navy, were out of the Baltic headed south, part of the fleet of Her Imperial Majesty Catherine the Great of Russia that was destined to battle the Turks in their home waters in the Mediterranean. The initiative in this imaginative enterprise came from the empress herself, and the appearance of the Russian fleet in the Mediterranean and its subsequent victory over the Turks at Chesmé in June 1770 did more to demonstrate to the other major powers of Europe the rise of Russian arms than any event since the victory of Peter the Great over Charles XII at Poltava in 1709. Moreover, the use of the Russian fleet in the Mediterranean in 1770 demonstrated that the Russian Empire possessed a range of methods to implement a foreign policy effectively that was on a par with the resources of the other Great Powers.

The Mediterranean campaign of 1769–70 was only part of Catherine's first war against the Turks, which ended a period of uneasy peace on the southern, steppe frontier that had lasted since the Treaty of Belgrade in 1739. In the earlier wars, before 1768, the regular Russian army had often been joined by Cossacks from the Don and Dnieper regions in a popular effort to

3

conquer and slay the Moslem Turks, and Russia secured substantial portions of steppe territory, which was of limited practical value as long as the seacoast to the south remained under Turkish control. While Turkish forts stood watch, the Crimean Tatars could organize raids into the territory to the north, seriously impeding the economic development of South Russia. But Russo-Turkish wars were never strictly localized. Austria and Poland often participated, and often the conflicts were part of a general European war.

Catherine's involvement in the affairs of Poland was a major factor in the outbreak of hostilities between Russia and the Ottoman Empire in 1768. Russian predominance in Poland had culminated in the "election" of Stanislas Poniatowski—a former lover of Catherine—as king in 1763. Polish resistance to Russian pressure on behalf of the dissident, mainly Orthodox minorities only increased Russian interference. Cossack patrols, in the process of suppressing rebellious Polish nobles, penetrated Ottoman territory. The Turkish sultan, encouraged by the French to believe that the time was right to settle old accounts with Russia, was provided with an excuse for declaring war in September 1768 and, following tradition, threw Alexis Obrezkov—the Russian envoy to Constantinople—into the Seven Towers fortress.

Russian military power had grown considerably, especially during the reign of Empress Elizabeth, while Russia's neighbors, particularly the Ottoman Empire and Poland, were at the same time declining rapidly in military prestige. In the Seven Years' War the Russian army received excellent training in modern military science and tactics and enhanced its reputation in battles such as Kunersdorf. But something else had been added to Russian power in the eighteenth century—a navy.

The Russian navy was founded in legend and in fact by Peter the Great and, though confined to the Baltic, had distinguished itself in engagements with Sweden. After suffering a serious eclipse after the death of Peter, the navy was rehabilitated by Elizabeth, and the Seven Years' War helped to bring the Baltic fleet back into prominence. The growth of the port of Saint Petersburg in the eighteenth century provided an additional basis for expansion; as more and more Russians gazed at ships and carried cargo on and off them, increasing numbers of foreigners considered the opportunities of employment in Russia. But periods of instability and court revolution, such as that of 1761–62, were more detrimental to the navy than to the army because ship building and ship maintenance demand long-range commitments of men and materials. In 1765 Catherine noted the general condition of the fleet: "We have ships, and men on them to abundance, but we have neither fleet nor sailors. . . . It must be confessed that they look like a herring-fleet which sets out every year from Holland, and not at all like a fleet of war."[1]

After having consolidated her position on the throne, Catherine took two important steps to improve the situation of the navy. A major ship construction program was under way by 1766, and, since Saint Petersburg had become the largest depot of naval stores in the world, good warships could be built cheaply and speedily. Also, taking advantage of friendly relations with England and the reduction of the British navy after the Seven Years' War by a cost-conscious government, Catherine was able to hire a large number of officers from the British Isles. The precise origin of the idea of sending the fleet around to the Mediterranean has not been traced, but the British officers recruited for the fleet very likely promoted the opportunity to make use of the fleet (and themselves) in a war against Turkey.

Nikita Panin, Catherine's foreign adviser, prepared a path for the fleet diplomatically by his efforts to secure a "northern accord" linking Russia with Prussia and Britain and the smaller North European states. In a treaty of alliance signed with Russia in 1764, Prussia agreed to a "Turkish Clause," which stipulated that Prussia would provide troops or a subsidy to Russia if requested in the event of an Ottoman attack on Russia. Negotiations for a political alliance between Russia and Britain stalled on the issue of the "Turkish Clause," which the British government, mindful of commercial interests in the Levant, would not allow, but a

---

1. Quoted in K. Waliszewski, *The Story of a Throne: Catherine II of Russia* (London, 1895), 1: 87–88.

mutually advantageous commercial treaty was signed in 1766.[2] Britain quietly encouraged Catherine's Near Eastern designs in hopes of painlessly arresting French gains in that area. France, allied with Austria, naturally opposed the "northern accord" and supported the Ottoman cause, but she was not prepared to enter a war that would probably involve Britain.

The overall command of the Russian Mediterranean campaign of 1769–70 was placed in the hands of Alexis Orlov, the intelligent and capable brother of Catherine's current lover, Gregory Orlov. The Orlovs had been instrumental in leading the Guard's revolt that brought Catherine to the throne and were now to be used in her military plans. Alexis was conveniently recuperating from an illness in Italy, where he could make arrangements for operational bases for the fleet.

The difficulties of the long voyage from Kronstadt and Revel, where the squadrons were assembled, through the Strait of Gibraltar to the eastern Mediterranean were eased by the use of the superior repair facilities of British and Italian ports. Without this assistance it is doubtful that many ships could have arrived at their destination in any shape to fight. Britain also encouraged more unemployed naval officers to enlist in Russian service. Although the fleet was under the direct command of a Russian, Admiral Spiridov, much of the naval action, especially at Chesmé, was directed by two Scottish officers, Samuel Greig and John Elphinston.[3]

---

2. The British envoy, Macartney, published a little known but revealing portrait of Russia, *An Account of Russia in the Year 1767* (London, 1768), but reported little on his negotiations. For an interesting analysis of Anglo-Russian relations during this time, see Dietrich Gerhard, *England und der Aufsteig Russlands: Zur Frage des Zusammenhanges der europäischen Staaten und ihres Ausgreifens in die aussereuropäische Welt in Politik und Wirtschaft des 18 Jahrhunderts* (Munich and Berlin, 1933).

3. Catherine's Mediterranean campaign has received little attention in the West. Two English historians have summarized the events: M. S. Anderson, "Great Britain and the Russo-Turkish War of 1768–74," *The English Historical Review* 49 (January 1954); 39–58, and "Great Britain and the Russian Fleet, 1769–70," *Slavonic and East European Review* 21 (December 1952); 148–64; and R. C. Anderson, *Naval Wars in the Levant, 1559–1853* (Princeton, 1952), pp. 278–304. But for a more complete cov-

On 6 July 1770, in the Bay of Chesmé along the Anatolian coast, the main Turkish fleet was trapped and completely destroyed through the use of fireships made awesomely effective by a strong west wind. The Russian command, surprised by its easy victory over the Turks and lacking further orders, failed to proceed with a quick strike at Constantinople, which was then quite vulnerable because of the deteriorated state of defenses along the Dardanelles. A sea attack without accompanying ground forces would have had little more than shock value, and the rapidity with which the Turks moved with French assistance to strengthen the defenses of the Dardanelles would probably have trapped the Russian fleet and reversed the verdict of Chesmé.

But the Russian fleet had a secondary mission in the Mediterranean. As a result of increasing contacts with the rest of the world and the concomitant appearance of a rudimentary national consciousness, many literate Russians had learned that the subject population of the Balkan peninsula was oppressed and possibly ready to revolt. This knowledge provided another motivation for southern expansion and enhanced the logic of sending a fleet far from its home bases into the waters of the Mediterranean. While most of the Slavic area of the Balkans was still beyond the reach of the Russian armies, the Mediterranean fleet could easily make contact with the Greeks. At the height of the Enlightenment the Greeks especially attracted the sympathies of the European world.

Catherine intsructed Orlov to encourage and support local revolts on the Greek islands and mainland.[4] The Greek response was stronger than anticipated, but the revolts failed because of

erage see Evgenii V. Tarle, *Chesmenskii boi i pervaia russkaia ekspeditsiia v Arkhipelag, 1769–1774* (Moscow, 1945). Firsthand accounts can be consulted in the following: *An Authentic Narrative of the Russian Expedition against the Turk by Sea and Land* (London, 1772); S. K. Greig, "Dnevnik," *Morskoi Sbornik* 2 (October-December 1849): 645–60, 715–30, 785–827; *Materialy dlia istorii Russkogo flota*, ed. F. Veselago, vol. 11 (Saint Petersburg, 1886); A. Sokolov, ed., "Dokumenty o Chesmenskoi bitve," *Morskoi Sbornik* 9 (June 1853): 473–83.

4. "Kniaz' Aleksei Gregor'evich Orlov," *Morskoi Sbornik* 9 (April 1853): 263–89.

oor leadership and insufficient weapons and supporting land
orces. Turkish fortresses on the islands and on the mainland,
ough dilapidated and undermanned, could withstand lengthy
ges, and the local pashas, who might be lukewarm in support
the sultan's interests north of the Black Sea but were quite
diligent in protecting their own affairs in Greece, quelled the
rebels with severe brutality. Some managed to escape into Russian service and later founded exile settlemens in the new Russian
territory on the Black Sea.

The Pugachev revolt on the home front, the expense of the
war, the threatening attitude of Sweden, and the waning enthusiasm of Britain influenced the decision to conclude a peace in
1774 that gave Russia important new territory and rights. By the
Treaty of Kuchuk-Kainarji Russia obtained for the first time a
small Black Sea coastline between the mouths of the Dniepr
and Bug rivers and additional territory on the Sea of Azov. The
area between these acquisitions, the Crimean (Tatar) Khanate,
was released from Turkish suzerainty and declared independent.
The treaty also awarded Russia the right of free commercial
navigation of Turkish waters including the Straits, thus opening
a direct Russian trade route to the Mediterranean for the first
time since the Turkic invasion of the steppe.

Russia might have acquired more territory, but she was sensitive to European opinion and was particularly concerned about
upsetting Austria, the other power with a direct interest in the
Balkans and the fate of the Ottoman Empire. Partly for this
reason, Russia agreed to release to Turkey the provinces of
Moldavia and Wallachia, which had been occupied by Russian
armies.[5] Another treaty provision, which was to cause problems
in the middle of the nineteenth century, gave the Russian ruler

---

5. E. I. Druzhinina, *Kuchuk-Kainardzhiiskii mir 1774 goda: ego podgotovka i zakliuchenie* (Moscow, 1955) is the best and most recent account
of the treaty. See also N. D. Chechulin, *Vneshniaia politika Rossii v nachale
tsarstvovaniia Ekateriny II, 1762–1774* (Saint Petersburg, 1896), 2: 359–
61. An English translation of the treaty may be found in J. C. Hurewitz, ed.,
*Diplomacy in the Near and Middle East: A Documentary Record, 1535–
1914* (Princeton, 1956), 1: 55–61. An excellent survey is: M. S. Anderson,
The Eastern Question, 1774–1923: A Study in International Relations
(London, 1966).

a vague authority to present petitions to the sultan on behalf of Ottoman Christian subjects. Even though the promise of great success at the beginning of the war was not fulfilled, Catherine was probably pleased that the treaty left an unsettled siuation that would almost inevitably result in continued Russian expansion to the south. Catherine also displayed shrewdness in following a policy of piecemeal expansion that would not alarm the other powers of Europe.

By the second half of the eighteenth century the great Western states, France and England, were developing an interest in the Mediterranean. The decline of Venice, the Ottoman Empire, Spain, and other Mediterranean states, simultaneously with the rise of colonial empires based on oceanic trade routes, had created an economic and political vacuum in the Mediterranean. The educated elite of these rival powers had been witnessing a rebirth of interest in the wellsprings of Western culture during the eighteenth century. France, after 1763 looking for an opportunity to recover from losses of prestige and colonies, was the first to take definite steps to establish commercial and political hegemony in the Mediterranean. Britain was busy consolidating and maintaining her empire and did not yet foresee the value of a route through the Mediterranean to India until Bonaparte pointed it out, but France was still the great rival and any political or economic gain for France was interpreted as England's loss. Russia and Austria were now joining the contest, attracted by spoils to be won from weakening neighbors and drawn in by the dynamics of European international relations.

After 1774 Russia was claiming, in effect, a political role equal to that of the other European powers. Leadership of the Armed Neutrality of 1780, which was directed against British naval practices in the Baltic and North Seas during the American Revolutionary War, emphasized Russia's new international position.[6] The defense of neutral rights and the Russian annexation of the Crimea in 1783 renewed the misgivings in Britain

---

6. For Anglo-Russian relations at the time of the Armed Neutrality, see especially Isabel de Madariaga, *Britain, Russia, and the Armed Neutrality of 1780: Sir James Harris's Mission to St. Petersburg during the American Revolution* (New Haven, 1962).

about the trustworthiness and value of this particular "continental ally." Russia under Catherine and her favorites was developing a broader and more independent and aggressive approach to international affairs. In contrast to earlier periods of Russian involvements with other European countries, such as during the Northern War (1700–1721) and the Seven Years' War (1756–62), these new policies did not plunge Russia directly into war.

France, Britain, Russia, and Austria increased their interest in the Mediterranean in the last decades of the eighteenth century also because of the general shift in the world political and economic situation. The change before 1770 was gradual, and a remarkable balance was maintained. But after 1770—and in this sense the Battle of Chesmé marks a real turning point—the shift was more rapid and the focus of the European powers more intense. The reasons for this were (1) the obviously rapid decline of Ottoman power, (2) the simultaneous development of social and political awareness among peoples within the Ottoman Empire and in other areas around the Mediterranean, (3) an increase in the commercial importance of the Mediterranean, to France because of mounting financial crisis at home, to Britain because of the loss of the North American colonies, and (4) the French Revolution. This new international situation opened the way for some spectacular Russian diplomatic and military projects.

Catherine's desire to play a leading role in world affairs led to the formulation by 1780 of a vague plan for disposal of the Ottoman Empire—the famous Greek Project. Russian successes in the most recent Russo-Turkish war had fostered the idea, but it was encouraged by Catherine's romantic inclinations and by her current favorite and adviser, Gregory Potemkin. The plan called for the resurrection of the Byzantine Empire under Catherine's second grandson (born in 1779 and appropriately named Constantine) with its capital at Constantinople. A kingdom of Dacia was to be created, probably for Potemkin, out of the Turkish-Romanian provinces, and Russian borders would be extended along the Black Sea coast and forward naval bases for the Russian fleet were to be established on islands in the Aegean

Sea. France, Britain, and Austria would share in the spoils, and a rump Turkey would be left in Anatolia.[7]

The accomplishment of this scheme depended upon the cooperation of Austria, the other European power bordering on the Ottoman Empire. Catherine's relations with the Austrian emperor, Joseph II, improved rapidly after the death of the anti-Russian Maria Theresa in 1780. In May 1781, a secret alliance was reached between the two courts. Although no specific territories were mentioned in the treaty, it was generally understood that Austria would expand into the western Balkans in return for her cooperation against the Ottoman Empire.

Despite the pressure of domestic problems, a considerable amount of Catherine's attention in the 1780's was devoted to the fulfillment of the Greek Project. The annexation of the Crimea in 1783 extended the Russian Black Sea coastline and added an important natural harbor at Sevastopol, which was to become the chief base of the rapidly growing Black Sea fleet. After 1783 Potemkin spent much of his time and the resources of the state developing the Black Sea coastal region. In 1787 he organized a state excursion through "New Russia" to the Black Sea to impress Catherine and a group of distinguished visitors that included the Austrian emperor. At the newly reconstructed fortress of Kherson on the estuary of the Bug the procession entered under a triumphal arch that bore an inscription in Greek: "The way to Byzantium."[8]

Soon after Catherine's visit to the Black Sea the Turks began hostilities. The annexation of the Crimea, growing Russian influence in Georgia, and finally the much publicized anti-Turkish plans of the Russian empress brought about the Turkish decision to act first. Catherine was ready—the Black Sea fleet set sail and the army marched across the Bug River into Turkish territory. Austria declared war in February 1788, and her armies moved toward Belgrade. The Baltic fleet was prepared to open a

---

7. Alfred L. P. Dennis, *Eastern Problems at the Close of the Eighteenth Century* (Cambridge, Mass., 1901), pp. 95–105.

8. Gladys Scott Thomson, *Catherine the Great and the Expansion of Russia* (Paper ed.; New York, 1962), pp. 144–45.

second naval front again in the Mediterranean, and Russian recruitment was started abroad to provide the trained officers that Russia needed for such an enterprise.[9] It seemed that "the sick man of Europe" had not long to live.

But this time the international situation favored the Turks. After Russia's leadership of the Armed Neutrality in 1780, Britain was no longer hospitable to Russian warships and even threatened action against them. The change in the British position was illustrated in a semiofficial yearbook, the *Annual Register:*

> England had had full leisure to ruminate upon, and sufficient cause to reprobate, that absurd and blind policy, under the influence of which she had drawn an uncertain ally, and an ever-to-be-suspected friend, from the bottom of the Bothnic Gulf to establish a new naval empire in the Mediterranean and the Archipelago.[10]

Much to Catherine's dismay, Sweden, allied with Turkey by an old alliance of 1739 and encouraged by Prussia and England, decided to declare war on Russia in July 1788. The war in the north forced Russia to abandon plans to send the Baltic fleet to the Mediterranean. Catherine was also worried at the same time by resurgent nationalism in Poland, and the Turks proved sufficiently fierce when holed up in a Danubian fortress to test the mettle of the most redoubtable Russian general, Suvorov. A threat of Prussian interference weakened the Austro-Russian alliance, and Leopold II, who succeeded his brother in February

---

9. About 1790, an English naval captain on half pay and a young French artillery officer who was distressed by the revolution considered entering Russian service. By deciding against this move, both Horatio Nelson and Napoleon Bonaparte missed serving with John Paul Jones against the Turks.

On the Second Turkish War, see R. C. Anderson, *Naval Wars in the Levant*, pp. 319–45; Samuel Bentham, "Notes on the Naval Encounters of the Russians and Turks in 1788," *United Service Journal*, 1829, pp. 333–39, and Sir Howard Cust, *Annals of the Wars of the Eighteenth Century* (London, 1859), 4: 23–35.

10. *Annual Register of 1788, or a View of the History, Politics, and Literature for the Year 1788* (London, 1789), p. 59. Edmund Burke may have been the author of this passage.

1790, agreed to negotiate a separate peace with the help of Prussian mediation. Left fighting alone, witnessing mounting hostility from Prussia and Britain, and concerned about events in France, Catherine concluded a peace at Jassy in January 1792. This treaty confirmed Russia's annexation of the Crimean khanate and extended her control of the Black Sea coastline to the Kuban River in the east and to the Dniester River in the west. Russia had now gained the entire northern shore of the Black Sea, which included the site of Odessa soon to be under construction.

But the Mediterranean was not entirely forgotten during this war. A group of Black Sea officers, headed by Admiral Mordvinov, sponsored a privateering expedition led by Captain Lambros Katzones, a former Greek pirate who had joined the Russian navy in 1770. Sailing initially from Venice and aided by Venetian officials, especially at Corfu, Katzones gathered a sizable volunteer fleet by the summer of 1789 to prey on Turkish merchant shipping with Russian letters of marque. Successes in the Adriatic and Aegean Seas caused a diversion of Turkish seapower into the Mediterranean, but Katzones was soon arrested by Austrian authorities for capturing neutral ships, and his activities were officially denounced in Saint Petersburg. Other privateer fleets materialized, however, and in 1790 Potemkin dispatched Rear Admiral Gibbs to take command and General Tomara to supervise shore arrangements, but shortage of funds hampered their attempts to control the unruly privateers. An important result of this Mediterranean "diversion" was the emigration to Russia of approximately five hundred Greeks and Adriatic Slavs.[11]

The results of Catherine's second Turkish war fell far short of the ambitious scope of the Greek Project. One reason for the

---

11. M. S. Anderson, "Russia in the Mediterranean, 1788–1791: A Little-Known Chapter in the History of Naval Warfare and Privateering," *Mariner's Mirror*, vol. 45 (February 1959): 27–34. Tomara reported that 400 Montenegrin families wanted to live in Russia's new territories along the Black Sea. Tomara to Bezborodko, 11 December 1791, in *Arkhiv Vorontsova* 20: 237–42.

failure to implement it may have been, as a Soviet scholar has suggested, that the Greek plan was never a real objective of Russian foreign policy because it conflicted with another goal—the protection of the interests of the Balkan Slavs (many of whom were to come under Austria according to the plan) and the achievement of their liberation from the Ottoman yoke.[12] Very little was known about the Balkan Slavs in Russia, however, and without a much more detailed investigation of the evidence, if enough exists, it appears impossible to classify Catherine as either a Grecophile or a Slavophile.

During the course of the Turkish war, Russia's international position underwent considerable change. Frederick William II of Prussia signed an alliance of friendship with the Porte on 31 January 1790 and supported the Swedish and Turkish causes. The new Habsburg emperor, Leopold II, under Prussian pressure, signed the Peace of Sistova with Turkey on 4 August 1791 and was hostile toward Russia. Thus Russia became estranged from Austria. In 1791, Britain, under William Pitt's leadership, considered a declaration of war on Russia after the capture of Ochakov. An important result of the Russo-Turkish and Russo-Swedish wars was that on the eve of a major European upheaval Russia was war-weary and was not only unaligned with any other European power but bore grudges against most of them. Ironically, the only major power that had not been directly hostile to Russia between 1788 and 1792 was France. Licking her wounds of war and vanity, Russia sat back to watch as Europe became embroiled in war and revolution.

Some analysts, both then and later, believed that after the Treaty of Jassy Russia should be satisfied with achieving what they maintained was a natural and ethnic frontier along the Black Sea. But in historical perspective it does not seem that coastlines have always made good natural frontiers. As soon as Russia had "driven to the sea," she was faced with the problem of competition for control of the water and, in the case of the

---

12. O. P. Markova, "O proiskhozhdenii tak nazyvaemogo grecheskogo proekta (80-e gody XVIII v.)," *Istoriia SSSR*, 1958, no. 4, pp. 75–78.

Black Sea, an exit to other waters. The two Turkish wars had given Russia a commanding position on the Black Sea, but she was still dependent upon the good will of the Ottoman Empire for passage of ships and goods through the Straits. Russia was forced to accept this disadvantage in the south until either an opportune military assault would cause the complete disintegration of the Ottoman Empire or the international situation and adroit diplomacy could force Ottoman dependency upon Russia.

The preoccupation of the other powers in a new international problem, the French Revolution, presented Russia with opportunities for pursuing either of the above courses. Austria and Prussia signed an alliance against France in February 1792, hoping to take advantage of her internal upheaval. France met this threat by attacking first, in April 1792, thus beginning a long series of costly worldwide conflicts. After the execution of Louis XVI in January 1793, hostilities spread. A month later the countries arrayed against France in the War of the First Coalition consisted of Austria, Prussia, Britain, Sardinia, Holland, and Spain.

Russia remained out of the war for the time being, despite pressure by Britain and Prussia, especially, for her participation. Russia was still recuperating from the recent conflicts with the Ottoman Empire and Sweden, and in 1792 a revolt in Poland had to be crushed that was, at least in part, an offshoot of the French Revolution. Catherine agreed to two final partitions of Poland in 1793 and 1795, thereby gaining extensive territory in the west. In the last year of her reign Catherine embarked on another grandiose scheme, the Oriental Project, which was promoted by her last and most youthful lover, Platon Zubov. The Oriental Project envisioned a massive assault beyond the southern frontier that would gain the key commercial and military points between Turkey and Tibet for Russia. The first attack, launched in the direction of the Caucasus upon Persia, was led by Platon's brother, Valerian Zubov, but Catherine died before any results were obtained, and her successor suspended hostilities. While the Polish partitions and the Oriental Project were being undertaken, the new Russian ambassador in Constantinople, Victor

Kochubei, assumed a sophisticated, friendly approach to the Turks, which was reciprocated. Russo-Turkish relations entered a new phase.

At the same time that her army was marching against Persia, Catherine decided somewhat reluctantly to enter actively into the war against France. The empress was naturally disturbed by the course of extremism and violence that the French Revolution had taken since 1792, and she was upset even more by the successes of the French armies in the field and the spread of revolution beyond France. By the summer of 1796, Prussia had been forced to sign a peace and Austria was being badly beaten in northern Italy. Britain desperately needed continental armies to replace the Prussian and bolster the Austrian, and was willing to pay generously for them with subsidies. Old animosities engendered by the Armed Neutrality and Russian southern expansion, even the current campaign against Persia, were forgotten by Britain in the emergency.[13] After prolonged subsidy negotiations, in August 1796 an army of 64,000 under Suvorov's command was ordered to march across the Austrian frontier "to slay the revolutionary dragon," and an advance squadron of the Baltic fleet set out to join the British fleet in the North Sea.

By the end of Catherine's reign, Russia's political posture in Europe had been considerably altered. Although the Turkish wars had been fought under a smoke screen of grandiose projects, the objectives realized were clearly in Russia's national interest. The value of the second and third partitions of Poland is more problematical; the western frontier was now firmly established by contact with other strong powers, and a potentially explosive area had, theoretically, been removed from the international scene.

Within Russia, westernization, in addition to widening the gap between peasant and noble, created discernible divisions in the highest echelons of Russian society, between the Saint Peters-

---

13. Judging from the reports of the Austrian ambassador dispatched during the summer of 1796, Russia's chief concern at this time was Poland— to assure maintenance of order and the solving of complicated financial problems (the debts of the Polish crown).

burg officials and the provincial gentry, and within these groups. The degree and effects of westernization varied considerably. By looking westward, many Russians were finding Russia. Westernization served as a catalyst for Russian national consciousness and created the contradictions that resulted in the "Russian dilemma," best represented by the famous Slavophile-Westernizer debate of the nineteenth century but also found in many leading Russians of the generation of the French Revolution and Napoleon. This development naturally affected foreign policy and made the interpretation of Russian national interests a complicated and debated issue: to what degree should withdrawal or involvement be pursued or resisted?

Economic factors were also changing and becoming more important at the end of the century. The growth of Russian industry and foreign trade in the second half of the eighteenth century at a rate comparable to that of the other countries of continental Europe meant that more and more Russians were dependent in some measure upon international trade for their livelihood.[14] The Baltic ports had become the principal suppliers of iron, hemp, and linen, especially sail cloth, and the favorable balance of trade that resulted was an important asset to the Russian Empire.[15] Foreign commerce was still concentrated around Saint

---

14. For a comparison of Russian economic progress with French, see Tarle, "Byla li ekaterininskaia Rossiia ekonomicheski otstaloiu stranoiu," in *Zapad i Rossiia: Stat'i i dokumenty iz istorii XVIII-XX vv.* (Petrograd, 1918), pp. 122–49. Tarle concludes that if Russia was backward, France was too.

15. The turnover of Russian trade was worth approximately 21 million rubles (exports 12 million, imports 9 million) in 1762, and 110 million rubles (exports 68 million, imports 42 million) in 1797. V. A. Butenko, *Kratkii ocherk istorii russkoi torgovli v sviazi s istoriei promyshlennosti* (Moscow, 1911), p. 85. Tarle, Florinsky, and other historians emphasize the unreliability of trade statistics for eighteenth-century Russia. While Florinsky believes that the advantage for Russia was less than the figures indicate, Tarle argues the opposite. On the basis of French archival material, Tarle cites the rather surprising fact that France in 1788 imported more from Russia than from any other continental country. Though also subject to error, this may provide a better perspective on Russian trade than the ruble figures. Tarle, *Zapad i Rossiia*, p. 135; *Michael T. Florinsky, Russia: A History and an Interpretation* (New York, 1955), 1: 564.

Petersburg, but the southern expansion introduced prospects for diversification.

The rapid consolidation and development of the new territories in the South established a base for increased trade with the Ottoman Empire and the Mediterranean. The new "Romanov" towns—Elizavetograd, Ekaterinoslav, Pavlograd, Alexandrovsk, and Konstantinograd—were located in the northern part of New Russia on the old steppe frontier, but they were economically oriented southward along the rivers to the newly acquired ports of Kherson, Ochakov, and Nikolaev.[16] A large proportion of state resources and the administrative talents of Potemkin and Zubov were concentrated upon populating the new lands, but areas farther to the east derived more direct benefit before 1796 from the opening up of the Black Sea. Taganrog, the old port on the Sea of Azov at the mouth of the Don, handled four times as much trade in 1797 as any other Russian port using the Black Sea.[17] The largest single item in the Russian trade with Constantinople between 1774 and 1796 was Ural iron, which was cheaper in Constantinople than in Saint Petersburg.[18]

Another factor that helped to shape a Mediterranean outlook in the South was the strategy employed by Catherine and Potemkin in awarding grants of land. Leading government officials such as Potemkin, Bezborodko, and Zubov were given the largest estates, but naval commanders such as Mordvinov, Ushakov, Ribas, and Greig also received sizable grants, which tended to tie them to this region. In 1786, when Prince Nassau-Siegen investigated the possibility of exporting the produce of his Polish estates through Black Sea ports, Catherine was sufficiently impressed to present him with a large estate in the Crimea, and in 1787 she appointed him to a high naval command on the Black Sea.[19] A number of Greeks who distinguished themselves in

---

16. E. I. Druzhinina, *Severnoe prichernomor'e v 1775–1800 gg.* (Moscow, 1959), pp. 77–81.

17. Grigorii Nebolsin, *Statisticheskiia zapiski o vneshnei torgovle Rossii* (Saint Petersburg, 1835) 2: 13–17.

18. Druzhinina, *Severnoe prichernomor'e*, p. 88.

19. Ibid., pp. 68, 119, et passim; F. Lashkov, *Istoricheskii ocherk krymsko-*

the Turkish wars—Alexiano, Metaxa, Mocenigo and others—
received land. A Soviet historian, Druzhinina, has noted the practice of issuing grants on condition of residence to a significant
number of Russian merchants.[20] It would appear that a landlord
aristocracy was developing in the South that was potentially more
commercially minded and less bound to tradition than in other
parts of the empire.

The change was dramatized by the rise of the port of Odessa.
In September 1789, General Ribas captured a small Tatar village
along the Black Sea in order to deny the Turks the use of its
protected harbor.[21] His reports after the war attracted the attention of Catherine and Zubov, who was in charge of constructing
a new line of defenses for the southwest corner of Russia. Ribas
was given the responsibility for enlarging the small Turkish fort
and for establishing a naval and commercial port. To ease a
critical labor shortage, he organized a Greek "division" from
those who had served in the war. The new name of Odessa,
originating with the Academy of Sciences, was conferred upon
the new town in 1796.[22] Odessa was much easier to reach by sea
than were Taganrog or Kherson, was less hindered by ice, and
could accommodate large ships from the Mediterranean; it was
also easier to reach by land from the Ukraine, and annexed Poland
and Austria. In 1796, 86 ships (49 Turkish, 34 Russian, and 3
Austrian) arrived at Odessa. A special commission reported in

tatarskago zemlevladeniia: sbornik dokumentov (Simferopol, 1897), pp.
131, 142; K. Miller, *Frantsuzskaia emigratsiia i Rossiia v tsarstvovanie Ekateriny II* (Paris, 1931), pp. 22–25.

20. *Severnoe prichernomor'e*, p. 166.

21. Don Joseph di Ribas-y-Boyons was born in 1749 in Naples, where
his father, a Spanish nobleman from Barcelona, was secretary of war for
the Kingdom of the Two Sicilies. On the way to inspect the estates of his
Irish mother in 1769, Ribas met Count Orlov in Livorno and joined the
Russian fleet. After the Archipelago campaign, he was transferred to the
army and commanded a regiment at the outbreak of the second Turkish
War. In recognition of his organization of a valuable Black Sea flotilla,
Ribas was shifted back to the navy in 1791 with the rank of vice admiral
and appointed commandant of the occupation zone around Odessa. A.
Skal'kovskii, *Pervoe tridtsatiletie istorii goroda Odessy, 1793–1823* (Odessa,
1837), pp. 8–38.

22. Ibid., pp. 38–43.

1797 that the male population was 3,455, including 337 in the Greek "division," 269 other Greeks, Albanians, and Moldavians, 33 Bulgarians, and 404 Black Sea Cossacks. In addition to the French and Austrian mercantile firms, traders were registered from Naples, Genoa, Constantinople, Tripoli, and the islands of the Archipelago. Exports in order of importance were grain, iron, hemp, cordage, leather, fish, caviar, and tallow; the chief imports were Turkish cloth, wines, and dried fruits.[23] Within three years of its founding, Odessa had become the second most important port in the South.

Russian progress southward was attended by a wide range of descriptive literature. Visitors to Russia increased dramatically in the second half of the eighteenth century. The temporary employment of army and navy officers, tutors, educators, and merchants often became permanent; others were attracted by curiosity and in search of good copy for the European reading public. At the same time special commissions, government bureaus, academies, and societies issued factual reports and analytic studies, of which some, as might be expected, were incomplete, inaccurate, or simply buried and lost, but others contained valuable raw material and circulated widely. Whether written by the celebrated Voltaire or by better informed travelers and scholars, books about Russia attracted a large reading audience. No longer remote, Russia became a side excursion on the Grand Tour.

The extra publicity given by Catherine to her Turkish wars and southern expansion, and the rising curiosity in Europe about

---

23. Ibid., pp. 50, 61–63; Mikhail Vol'skii, *Ocherk istorii khlebnoi torgovli novorossiiskago kraia s drevneishikh vremen do 1852 goda* (Odessa, 1854), pp. 57–61. Vol'skii notes that France and England both became regular importers of grain only after 1790. Western demand thus coincided with Russia's Black Sea export capability. For French and Austrian commercial activities in the Black Sea, see Baron de Saint-Joseph Anthoine, *Essai historique sur le commerce et la navigation de la Mer-Noire* (2d ed.; Paris, 1820); Sicard (aîné), *Lettres sur Odessa* (Saint Petersburg, 1812); and Hans Halm, *Habsburgischer Osthandel im 18. Jahrhundert: Österreich und Neurussland (II): Donauhandel und -schiffahrt 1781–1787*, Veröffentlichungen des Osteuropas-Institutes München, vol. 7 (Munich, 1954).

all of that little-known "uncivilized" world east of Rome, combined to focus attention on the Black Sea area. Lady Craven's book about her travels through the Crimea in 1786, though of limited value to the present-day historian, was published in several editions including a Russian one in 1795.[24] And scholars such as Pallas, Muller, Storch, Pleshcheev, and LeClerc devoted special attention to the southern territories. Civil and military staffs could now obtain access to a whole library of maps, atlases, and descriptive books, and when a Russian army marched, or a fleet sailed, many people within Russia and abroad would know where it was. The level of publication in Russia at the end of the eighteenth century suggests the conclusion that in the formulation of foreign policy for the empire more attention should be paid to public opinion.

As Russia became more a part of Europe, the opportunities to wage successful limited wars diminished while the chances of involvement in major conflict increased. Could Russia materially afford a major war? The successes of the army and navy in battles against Sweden and the Ottoman Empire were not as great as might have been expected, and they had not been tested by another major European power since the Seven Years' War. Available manpower was limited by serfdom, as the Pugachev revolt had shown, and the tremendous extent of the empire hampered efficient concentration of forces; extended military occupations and the establishment of new administrations absorbed both men and money. Although an increase in commercial and industrial activity made higher direct taxes feasible and raised revenues from customs, mines, and indirect taxes, imperial court luxury and wasteful administrative projects, in which, for example, the surveying of the Russian land itself cost 5,400,000 rubles, caused expenditures to exceed revenues throughout Catherine's reign.[25] The costly development of South Russia

---

24. Druzhinina, *Severnoe prichernomor'e*, p. 21.
25. Florinsky, 1: 558.
Significant increases in poll tax from annexed population came only with the Second and Third Partitions and were not realized in Catherine's reign. Storch lists the entire population of the annexations of 1774, 1783, and

and the debts inherited from the Polish crown added to Russia's own indebtedness, which reached an impressive figure of 215,-000,000 rubles in 1796 while annual income and expenditure were 55,400,000 and 78,200,000 rubles respectively.[26] Because of a long, undelimited frontier, Russia was fighting in the Caucasus and expanding into America while most of Europe was in upheaval. In balance, Russian interests in 1796 could probably be served best by a cautious foreign policy and a concentration on internal consolidation and reform.

1792 at 214,318, whereas the three partitions of Poland added 6,767,953 (total population of the empire in 1796: 36,152,000). Henri Storch, *Tableau historique et statistique de l'empire de Russie à la fin du dix-huitième siècle* (Basle and Leipzig, 1802), I, n. 22.

26. Florinsky, 1: 566–68. For an analysis of Catherine's trade policy see N. N. Firsov, *Pravitel'stvo i obshchestvo v ikh otnosheniiakh k vneshnei torgovle Rossii v tsarstvovanie imperatritsy Ekateriny II: ocherki iz istorii torgovoi politiki* (Kazan, 1902).

2

A Crusader and His Knights

The man who succeeded to the Russian throne in 1796 is one of the most controversial figures in Russian history. Most contemporary observers—at least those who recorded their opinions in memoirs—vehemently attacked Paul, portraying him as a half-crazy potentate whose reign represented an unfortunate interruption in the course of imperial Russian history and a sorry contrast to the glorious reigns of Catherine II and Alexander I. This view of Paul, standard throughout the nineteenth century, was popular with the Russian nobility and was promoted by the Romanovs themselves. It justified Paul's murder in March 1801 as a matter of obvious necessity.[1]

---

1. Most typical of this group of sources is N. K. Shil'der, *Imperator Pavel I: istoriko-biograficheskii ocherk* (Saint Petersburg, 1901). K. Waliszewski, *Paul the First of Russia, Son of Catherine the Great* (London, 1913; Russian ed., 1914) represents an example of the negative type heavily relied upon in general English language texts, probably since it also was published in English and French editions. An example of a negative and unscholarly approach to Paul is E. M. Almedingen, *So Dark a Stream: A Study of the Emperor Paul I of Russia, 1754–1801* (London, 1959). Other noted historians who have approached Paul in a negative light in their works are A. A. Brikner (Brückner), V. I. Semevskii, N. D. Chechulin, A. A. Kizevetter, M. N. Pokrovskii, M. K. Liubavskii, A. A. Kornilov, and P. I. Kovalevskii. For a discussion of the Russian literature on Paul, see M. V. Klochkov, *Ocherki pravitel'stvennoi deiatel'nosti vremeni Pavla I* (Petrograd, 1916), pp. 46–73, and Valentin Graf Zubow, *Zar Paul I: Mensch und Schicksal* (Stuttgart, 1963), pp. 258–73.

A smaller number of contemporaries and some later historians, though agreeing with some of the criticisms leveled at Paul, took a generally favorable view. They depicted him as a tragic victim of his times and of his own ideals who was unjustly maligned by the supporters of Catherine and Alexander. Paul's defenders point out his attempts to lessen the burdens of the peasantry and to reduce the corruption rampant in government administration, and emphasize his unselfish, idealistic foreign policy and the resounding victories of Russian arms during his reign.[2] In the early twentieth century, several historians, using newly-released archival materials, were able to make important reappraisals of Paul's reign.[3]

Soviet historians have tended to treat Paul more favorably than did prerevolutionary writers. In part, this can be attributed to a reaction against the historians of the old regime. Paul's restrictions on the "spoiled" nobility, his efforts to curb abuses of the peasants, and his authoritarian manner toward the army have been stressed by the Soviet rewriters of history. Above all they have admired the independence and flexibility of Russian foreign policy during Paul's reign, but the personality and quirks of character of the sovereign have naturally been overshadowed in the deterministic approach.[4]

---

2. The military achievements as well as personal qualities of the monarch are praised by D. A. Miliutin, *Istoriia voiny 1799 goda mezhdu Rossiei i Frantsiei v tsarstvovanie Imperatora Pavla I*, 5 vols. (Saint Petersburg, 1852–53). M. I. Semevskii, D. F. Kobeko, and P. N. Butsinskii are also favorable to Paul. See Klochkov, pp. 74–80.

3. E. S. Shumigorskii, *Imperator Pavel I—zhizn' i tsarstvovanie* (Saint Petersburg, 1907) is the best example. See also his biographies of Paul's wife and mistress: *Imperatritsa Mariia Fedorovna* (Saint Petersburg, 1892) and *Ekaterina Ivanovna Nelidova* (Saint Petersburg, 1898). *Kantsler Kniaz' Aleksandr Andreevich Bezborodko v sviazi s sobytiiami ego vremeni*, pt. 2, ed. N. Grigorovich (Saint Petersburg, 1881), vol. 29 of *Sbornik Imperatorskago Russkago Istoricheskago Obshchestva* (hereafter cited as SIRIO), and Klochkov, who provides the best historiography of the man and his period up to 1916, can also be classed in the group. See Klochkov, pp. 80–91.

4. In order of their appearance the following works provide examples of the best Soviet scholarship on Paul: P. Sadikov, "Neskol'ko marterialov dlia istorii mer pravitel'stva Imperatora Pavla I protiv proniknoveniia v Rossiiu idei velikoi frantsuzskoi revoliutsii," *Dela i Dni: Istoricheskii Zhurnal*, III

Paul wanted to consolidate the Russian Empire, to restore the shaky Romanov dynasty to complete power, which he felt had been undermined by Catherine's favorites, and to carry out basic administrative and social reforms that would rationalize Russian government and regulate Russian society. He believed that Russia should be neutral in the conflict between France and England but should try to prevent the spread of war on the continent into areas that would threaten Russian security. As his instructions to ambassadors in early 1797 show, Paul wanted to build defensive alliances on the northern and southern flanks of Europe, and to avoid commitments to the major powers. Though he would have preferred an independent Poland closely allied with Russia, the partitioning of Poland was now a fact beyond his immediate control. If it became necessary for Russia to act militarily, she should do so quickly and decisively with a disciplined, hard-striking army in the manner of Frederick the Great. In this rather narrow approach, Paul ignored the fact that other powers were more vulnerable than Russia to French ideas and armies; that this was an "age of democratic revolution." He did recognize, however, that liberal and radical ideas threatened the stability of church and state, and his major objective, which entwined his domestic and foreign policies, was to eliminate these threats, first by curbing them at home with a regime of law and order.

Because Russian foreign policy in the imperial period was formulated mainly by the autocrat himself, the personal characteristics and whims of the ruler affected that policy.[5] Whatever may be said about Paul's sanity, he was very strong-willed, and

---

(1920), 391–397; M. Balabanov, *Rossiia i velikaia frantsuzskaia revoliutsiia* (Kiev, 1923); R. S. Lanin, "Vneshniaia politika Pavla I v 1796–1798 gg.," *Uchenye Zapiski, LGU. seriia istoricheskikh nauk*, vol. 10 (Leningrad, 1941); V. I. Samoilov, *Vnutrenniaia i vneshniaia politika Pavla I (1797–1801)* (Khlebnikogo, 1946); A. V. Fadeev, *Doreformennaia Rossiia (1800–1861)* (Moscow, 1960).

5. For an analysis of the role of the tsar in the formulation of Russian foreign policy, see Robert C. Tucker, "Autocrats and Oligarchs" in *Soviet Foreign Policy: Essays in Historical Perspective*, ed. Ivo J. Lederer (New Haven and London, 1962), pp. 171–95.

that played a very important role in directing Russia's foreign affairs, especially in the Mediterranean. To understand Paul's subjective interpretation of Russian interests in the Mediterranean during the period from 1797 to 1801, we must examine Paul's background and philosophy.

Throughout the last twenty years of Catherine's reign, from the time Paul came of age in 1776, he waited impatiently to ascend the throne. He supported his mother's policies officially but grew more and more restless in his private little world at Gatchina, about thirty miles from Saint Petersburg, where, after 1783, he maintained a court of favorites and drilled a small "army" modeled after the Prussian. His advice on major policy matters was never sought, and he was allowed to play little part in the government. Although the relationship between Paul and his mother was quite strained, it did not endanger his position as heir until the last few years. Paul's presence was useful to Catherine—to justify her accession to the "regency" (after the overthrow of Peter III), to discourage favorites from usurping the throne for themselves or their children (by Catherine), and to provide additional heirs to the Romanov (Catherinian) line.[6]

Paul's unhappy first marriage to Princess Wilhelmina of Hesse-Darmstadt ended with her death in childbirth in 1776. A

---

6. The problem of Paul's legitimacy is important in the treatment of his personality. According to many sources, his father was not Catherine's husband, Peter III, but Sergei Saltykov, an intimate of the grand-ducal court. However, a number of striking similarities between Peter III and Paul can be cited—ungainliness, bad temper, and affinity for Prussian military style—while Saltykov was tall and handsome. A few historians have also reported the rumor that Catherine's baby by Saltykov was stillborn (or a girl), and that the baby of a Karelian servant girl from the town of Kotka was substituted. Nikita Panin, in 1760 and 1761, urged Empress Elizabeth to utilize the succession law of Peter the Great to name Paul her successor with Catherine as regent, but she failed to do so. Then the tide nearly shifted drastically for Catherine and her son; Peter III is credited with planning to have Catherine denounced as an adultress and Paul as an illegitimate son, to have the marriage declared void, and to throw both mother and son into prison. Sablukoff, "Reminiscences of the Court and Times of Paul I of Russia, up to the Period of His Death: from the Papers of a Deceased Russian General Officer," *Fraser's Magazine* 72 (August 1865): 229-30.

second marriage to a Württemberg princess, whose Russian name was Maria Fedorovna, was arranged soon afterwards. Two sons, Alexander and Constantine, were born in 1777 and 1779 respectively. These infants were taken away from Paul by their grandmother (just as Paul had been removed from Catherine by Elizabeth); nevertheless, Paul and Maria Fedorovna, to whom several more children were born, presided over the first Romanov family household since the time of Peter the Great.[7]

The preparation of the Grand Duke Paul for the difficult task of ruling Russia was begun by Empress Elizabeth. Count Nikita Panin was appointed chief tutor and, despite numerous obstacles, did a creditable job. As a result, Paul obtained a formal education that surpassed that of most of his predecessors on the Russian throne and equaled that of most of his successors. The grand duke also had several well-informed young friends who corresponded with him about world affairs and later visited his family residence at Pavlovsk or his model state at Gatchina. Paul broadened this experience by his own extensive reading and through the limited administrative training gained by directing the activities at Gatchina.[8]

Paul received a firsthand view of the European scene in 1781 and 1782, when he and his wife made a grand excursion through most of the capitals of continental Europe. Traveling incognito as Count and Countess of the North, they were nonetheless fêted everywhere as imperial dignitaries. During their tour of Italy, with stops at Venice, Bologna, Padua, Naples, Rome, Genoa, and Turin, the grand duke got his first glimpses of the Mediterranean.

---

7. Waliszewski, *Paul the First of Russia, the Son of Catherine the Great* (London, 1913), pp. 16–19.

8. The one outstanding work on Paul's life before 1796 is by D. F. Kobeko, *Tsesarevich Pavel Petrovich (1754–1796)* (Saint Petersburg, 1882). Another book by Pierre Morane, *Paul Ier de Russie, avant l'avènement, 1754–1796* (Paris, 1907), is more psychological in approach. See also Alexander Kurakin's long, interesting letters to Paul written from Leyden in 1770 to 1774 about the government and society of Holland, France, and England in *Arkhiv Kniazia F. A. Kurakina*, ed. V. N. Smol'ianov (Saratov, 1898–1904), vols. 5–10.

Catherine, as usual, kept the heir under close surveillance, and his words and actions were reported back to Saint Petersburg. Although Paul must have been aware of this, he seemed quite free in his conversations with foreign monarchs and ministers, upon whom he made a generally good impression.[9]

Catherine's treatment of Paul undoubtedly contributed to the development of some of his undesirable personality traits, especially his obsessive fear and suspicion of conspiracy. She maintained spies at the grand-ducal court to watch his movements. The relationship between mother and son, never very close, became more strained as Catherine grew older and as Paul's impatience to reign increased, but it is easy to exaggerate this rift. Although there were several opportunities, Paul was never party to a movement to dethrone Catherine. He approved the broad outline of her policies. His chief criticisms were directed at her administration of the army and navy, her various lovers, whose temporary influence greatly surpassed his own, and the extravagant spending of state resources on frivolous court affairs and ambitious foreign enterprises. Had he been given a part in this government, he would perhaps have been more willing to defend its policies.

In the last few years of Catherine's reign, rumors circulated in Saint Petersburg that the empress planned to remove Paul from the line of succession and replace him with Alexander, and that an important manifesto pertaining to the change was to be issued on 12 January 1797.[10] If the empress did consider such a course, Bezborodko, one of her most experienced advisers, would have cautioned against it, and Catherine herself must have realized that the years of effort expended in making Russia great might be tarnished if they ended with an event similar to the one which began her reign. Moreover, Alexander, the logical choice after Paul, was still in his teens and, surprisingly, coming under

---

9. A good account of Paul's trip abroad can be found in the work of Kobeko and in C. de Grunwald, *L'assassinat de Paul Ier, tsar de Russie* (Paris, 1960), pp. 48–53.

10. There was also a report that it was to be proclaimed even earlier than the New Year, on 24 November, the day of Saint Catherine. Grunwald, p. 90.

the influence of the military atmosphere of Gatchina; he had developed respect and admiration for his father.

When the news of Catherine's stroke reached Paul at Pavlovsk in November 1796, he was at first terrified by the fact that the long-awaited moment had arrived and by the fear that his great ambition to rule might still be thwarted, but before her death the next day, Paul had introduced his loyal Gatchina guard into the Winter Palace and had secured the succession. Paul's first acts as ruler were no more out of the ordinary than might be expected under the circumstances. A tight secrecy was clamped on the activities of the court while papers were searched, oaths were taken, and the control of key government departments was guaranteed. Foreign observers were shocked by the bizarre funeral staged for Peter III but pleased by Paul's friendly and intelligent conversation at official receptions.[11]

Paul immediately moved to stop the war against Persia, to limit the *barshchina* (labor required of serfs on landlord estates) to three days a week, and to establish a succession law (through the eldest son). Paul also began two major tasks that were to dominate his reign—the reorganization of the central government and the reeducation of the nobility for loyal and efficient service. Much of the administrative machinery in Russia had been allowed to deteriorate under the rule of Catherine and her favorites, and by strengthening the central apparatus of the state, Paul intended to immunize Russia against what had happened in France. According to Klochkov, Paul's greatest and most lasting accomplishment was this reform, a long and arduous job which was far from complete at his death.[12]

---

11. The best published firsthand account of the change from Catherine to Paul is Count Stedingk's report to Gustavus III, dated 17 November 1796, but continuing as a diary until 26 November since couriers were not allowed passports, in Anna Brevern de la Gardie, ed., *Un ambassadeur de Suède à la cour de Catherine II: Feld-Maréchal Comte de Stedingk, choix de dépêches diplomatiques, rapports secrets et lettres particulières de 1790 à 1796* (Stockholm, 1919), 2: 215–24. In manuscript see Cobenzl to Thugut, 25 November 1796, HHSA, 84 Russlands II Berichte.

12. Klochkov, pp. 570–84. The administrative reforms led to a reorganization of the College of Foreign Affairs, but the formulation of foreign policy was still in the hands of the tsar and his chief advisers, and the traditional diplomatic service was left relatively undisturbed.

The first actions of the new emperor proved that he was a true follower of the absolutist principles of Ivan the Terrible and Peter the Great, that he was an autocrat who would order noble and peasant alike to do his bidding. But the Russian nobility, especially in and about Saint Petersburg and Moscow, had been exposed to the ideas of the Enlightenment and had become familiar with the relative freedom of Western aristocracies. Catherine, recognizing the debt that she owed the nobility for supporting her claim to rule, had favored this class throughout her reign and, in 1785, issued the Charter of Nobility, which guaranteed special privileges. Paul tried to reverse this process and to rededicate the nobility to the service of the tsar, the church, and the state, but he achieved little success.[13]

Probably Paul's greatest mistake at the beginning was acting too hastily. Having been denied the scepter for so long, he understandably wanted to effect rapid changes. His generosity and clemency was nullified by a flurry of petty and insulting measures that directly affected the lives of the nobles, who were already prepared to greet the efforts of the new ruler with condescension or hostility. This reception only angered Paul into more extreme measures. Paul lacked what was one of the most marked qualities of his successors—patience.

In the first two years of his reign, Paul was fortunate to have a chancellor with experience and intelligence, Prince Alexander Bezborodko. This statesman, a protégé of Potemkin and successor to Panin, had been one of Catherine's most trusted advisers but had been eclipsed in the last years of her rule by Platon Zubov. Though often lazy and quick-tempered, Bezborodko was invaluable to Paul in the first months, helping him to examine state papers and smoothing over the transition.[14]

Largely as a result of Bezborodko's efforts, there were fewer

---

13. Many writers have emphasized Paul's knightly proclivities. See, for example, Shumigorskii, *Imperator Pavel I*, pp. 42–46, 163–66.

14. Grigorovich, pp. 349–54. Some sources claim that Bezborodko or Alexander Kurakin assisted Paul in locating and destroying the documents that replaced Paul by Alexander in the line of succession, but this cannot be proved. Zubow, p. 35.

disruptions in government than might have been expected in the shift from Catherine to Paul. The Zubovs and their friends were dismissed from positions of importance and awarded large estates. Paul's intimates were appointed to high offices, but many of the old bureaucrats remained. The greatest change was in administrative practice; almost every matter, even of very minor consequence, was passed on to the emperor himself, and little responsibility was delegated, particularly after the death of Bezborodko in the spring of 1799. His successors in the highest posts of chancellor and vice-chancellor and the men who served as foreign advisers—Victor Kochubei, Fedor Rostopchin, Alexander Kurakin, Nikita (Petrovich) Panin, and Peter Pahlen—were of limited experience and varied ability. None of them commanded either outstanding public respect or the complete confidence of Paul. The emperor, who admired the French king Henry IV, once remarked, "If only I had a Sully!"[15]

The Russian diplomats abroad, however, were experienced and highly respected. The senior ambassadors, Simon Vorontsov in London and Alexander Razumovsky in Vienna, had been completely assimilated into their respective foreign social environments and were often partial to the courts they attended. On the other hand, foreign representatives in Saint Petersburg—less talented on the whole—remained strongly committed to the causes of the governments they served. The dean of the diplomatic colony in the capital was Duke Antonio Maresca Serracapriola, ambassador from the Kingdom of the Two Sicilies. He and Count Curt von Stedingk from Sweden were the only foreign envoys to remain on close terms with Paul throughout his brief reign. Many of the others were unhappy in Saint Petersburg, and their desires for recall may have prompted some of their indiscretions.

French émigrés had already arrived in Saint Petersburg in considerable numbers before Catherine's death. The influx

---

15. Paul had studied carefully the memoirs of the French statesman of the seventeenth century and made revealing notations in his copy. Klochkov, pp. 116–117; Zubow, p. 21.

increased after 1796 following the invitation to Louis XVIII and Prince Condé to take refuge on Russian territory. Most of these wandering exiles were useless encumbrances to the Russian court, but some were appointed to important administrative posts and served Russia well.[16] Their influence upon foreign policy is difficult to measure; generally, they supported Paul's principles of autocracy and his fantasies of knighthood. Those French émigrés who belonged to ecclesiastic orders or the Knights of Malta were certainly influential in involving Russia in Mediterranean affairs.

At the beginning of his reign, Paul had no special plans for the Mediterranean or for South Russia. His prejudice against Potemkin and Zubov probably influenced his decision to reduce their old "royal fief," the Novorossisk administration (which had consisted of three provinces) to a single province and to transfer the northern part back to the Ukraine. The names of Tavricheskii and Ekaterinoslavskii were thus removed from their prominent place on the map of Russia. The policy of subsidizing the development of the new territories was ended by Paul, and the port of Odessa especially suffered from the curtailment of construction on the shipyards, the end of its privileged customs' status, and the removal of Ribas to Saint Petersburg. In an effort to win the favor of the new tsar, the merchants of Odessa sent 3,000 oranges as a gift, but Paul was not yet interested in such practical matters as trade.[17] He had set his sights on a "higher," more ideological objective.

RUSSIA AND THE ORDER OF MALTA

Paul's devotion to the Order of Saint John of Jerusalem (now officially known as the Sovereign Military Order of Malta) con-

---

16. For treatments of the French émigrés in Russia, see L. Pingaud, *Les Français en Russie et les Russes en France* (Paris, 1886), pp. 206–45, and K. Miller, *Frantsuzskaia emigratsiia i Rossiia v tsarstvovanie Ekateriny II* (Paris, 1931).

17. Skal'kovskii, pp. 55–58, 67, 85.

tributed significantly to the character of Russia's interest in the Mediterranean during his reign. The order was founded during the Crusades as a benevolent fraternity of knights devoted to the protection of pilgrims to the Holy Land. During the rise of Turkish power in the eastern Mediterranean, the knights fought valiantly as the rearguard of Christian Europe. The order's citadel for holding back the Turks was the beautiful Greek island of Rhodes. The knights, however, were dislodged from Rhodes by the Turks and were given a refuge by Emperor Charles V in 1530 on the smaller and less attractive island of Malta.[18] From Malta the order continued its war against the Moslems through territorial units called *langues* and their subdivisions, the priories, located on the continent. The main bases of these *langues* were in Catholic southern Europe—in Spain, France, and Italy—but priories existed farther north, in the British Isles, Bavaria, Bohemia, and Poland. The order's revenue consisted of annual taxes collected from the priories, which were in turn supported by gifts from wealthy nobles and monarchs, and of proceeds from trade, privateering, and miscellaneous services. The general economic decline of the Mediterranean area reduced the income of the order, and the rise of the Barbary pirates weakened its naval position.

By the last quarter of the century the Order of Malta was in poor condition to receive the shock of the French Revolution. The seizure of the rich properties of the *langues* of Auvergne, Provence, and France (a separate *langue* in central France) by acts of the French Legislative Assembly in 1791 and 1792 deprived the order of three-fifths of its revenue and eliminated its favorable balance of trade with the continent.[19] By 1797, internal

---

18. A. F. Bychkov, comp., "Depeshi Grafa Litty poslannika Mal'tiiskago Ordena v Peterburg pisannyia v kontse 1796 i nachale 1797 goda," *SIRIO* 2 (1868): 184. The Sovereign Military Order of Malta is now housed in Rome and, like the Vatican, enjoys a status of extraterritorial sovereignty within the Italian state. An old but still reliable history of the order is M. Miège, *Histoire de Malta*, 3 vols. (Paris, 1840).

19. Bychkov, in *SIRIO* 2: 175; Captain Eric Brockman, "Background to Betrayal (June 1798)," *Annales de l'Ordre Souverain Militaire de Malte* 8, no. 3 (1960): 9–24.

dissension had further weakened this outpost of militant Christianity. The French Revolution appealed to the latent crusading spirit of some of the knights; others were simply disillusioned by the loss of private fortunes in the continental upheaval and by the rapid decline of the order.

Early Russian contacts with the Maltese knights had been limited to a few isolated embassies. Peter the Great, interested in the possibility of securing an alliance against the Ottoman Empire, sent Count Boris Sheremetev to Malta in 1697, but nothing resulted from the mission except that the emissary became an honorary knight.[20] In hopes of securing aid for the Mediterranean fleet, Catherine appointed a Venetian, Marquis George Cavalcabo, as Russian chargé d'affaires on Malta in June 1769, but the assistance was insignificant since the majority of the knights, of French, Italian, and Spanish blood, were still prejudiced against Orthodoxy and Russia. The order was also approached by Catherine in connection with her designs to implement the Greek Project. Captain Antonio Psaro, a Greek in Russian service, was dispatched to Malta in 1784, and this time the Russian envoy received a grand welcome. As a result of this overture and desperate circumstances on the island, a few knights entered Russian service. Most notable of these were Count Giulio Litta and Admiral Ribas.[21] But even if Catherine had been able to send the Baltic fleet to the Mediterranean in 1788, Malta would probably have not become a Russian base.

Because of the poor economic position of the order in the 1790s, the popular and easygoing Grand Master de Rohan decided to send Giulio Litta back to Russia as a special emissary in quest of financial support. The purpose of Litta's mission was to settle the old problem of the Ostrogski estates in favor of the

---

20. Bychkov, in *SIRIO* 2: 173; I. K. Antoshevskii, *Derzhavnyi orden Sviatago Ioanna Ierusalimskago imenuemyi Mal'tiiskim v Rossii* (Saint Petersburg, 1914), p. 41.
21. Vicomte L. F. de Villeneuve-Bargemont, *Monuments des Grands-Maîtres de l'Ordre de Saint-Jean de Jérusalem* (Paris, 1829), 2: 267; P. Pierling, *La Russie et le Saint-Siège: Etudes diplomatiques*, vol. 5: *Catherine II—Paul Ier—Alexandre I* (Paris, 1912), p. 193.

order. Janusz Ostrogski, a wealthy Polish nobleman living in Volynia, had willed in 1609 that his extensive lands were to pass to the Order of Saint John if ever his direct line died out. The knights naturally tried to take it over when the last descendant of Janusz Ostrogski died in the early part of the eighteenth century. There were legal complications, however, and the Polish Diet supported the claims of the Czartoryski family, administrators of part of the disputed territory, and refused to uphold those of the order. Matters rested until the first partition of Poland. At the intercession of Austria, backed by Russia and Prussia, the Diet was forced, first in legislative acts and then by a treaty concluded in 1775, to award an annual allowance for the support of the Polish priory of the order.[22]

The situation changed when the bulk of the Ostrogski estate passed to Russia in the second partition of Poland in 1793. Influenced perhaps by the handsome young Czartoryski brothers then at her court, Catherine ignored the laws passed by the Diet, leaving the order once again without this income. Also, the Polish priory was awkwardly placed on Russian territory. Experienced in Russian ways and known to the Empress, Litta was an obvious choice to be sent by the order to Saint Petersburg, where he presented his credentials on 18 October 1795.[23] Negotiations were conducted in a desultory fashion because Catherine had little interest at the time in Maltese affairs and Litta did not get along with Zubov.

In order to understand the dramatic change that occurred in Russo-Maltese relations after the accession of Paul, it is necessary to examine Paul's religious views. This is a difficult task, since few historians have explored the subject and source material is scanty. Most writers agree, however, that Paul was deeply

---

22. Bychkov, in *SIRIO* 2: 166; Grigorovich, pp. 366–67. See also William Hardman, *A History of Malta during the Period of the French and British Occupations, 1798–1815*, ed. J. Holland Rose (London, 1909), p. 361.

23. Bychkov, in *SIRIO* 2: 166; Guiseppe Greppi, *Un Gentiluomo milanese guerriero-diplomatico, 1763–1839, appunti biografici sul Bali Conte Giulio Litta Visconti Arese* (Milan, 1896).

religious. His early theological education was entrusted to a noted Russian churchman, Platon, who had risen to the office of metropolitan of Moscow in 1796. Paul read widely in religious works, especially church histories, and developed, in the 1770s, a serious interest in Freemasonry and Martinism.[24] Though remaining in practice a strict adherent of Russian Orthodoxy, he was surprisingly tolerant of other denominations and sects. The Old Believers, for example, were granted freedom to worship and to build churches, even in Moscow, during his reign.

After his accession Paul carried out a number of consequential reforms of church administration that provide a clue to his views. He granted small parcels of land to local churches and various church offices, reversing a long trend of curbing the holding of land by the church. He also established new seminaries in Saint Petersburg and Kazan and awarded lavish grants to others. Another series of measures attempted to eliminate cleavages within the Orthodox Church and to integrate the church with the state administration. Paul decreed that half of the high church posts, as they became available, were to be awarded to members of the "white" clergy (the priests) rather than have all such posts awarded to the "black" clergy (the monks) as had been the custom. Both groups were to be subject to the Table of Ranks in the same manner as civil and military servants of the state. The sons of priests, excluding the one who customarily succeeded his father, were encouraged to enter military or civil service.[25] Other sects and religions that were officially recognized were subject to the same extensive state regulation and inspection. Paul seemed to be headed toward a fusion of church and state, of religion and politics.

Paul had been attracted to the Order of Malta since his youth,

---

24. Paul may have become a Mason in 1776, when several of his friends were initiated, during the visit of Gustavus III in 1777 (Paul's portrait is in a gallery of Masons in Stockholm), or during his trip abroad in 1781–82. Paul's dedication of a church on 24 June 1778, a Masonic holiday, is supposed to have some significance. See P. Pekarskii, *Dopolneniia k istorii masonstva v Rossii XVIII stoletiia* (Saint Petersburg, 1869).

25. Waliszewski, pp. 122–24, 175–80.

when he had read a colorful history of the knights by Vertot. The order represented to Paul a means by which an ideological and political union of all nations, classes, and confessions might be forged, not only to resist revolution, but also to lead a counter-revolution against liberal and atheistic movements. In Russia the order might regenerate the nobility, inspire it to greater sacrifices for the autocracy, and destroy the demoralizing tendencies of the Enlightenment. Paul's goal was to rejuvenate the conservative attributes of knighthood not only in Russia but in all Europe and to lead this united force against the "destructive" ideas of the French Revolution.[27]

Count Litta was pleasantly surprised by the favorable results of his first conferences with the new emperor on 26 and 30 December 1796. On the thirtieth, Litta wrote back to Malta: "The emperor desires that the Order of Malta be established here in a manner that would give it the same respect and consideration that it enjoys by right in the territories of other powers."[28] The duke of Serracapriola, the ambassador from the king of the Two Sicilies, who was the legal suzerain of the island of Malta, assisted Litta in the negotiations. Bezborodko and Alexander Kurakin handled the details for Russia.

On 15 January 1797 the first convention to be signed by Paul with a foreign government was concluded between him and the grand master. The terms of the Polish treaty of 1775 were renewed, and the Grand Priory of Poland was reconstituted as the Grand Priory of Russia (article 4 of the convention). The annual subsidy Poland had paid to the order was raised from 120,000 to 300,000 zloty (article 3). This figure was augmented by a favorable rate of exchange to the ruble and by a provision

---

26. Pierling, 5: 195. For strange but colorful reading, see Abbé de Vertot, *Histoire des Chevaliers Hospitaliers de S. Jean de Jérusalem,* 7 vols. (Paris, 1761).

27. Klochkov, pp. 80–82. A number of historians have investigated Paul's involvement with the Knights of Malta. For special studies see Evgenii Karnovich, *Mal'tiiskie rytsari v Rossii : istoricheskaia povest' iz vremen imperatora Pavla Pervago* (Saint Petersburg, 1897), and Antoshevskii (see note 20 above).

28 Bychkov, in *SIRIO* 2: 201.

.ch made payments retroactive to the second partition.[29] .i a long dispatch of 18 January 1797 to the grand master, Litta praised Paul: "This prince is entirely devoted to the duties of the throne; without exception his actions constantly serve the state and the people; the fixed principle of all of his disposition is the dignity of the empire, and the welfare of his subjects. . . . The Order of Malta, a model and example by its institution and conduct, is for him an object of respect and affection."[30] Litta added, however, that the Russian emperor was not pleased to have the Russian priory, like the previous Polish priory, incorporated into the Anglo-Bavarian *Langue*, and suggested that a sixth *langue*, a "Langue du Nord," be established to accommodate Paul.[31]

A mission was immediately organized to represent Russia at Malta. At first Psaro was nominated by Bezborodko to head the new embassy, but for reasons left unclear, O'Hara—an Irishman in Russian service who was known to Rohan—was selected. Bailli Fornone, a friend of Litta's, was dispatched in advance with a copy of the convention, but on his way to Malta he was captured by General Bonaparte.[32] Thus, Paul's special interest in the Order of Malta immediately became known to the French. O'Hara arrived at Malta with the original of the convention just after the death of Rohan in July 1797.[33] The election of a new grand master offered an opportunity for foreign interference, but Paul was still too far away and too weak in influence to affect the choice. Ferdinand von Hompesch, the Austrian nominee, was selected—an indication of the relative rise of Germans in the ranks of the order after 1789.

French interest in the declining order had also revived, how-

29. *Konventsiia zakliuchennaia mezhdu ego Velichestvom Imperatorom Vserossiiskim i derzhavnym ordenom Mal'tiiskim i Ego Preimushchestvom Gros-Meisterom* (Saint Petersburg, 1798).

30. Bychkov, in *SIRIO* 2: 227; also Pierling, 5: 199.

31. Bychkov, in *SIRIO* 2: 221.

32. G. Litta to the Grand Master de Rohan, 5 February 1797, ibid., 197. See also Frederick W. Ryan, *The House of the Temple: A Study of Malta and Its Knights in the French Revolution* (London, 1930), p. 243.

33. Greppi, p. 105.

ever, and Bonaparte thought that Pope Pius VI could be brib
into supporting a Spanish candidate who would be pro-French.
While campaigning in Italy in 1797, he wrote to the Executive
Directory:

> The island of Malta is of major interest for us. The Grand
> Master is dying, and it looks as though his successor will
> be a German. It would take 500,000 or 600,000 francs to
> have a Spaniard made Grand Master. Would it not be
> possible to persuade the Prince of Peace to take steps to
> that end, which is most important? Valetta has 37,000 in-
> habitants who are very well disposed towards the French;
> there are no longer any English in the Mediterranean; why
> should not our fleet or the Spanish, before going into the
> Atlantic, sail to Valetta and occupy it? There are only 500
> knights and the regiment of the Order is only 600 strong.
> If we do not, Malta will fall into the power of the King of
> Naples. This little island is worth any price to us.[34]

BONAPARTE AT MALTA

The French commander's interest in the Mediterranean grew
rapidly during 1797. In November he sent a special agent,
Poussielgue, to Malta "on the pretext of inspecting our estab-
lishments in the Levant, but, in reality, to give the final touches
to our plan for that island."[35] Poussielgue paved the way for

---

34. Bonaparte to the Executive Directory, 26 May 1797, in *Letters and Documents of Napoleon*, ed. and trans. John Eldred Howard, vol. I: *The Rise to Power* (London, 1961), p. 191. Bonaparte's plan for the seizure of Malta "before going into the Atlantic" suggests that Malta came before Egypt in his thinking. Did the problem of the election of a new grand master, coming as it did at the very time of major French military and diplomatic successes in Italy, turn the general's thoughts in that direction, was he already trying to turn the Directory's sights toward Egypt by holding up a juicy plum, or was he merely easing the way for the approval of the occupation of the Ionian Islands?

35. Bonaparte to the Directory, 12 November 1797, ibid., 1: 208. Bonaparte's eastern projects were supported and even expanded in Paris by Talleyrand, who had become minister of foreign affairs in July. Learning in early September of the election of Hompesch, the Austrian nominee, as grand master, Talleyrand ordered Bonaparte to prevent an Austrian occupation of the island as a counter to the French occupation of the Ionians. The

ᴏsequent French action by gathering information and distributing bribes to some of the disillusioned French knights. Bonaparte then waited for an opportunity to create an incident.

On 24 February 1798, Admiral Brueys, commander of a French squadron in the Mediterranean, left Corfu with a fleet of decrepit ships assembled in the Adriatic from the navy of the defunct Venetian Republic. He stopped at Malta on his way to join the French expeditionary force at Toulon and asked permission to take on water. Because there was a scarcity of water on the island, the grand master replied that, according to custom, only four ships could enter the harbor at one time for this purpose.[36] This stipulation was construed as an unfriendly defiance of the French navy, although Brueys did not respond with force at this time because of the weakness of his squadron. On 12 April on Bonaparte's initiative, the Directory declared that "the Order of Malta has of its own volition adopted a hostile attitude towards France" by sheltering émigré enemies of the revolution and threatening to hand the island over to Britain, and it instructed "the Commander in Chief of the Army of the East . . . to occupy the island of Malta. To this end he will at once direct against it the land and sea forces under his command."[37]

Bonaparte's great expedition destined for Egypt left Toulon on 19 May 1798 and arrived at Malta on 9 June having escaped Nelson's detection. The huge old fortresses of the island required

---

Directory not only approved the seizure of Malta (on 27 September), but ordered that it be done immediately (on 3 October). Bonaparte, however, was busy at Campoformio. This helps to explain the timing. Since a French attack, probably from the Ionians, was expected to follow shortly afterwards, Poussielgue was given more money and power than might otherwise have been the case. But after Campoformio the Directory's attention turned to the project for the invasion of England, and Bonaparte was called to Paris at the end of November. See François Charles-Roux, *Les origines de l'expédition d'Egypte* (Paris, 1910), pp. 294–307, and Albert Sorel, *Bonaparte et Hoche en 1797* (Paris, 1896).

36. Le Bailli Comte Michel de Pierredon, *Exposition de l'histoire de l'Ordre Souverain de Malte au bénéfice du pavillon des lépreux* (Paris, 1929), p. 15.

37. The Directory to Bonaparte, in *Letters and Documents of Napoleon* 1: 233.

about 30,000 men for a proper defense, but at that time there were, on the island, only 282 knights, a Maltese infantry regiment of 2,000, 200 of the grand master's personal guards, 550 sailors, 550 galley crewmen, 700 artillery men, and 13,000 rather unreliable local militia—a rough total of 17,000.[38] Even a force of this size should have held out with no great difficulty until the English arrived or until Bonaparte decided to hurry on to his destination, Egypt, but the defense was unorganized, leadership was uncertain, and French money had apparently won over several important knights.[39] The grand master's refusal to acquiesce to Bonaparte's request for water for his tremendous fleet of over 400 brought a feigned rage of indignation from the French commander. Caruson, the French consul on the island, replied in Bonaparte's name:

> Eminence, having been called upon to carry aboard the flagship the reply of Your Eminence to the request that the squadron be permitted to take on water, the Commander-in-Chief Bonaparte is indignant that permission to water should be accorded only to two ships at a time; what length of time, indeed, would it not take for 500 or 600 sail to procure in this way the water and other things they urgently need? This refusal has surprised General Bonaparte the

38. Luigi Rangoni-Machiavelli, "LXX—Fra Ferninando von Hompesch, 1798–1799," *Revista del Sovrano Militare Ordine di Malta* 14, no. 3 (1960): 10. Miège, 3: 35, writing in 1840, gives the same total, but another source lists 332 knights present on the island when the French fleet appeared: 200 French, 90 Italian, 25 Spanish, 8 Portuguese, 4 German, and 5 Bavarian (one unaccounted for). F. Giuseppe Terrinoni, *Memoire Storiche della resa di Malta ai francesi nel 1798* (Rome, 1867), p. 24. It is important to note that the number of French knights on the island was quite disproportionate to the number of rank and file knights in the continental priories.

39. A historian of the Egyptian expedition, J. Christopher Herold, notes: "Hompesch's ignorance and irresolution, combined with the confusion created by a handful of disaffected men, led to the decision . . . to sue for an armistice. For twenty-four hours, the course of modern history depended on some 300 men, warrior monks, quaint relics of the Age of Crusades." *Bonaparte in Egypt* (New York, 1962). The problem was not so much "Hompesch's ignorance and irresolution," since he knew about the approach of the French and of the disaffection of some of the knights, but the fact that a number of these "quaint relics" were attracted to the French cause.

more, since he is aware of the preference granted to the English and of the proclamation issued by Your Eminence's predecessor.

General Bonaparte is resolved to secure by force what ought to have been accorded to him in the name of hospitality which is the basis of your Order.[40]

On 10 June fifteen thousand French troops landed and with little opposition occupied the key forts. Hompesch quickly decided to come to terms. According to the recollections of Doublet, one of the Maltese negotiators for surrender, Bonaparte considered the order's recent convention with Russia a reason for the harsh terms that he claimed he had to impose.[41] This seems to have been only another pretext. He had much more to fear from the island's use as a base by the British or Neapolitan fleets. Although the island lacked wood and water supplies adequate for a large naval station, it was ideal as a strategic coordinating post for commerce, communications, and corsair activities in the central Mediterranean, and with respect to the Egyptian campaign it was important to deprive the British of these advantages.

From Bonaparte's actions after occupying the island it appears that another of his motives for taking Malta was the seizure of the remaining wealth and treasury of the knights. He realized that the Directory was financially hard-pressed at home, and that the gold and silver plate, valued at 6,000,000 francs, promptly melted down and stowed aboard the *Orient*, would be useful, perhaps indispensable, in financing the Egyptian campaign. Some of the treasure was sent back to France, part of it paid the expenses of scattering the remnants of the order, and some was forwarded to strategic French bases such as Corfu.[42] Bonaparte

40. Caruson to the grand master, 10 June 1798, in *Letters and Documents of Napoleon* 1: 233. Caruson was a former knight of the order.

41. Brockman, *Annales de l'OSMM* 8: 17; Pierre-Jean-Louis-Ovide Doublet, *Mémoires historiques sur l'invasion et l'occupation de Malte par une armée française, en 1798* (Paris, 1883), p. 173. For Hompesch's own defense, see "Précis de la Révolution de Malte," in Historical Manuscripts Commission, *Report on the Manuscripts of J. B. Fortescue, Esq., preserved at Dropmore* (Hereafter cited as *Dropmore*) (London, 1905) 7: 367–76.

42. Order of Bonaparte, 13 June 1798, in *Letters and Documents of*

also stated that a subsidiary purpose in taking the island was to impress the Turks by liquidating an old enemy of theirs.[43] After seizing and garrisoning this strategic point in the Mediterranean by outmaneuvering the British fleet, he proceeded with the Egyptian campaign.

PAUL BECOMES GRAND MASTER

The news of the fall of Malta to the French reached Saint Petersburg in July and placed the seal upon the emperor's determination to send an expedition of Russian forces into the Mediterranean. Litta immediately drew up plans for a blockade of the island. The nature of the surrender, rather than the unsurprising capture itself, produced a chain of remarkable events in Saint Petersburg.

A letter purporting to be from the respected Bailli de Tigné, in captivity on Malta at the time, to Bailli Litta in Saint Petersburg accused Hompesch of treason to the Order of Malta for selling out to the French. The result of this accusation was a declaration drawn up by the Russian priory and ratified by Paul on 10 September denouncing Hompesch. Although the letter was later suspected of being a forgery, the publicity given to it at the time by Russia caused many of the knights in exile to favor deposing Hompesch and offering the grand mastership to Paul.[44]

Napoleon 1: 241; Terrinoni, p. 47. Most of the treasure went down with the *Orient* in the famous Battle of the Nile (Abukir). In recent years a complex four-way legal battle between France, England, the United Arab Republic, and SMOM (The Sovereign Military Order of Malta) has been taking place over the possible recovery of the treasure by divers. Bonaparte and the scholars who accompanied him were also interested in the Maltese archives, much of which also went down on the *Orient* to the misfortune of historians of the order.

43. Bonaparte to the Grand Vizir, 17 August 1798, in *Letters and Documents of Napoleon* 1: 300.

44. Brockman, *Annales de l'OSMM* 8: 21. Another letter to Litta written at about the same time (22 June) by Bailli de Loras from Sicily appears to be more genuine although it was given less attention. Loras believed that the island could have held out for eight days, time enough for the English to relieve it. Excerpts from the letters of Loras and Tigné

Paul's subsequent "election" as seventieth grand master on 9 November 1798 has often been considered illegal because no precedent existed for the deposition of a grand master, not all priories participated in the election, it was not ratified by the pope, and, above all, Paul was the first (and only) non-Catholic grand master. Many of the knights from Malta had given up hope and returned to their homelands. Only a few representatives of the continental priories managed to reach Saint Petersburg in time to vote in the election by a council formally convoked by a group of French émigré knights. Though certainly irregular, this election was probably no more fraudulent than some of those in the past.[45] Many of the knights—even those who could not get to Saint Petersburg—realized the advantages of choosing a grand master who was dedicated to the causes of the order and backed by the resources of the Russian Empire.[46]

The British underestimated the ideological factor and interpreted Paul's acceptance of the title as a measure to improve the Russian military position in the Mediterranean by securing a

are in: items 3 & 4, respectively, of enclosure 8, Cobenzl to Thugut, 9 September 1798 (no. 48), HHSA, 88 Russland II Berichte (III–IX, 1798).

45. Michel de Taube, *L'Empereur Paul Ier de Russie, Grand Maître de l'Ordre de Malte et son "Grand Prieuré Russe" de l'Ordre de Saint-Jean-de-Jérusalem* (Paris, 1955), pp. 9–17. The official historians of the order, for example, Miège, Terrinoni, and Pierredon, were Catholic knights who interpreted the election as illegal. Taube, however, disagrees. Maisonneuve, Paul's own official historian, argued that Hompesch's election had been secured by Austrian money. *Annales historiques de l'Ordre Souverain de St. Jean de Jérusalem depuis l'année 1725 jusqu'au moment présent* (Saint Petersburg, 1799), p. 89.

46. Whitworth, the British ambassador, wrote to Paget at the time he was negotiating a convention with Russia (28 December 1798), "You have I daresay been as much bored where you are [Naples] as I have been with the affairs of the Order of Malta. You know how we have proceeded against the late Grand Master Hompesch and that we have kicked him downstairs and got into his place. I confess for my own part I am decidedly an anti-Hompesch, and I think the Order, in gaining such a support as the Emperor of Russia, at a moment when every Government where it has possession considered the game as up, and its property as lawfull pillage, has made no bad bargain." *The Paget-Papers: Diplomatic and Other Correspondence of the Right Hon. Sir Arthur Paget, G.C.B., 1794–1807*, ed. Sir Augustus B. Paget (London, 1896), 1: 144.

strategic naval base in that region. But any Russian admiral familiar with the usual condition of Russian ships, or even Paul himself, must have recognized that the island of Malta alone, with little timber, water, or other resources, was ill-suited as a forward post for the Russian fleet. There is no evidence that Paul's motive was purely one of territorial expansion. He voiced no intention of displacing the official suzerain, the king of Naples. Bonaparte observed in his dispatch of 17 June 1798 to the Directory:

> You will find attached the original of the treaty which the Order of Malta had just concluded with Russia. It had been ratified only five days, and the courier [Fornone], who was the man I arrested two years ago at Ancona, had not yet left. Thus His Majesty the Emperor of Russia owes us his thanks, for the occupation of Malta saves his treasury 400,-000 rubles. We have understood the interests of his nation better than himself.
>
> If his aim was to prepare the way to establish himself in the port of Malta, it seems to me that His Majesty should have done things a little more secretly and not made his plans so easily discoverable. But, in any case, we now have in the centre of the Mediterranean the strongest fortress in Europe and it will cost anyone dear to dislodge us.[47]

But Bonaparte, too, missed the main point of Paul's interest in Malta. The tsar was paying not for the island but for the order, which Bonaparte valued very little. The French general, by seizing the island in the way he did, ruined the reputation of Hompesch and delivered the order into the outstretched arms of the Russian emperor.

Although he now acted in a dual role as Russian tsar and Maltese grand master, Paul did not separate the foreign policy aims of the two. The new grand master gave the Order of Saint John of Jerusalem a more universal character by establishing a Russian Orthodox priory in addition to the Russian (formerly Polish) Catholic priory. The purpose of the creation of the new priory was to promote the attributes of militant dedication and

---

47. *Letters and Documents of Napoleon* 1: 243.

service, which he believed the knights possessed, in the Russian nobility. The new grand master liberally distributed command- eries, the lowest subdivisions of the order, to leading Russian no- ble families. When the officers of the Grand Council of the order were appointed, Russians predominated, although there were many émigré members of the order on hand in Saint Petersburg at the time. One of the first actions of the council was to define the struggle against France as a war against the infidel.[48] Thus, the Order of Saint John was the vanguard of the counterrevo- lution.

PAUL AND ROME

The relations between Paul and the Roman Catholic Church and their effect upon the development of Paul's policies have been much debated and are still controversial. The arrival in Moscow on 1 April 1797, of a papal nuncio, Archbishop Lorenzo Litta, for the coronation, created a considerable stir because he was accorded the honor of first rank among the diplomatic corps and because of the long audience granted him on 10 April, two days after Paul's own arrival. Later, in Saint Petersburg, Litta, with the help of his brother, Giulio, negotiated with Paul and Bezborodko and Alexander Kurakin for the restoration of the prepartition rights of the Catholic and Uniate churches in the Polish provinces.[49]

In Rome, Pius VI, who had impressed Paul when they met in 1782, consulted his advisers Cardinals Gerdil and Antonelli about the problems of advancing the cause of Catholicism in Russia. Cardinal Gerdil wrote a long memoir on the possibility of reunion

---

48. "Protocole du Sacré Conseil de l'Ordre Souverain de St. Jean de Jérusalem," Saint Petersburg, Fifth Session at Gatchina, 19 September 1799, p. 39 (unpublished manuscript in the Archives of the Sovereign Military Order of Malta, Rome).

49. M. J. Rouët de Journel, S.J., *Nonciatures de Russie d'après les docu- ments authentiques: Nonciature de Litta*, 1797–1799, Studi i Testi, No. 165 (Vatican City, 1943), pp. xii–xiii, 24–50. For Litta's reception in Russia, see Cobenzl to Thugut, 3 and 13 April 1797, HHSA, 85 Russland II Berichte.

of the Eastern and Western churches. Cardinal Antonelli, however, warned the pope of two dangers—first, the natural intolerance of the Russian autocratic system, which was traditionally opposed to the Latin rite; and second, the character of the leading Catholic in Russia, the archbishop of Mogilev, Siestrzencewicz-Bohusz, whom he described as "an intelligent and even learned man, but possessing a servile and ambitious character, coming from Protestantism to the Roman Church and never acquiring a truly Catholic soul."[50] This proved to be an accurate portrait of the Polish-Lithuanian Siestrzencewicz-Bohusz, the man who had been selected by Catherine to head the Roman Catholic Church in Russia. At first he supported Lorenzo Litta's program, hoping to gain his favor and obtain a cardinal's hat. He then turned against Litta, who had become his chief rival for power within the church and, by adhering to all Paul's demands, thus courting his favor, the archbishop succeeded in undermining the nuncio's position.

After frustrating delays most of Litta's proposals for reform of the administration of the Catholic Church were implemented in imperial ukases in early May, 1798. The five Latin bishoprics and the three Uniate bishoprics were reestablished, but one significant problem was left unsolved—free and unhindered contact between church prelates and Rome. At a conference with Kurakin on 12 May 1798, Litta found the ukases to be acceptable to the church, but later he discovered that they contained an entire clause (Article XII) that had not appeared in the ministerial notes at the conference.[51] This article forbade the clergy to correspond with persons abroad except under imperial censorship, and, since the interdiction had already become law, Litta was forced to take a stand in opposition to an established state policy. A difficulty concerning the head of the Department

---

50. Doria to Litta, 8 July 1797, Rouët de Journel, p. 85; Pierling, 5: 184–86, 250.

51. Pierling, 5: 243–44; Rouët de Journel, p. xxxvii. Litta's greatest problem was lack of money. If the hard-pressed See in Rome had been able to provide Litta with enough to live in style and for the usual bribes, his tasks would have been greatly simplified.

of Catholic Affairs of the College of Justice was resolved by substituting Siestrzencewicz for the Lutheran president.[52] Communications with Rome were so slow that Litta finally gave up waiting for ratification and on his own authority published, in August 1798, at the Jesuit monastery of Polotsk, the new regulations for the Catholic Church in Russia, which remained in force for many years (and was republished in 1855).[53]

Papal approval of the tsar's assumption of the title of grand master was yet to be obtained. The pope was influenced by the Spanish and Roman priories of the order, which refused to recognize the deposition of Hompesch as legal. A *pro memoria* of the pope arrived in Saint Petersburg on 17 April 1799, presenting the official view that the election could not be approved because Paul was not Catholic. An accompanying letter in cipher instructed Litta to tone down or withhold this decision, depending on the circumstances. The *pro memoria*, however, had come by Russian courier from Vienna, where Ambassador Alexander Razumovsky had opened it and passed on the information in the unciphered part.[54] Angered by this setback from the pope, the tsar placed full blame on Lorenzo Litta, expelled him from the country, and forced his brother to retire to his estates. This left the Roman Church in the hands of Siestrzencewicz.[55]

Despite the Litta-Maltese episode Paul continued to evince an interest in Catholic affairs, and the Papacy could not afford to antagonize a potential ally in a ·time of trouble. The Jesuits, especially, enjoyed the tsar's protection and patronage, and, in the last year of Paul's reign, when he was under the influence of Father Paul Gruber, the Jesuits' role in education advanced rapidly. The University of Vilna was turned over to them, and a

---

52. Adrien Boudou, S.J., *Le Saint-Siège et la Russie: Leurs relations diplomatiques au XIX siècle*, vol. I: 1814–1847, 2d ed. (Paris, 1922), p. 18.

53. Rouët de Journel, p. xli.

54. Ibid., p. lx; Giuseppe Berti, *Russia e stati italiani nel Risorgimento* (Turin, 1957), p. 170.

55. Rouët de Journel, pp. lxi–lxiiv. Joseph de Maistre reported that at a public audience in March, before the arrival of the *pro memoria* and before the expulsion of Litta, Siestrzencewicz, while standing beside Paul, hurled defiance at Litta with the words: "Voilà mon Pape, à moi." Ibid., p. lix.

Jesuit college was founded in Saint Petersburg. Gruber was instrumental in securing the dismissal of Siestrzencewicz in November 1800. And on 24 January 1801, on the tsar's insistence, Pius VII legalized—for the first time anywhere since 1773—the existence of the Jesuit Order in Russia.[56] Here the Jesuits began the road to recovery by becoming, in Paul's mind, the educational and spiritual complement to the Maltese military and social order.

Evidence has been uncovered that in late 1800 Paul secretly proposed the unification of the Eastern and Western Churches, using Serracapriola and the king of Naples as intermediaries. The idea was supported by Father Gruber and the Orthodox Metropolitan Ambrose of Saint Petersburg. Paul is supposed to have had two important conferences with Serracapriola in late November and to have written to Ferdinand IV and Acton in Naples on the subject. The text of a note of Serracapriola describing one of these conferences was discovered by the Vatican historian Rouët de Journel. He also notes that in the Vatican Archives is a letter dated 6 February 1801 from Cardinal Ruffo—the brave liberator of Naples from the French who would have been a logical intermediary from Ferdinand IV—to Cardinal Consalvi, the papal secretary, requesting a papal audience that evening to discuss a matter of "great importance."[57] Proof is lacking, however, that Pius VII seriously considered this proposal, especially since he had not acted on Paul's offer of asylum. Paul was murdered soon afterwards, and the question of reunion was dropped by his successor. Another report that Paul was converted

---

56. On 10 October 1800, Paul told Gruber, "Pour arrêter le flot de l'impiété, de l'illuminisme et du jacobinisme dans mon empire, je ne vois d'autres moyens que de confier l'éducation de la jeunesse aux jésuites. C'est par l'enfance qu'il faut commencer. Il faut reprendre l'édifice par le fondement, sinon tout croulera, et il ne restera plus ni religion, ni gouvernement." On 11 October the University of Vilna and the main Catholic church of Saint Petersburg, Saint Catherine's, were turned over to the Jesuits. Pierling, 5: 303; M. I. Moroshkin, *Iezuity v Rossii s tsarstvovaniia Ekateriny II i do nashego vremeni* (Saint Petersburg, 1867–70), 1: 324–35.

57. Rouët de Journel, "L'Imperatore Paulo I e la riunione della chiese," *La Civiltà Cattolica*, Anno 110 (September 1960), pp. 604–14.

to Catholicism shortly before his death is not convincingly documented.[58] Conversion would probably have accompanied a unification of the churches and a visit by the pope. Perhaps something of this nature was on his mind. The Kazan Cathedral on Nevsky Prospect in Saint Petersburg, patterned after Saint Peter's in Rome, was planned by the architect Voronikhin in the last year of Paul's reign.

Did Paul plan to give the Eastern Church to the pope in return for the pope's recognition of him as grand master? The project to reunite the churches would have been a logical outgrowth of Paul's position as grand master of the Order of Malta, his sympathy towards the Jesuits, and his personal ambition to be a savior of the Old Order in Europe, but it would be rash to assume that Paul carried his projects so far as to imagine himself in the role of a Holy Roman Emperor. More likely he thought of himself as a Richard the Lion-Hearted, as the leading knight of a militant church. As his flirtations with the Masons and his liberal attitude toward the Old Believers demonstrate, ritual and dedication were what mattered, not doctrinal issues. The "Catholic tendencies" of the nineteenth-century Romanovs originated with Paul; one might even discover the germ of the Holy Alliance in Paul's ideas.

The time and energy that Paul devoted to the Order of Malta and the Catholic Church were an integral part of his plans to support the legitimate institutions of Europe. The Order of Malta and the Papacy drew his attention to their threatened homelands in the Mediterranean area. Although Paul hoped to bolster the monarchies of Europe, increase the strength of the Christian religion, and end the menace of revolution, he naturally thought first of his own throne and religion and the immediate danger to Russia. His administrators and diplomats,

---

58. Ibid, p. 613. Michel de Taube presents the argument for the emperor's conversion in *L'Empereur Paul Ier de Russie*, pp. 33–34. Taube also maintains that Alexander I, as well as Constantine, was converted to Catholicism. His article, "Le Tsar Paul Ier et l'Ordre de Malte en Russie," *Revue d'histoire moderne* 5 (1930): 161–77, is the best single survey of Paul's relations with Malta despite the author's rather subjective conclusions.

likewise, were usually concerned with the best interests of Russia, and some, like Alexander Razumovsky, thought the Order of Malta a ridiculous fantasy of an emperor who was out of step with his times.[59] Paul's ideological goal—the development of an international movement that militantly supported the basic institutions of church and state—conflicted with the traditional interests of the Russian state, such as territorial expansion at the expense of the Ottoman Empire. But it harmonized with a new interpretation of Russian interest in the South, formed by "practical" men like Victor Kochubei, which called for friendly cooperation with the Turks.

---

59. A. A. Vasil'chikov, *Semeistvo Razumovskikh*, vol. 3: *Svetleishii Kniaz' Andrei Kirilovich* (Saint Petersburg, 1882), pt. 1, pp. 284, 308.

3

The Crusade

Between the signing of the convention with the Order of Malta in January 1797 and the installation of Paul as grand master in December 1798, Russia became committed to a crusade to remove the French from the eastern and central Mediterranean, and emerged as co-leader, with England, of the Second Coalition. Although Paul's ideological views shaped the nature of the Russian involvement in the Mediterranean, they should not be overemphasized as a causative factor. The victories of French armies in Italy drastically altered the political situation in the Mediterranean. Austria was militarily defeated and ready for peace. French prestige added force to the flow of revolutionary ideas into the semifeudal princedoms of Germany and Italy. As a result, practically all of central and southern Europe was unstable, while in the Ottoman Empire, where the central government was divided and weakened by the reforming attempts of Selim III, rebellious pashas spread a reign of terror over a major part of the Balkans.

Yet the Russian emperor, guided and influenced by Bezborodko, pursued a policy of peace. He needed time to establish his position on the throne more firmly, to improve the state of finances, and to reform the army. In January 1797, Paul ordered negotiations for a resumption of normal relations to begin in Berlin, but the Russian envoy, Kolychev, was less than half-hearted in his efforts. Peaceful intentions were declared to all governments and were especially emphasized in the instructions to Victor Kochubei, the ambassador in Constantinople.[1] The tsar flatly turned aside the efforts of Charles Whitworth, the English ambassador, to secure the army that Catherine had promised to send.

Preparations for the coronation in Moscow occupied most of March and April, but as soon as the ceremonies were over Paul initiated a more active foreign policy by calling a special conference of ambassadors at Bezborodko's house in Moscow on 3 May and proposing a general European peace congress to meet at Leipzig. He even named Simon Vorontsov, the ambassador in London, to lead the Russian delegation, and announced that Panin and Repnin would leave for Berlin immediately to negotiate separately with the French. Paul told the Austrian ambassador that if the French refused all reasonable offers, a Russian army of 60,000 would be sent.[2] But, unknown to Paul, Austria had agreed at Leoben on 18 April to negotiate a separate peace.

Before Franco-Russian talks could begin in Berlin, Paul improved his posture toward England: a trade treaty that had caused troublesome negotiations for ten years was signed on 11 May; in June Paul gave in to Vorontsov's insistence that the Russian squadron sent by Catherine the year before be left in the North Sea, where it provided assistance to the Royal Navy in quelling a serious mutiny later in 1797.[3] Paul's peace campaign may have had some influence on the English decision to begin separate negotiations with France at Lille in July. Both England and Austria preferred to treat separately rather than attend a general congress.

---

1. Cobenzl to Thugut, 3 January 1797 (no. 1), HHSA, 85 Russland II Berichte; R. S. Lanin, "Vneshniaia politika Pavla I v 1796–1798 gg.," *Uchenye Zapiski, Leningradskii Gosudarstvennyi Universitet, seriia istoricheskikh nauk* 10 (1941): p. 8.

2. Cobenzl to Thugut, 4 May 1797 (no. 29), HHSA, 85 Russland II Berichte.

3. Lanin, p. 17; A. M. Stanislavskaia, *Russo-angliiskie otnosheniia i problemy sredizemnomor'ia, 1798–1807* (Moscow, 1962), p. 81; Conrad Gill, *The Naval Mutinies of 1797* (Manchester, 1913), p. 177.

Nikita (Petrovich) Panin's negotiations with the special French emissary in Berlin proved rather fruitless partly because of Panin's anglophile tendencies. In fact, most of Paul's advisers and diplomats were becoming aligned during 1797 on one of two sides: that of peace, withdrawal, and perhaps accord with France, and that of war, involvement, and perhaps accord with England. The "peace party" held the high ground in Saint Petersburg in the summer of 1797, led by Bezborodko and Alexander Kurakin. Victor Kochubei, who was summoned from Constantinople in June to head the College of Foreign Affairs, was also an adherent to the view that Russia should concentrate on internal affairs. The "war party" consisted of the leading diplomats abroad—Vorontsov, Panin, Razumovsky in Vienna, and Vasili Tomara, the new ambassador to the Ottoman Porte—and Fedor Rostopchin, who at this time favored Russian involvement in Europe mainly because of personal animosity toward Bezborodko and his friends.[4] Because Paul consulted his advisers infrequently but read his ambassadors' reports thoroughly, the latter party may have had the long-run advantage.

But most of Paul's attention, during the summer months of 1797, was absorbed by domestic troubles—continued peasant unrest after the serious outbreak in February, complicated postpartition problems in Poland, a financial crisis heightened by the expense of the coronation, and opposition to army and administrative reforms manifested by a large number of retirements from civil and military service. The Austrian representative doubted Russia's ability to fight in a European war.[5] And Paul seems to have been completely unaware of what was going on in the Mediterranean that summer.[6] The French had beaten the Russians to Greece.

---

4. Stanislavskaia, pp. 91–96.

5. Dietrichstein to Thugut, 17 August 1797 (no. 49), HHSA, 85 Russland II Berichte. The Austrian ambassador, Cobenzl, returned to Vienna in July and became one of the chief negotiators at Campoformio and Rastadt. Dietrichstein was a temporary replacement who had been sent to Russia as a special envoy to the coronation. Both Dietrichstein and Cobenzl were able reporters of the Russian scene.

6. Several reasons can be offered for this situation: the suddenness of Bonaparte's seizure of the Ionians, the secrecy that surrounded the expedition

On 26 May 1797, Bonaparte ordered General Gentili with approximately 1500 French soldiers, 500 Venetian militia, and a squadron of the fleet to occupy Corfu, Zante, Cephalonia, and the other Ionian Islands.[7] In his instructions to Gentili, the general wrote, "If the inhabitants of the region are prone to independence, flatter them, and in the various proclamations that you issue do not fail to speak of Greece, Athens, and Sparta."[8] By the time the French occupation force reached Corfu (27 June), Bonaparte was reaffirming the importance of this foothold in the eastern Mediterranean to the Directory.

> The islands of Corfu, Zante, and Cephalonia are more important for us than the whole of Italy. If we were forced to choose, I believe it would be better to restore Italy to the Emperor and keep the four islands, which are a source of wealth and prosperity to our trade. The Turkish Empire is crumbling day by day, and the possession of these islands will put us in a position to support it as much as possible or to take advantage of it.[9]

Bonaparte had discovered that the Ionian Islands did indeed occupy an important strategic gateway to the eastern Mediterranean, and, as a result of Venetian economic development years before, possessed a lively trade based upon the production of olive oil, dried currants, and wines. But the French commander was probably more interested in the political importance of the islands. At the end of July, Bonaparte dispatched to Greece two agents, Dino and Nicolo Stephanopouli, to win Greek friendship, and, what was more practical, to draw up a plan for the conquest of the Morea (the Ottoman Peloponnese).[10]

---

and the negotiations at Campoformio, the interruption of communications across the Balkans by the disturbances of Pasvan-oglu, and the change in ambassadors at Constantinople, resulting in a break in regular communications. This case seems to prove that Russian contacts in the Balkans were practically nonexistent at this time.

7. Bonaparte to the Executive Directory, 26 May 1797, in *Letters and Documents of Napoleon*, 1: 190.

8. Jean Savant, "Napoléon et la libération de la Grèce," *L'Hellénisme contemporain* (July–October, 1960), p. 321.

9. Bonaparte to the Executive Directory, 29 July 1797, in *Letters and Documents of Napoleon*, 1: 199.

10. The Stephanopouli were Greeks from Corsica. For an account of

Bonaparte carried out the "Ionian campaign" entirely on his own initiative, without authority from Paris and in technical violation of the preliminary peace of Leoben. He acted to seal the demise of the Venetian Republic and to assure French presence on the Ottoman frontier. It was a characteristically impulsive move that took little consideration of possible reaction. The Directory had to be persuaded to approve the occupation; Bonaparte's long letter of 16 August reaffirmed the importance of the Ionians for communication "with the pashas of Albania" and for either supporting the Ottoman Empire or "taking our share."[11] His ally in Paris, Talleyrand, reported back on 23 August that the Directory approved, agreed with their "importance for Albania, Greece, and Macedonia [!]," and, apparently having consulted a map, pointed out that the island of Cerigo, off the southern tip of Greece, should also be occupied.[12]

On 13 September, Bonaparte wrote to Talleyrand, "From now on the great maxim of the Republic must be never to give up Corfu, Zante, etc. On the contrary, we ought to establish ourselves there firmly. They contain immense commercial resources and will be of great importance to us in the future movements of Europe."[13] It is a measure of the influence of Bonaparte and Talleyrand that the Directory incorporated the Ionian Islands and their continental tributaries into the French Republic as the départements of Ithaca, Corfu, and the Aegean, thereby extending the borders of France to the Aegean Sea and into the Balkan Peninsula. Ludwig Cobenzl, the Austrian ambassador to Russia, serving on special assignment at Campoformio agreed to the French fait accompli and the Austrian acquisition of the Venetian territory in Istria and Dalmatia.

Paul learned only in early October 1797 of the French appear-

---

their journey, see Dino and Nicolo Stephanopouli, *Voyage de Dino et Nicolo Stephanopouli en Grèce, pendant les années 1797 et 1798 d'après deux missions, dont l'une du Gouvernement français, et l'autre du général en chef Buonaparte,* ed. professors of the Prytane (Paris, year VIII [1800]).

11. François Charles-Roux, *Les origines de l'expédition d'Egypte* (Paris, 1910), p. 298.

12. Ibid., pp. 299–300.

13. In *Letters and Documents of Napoleon,* 1: 201.

ance in the Ionians from a report that the Russian consul at Zante, Zagorskii, had been arrested; but the extent of the French occupation was not realized, and the Russian response was limited to a strong protest through Panin in Berlin and an alert of the Black Sea fleet.[14] The emperor was led to believe by fragmentary reports of the peace negotiations that the Venetian Republic would survive either independent or as a dependency of Austria. The first news of the signing of the Treaty of Campoformio (17 October) reached Saint Petersburg on 14 November, but the details of terms were confused and contradictory. It appeared that France gained not only the Ionian Islands but also Istria and Dalmatia. That the Austrian envoy could not supply him with a complete treaty exasperated Paul, who was obviously quite alarmed. Bezborodko held a long conference with Dietrichstein on 20 November explaining Paul's displeasure that Russia had not been consulted "in matters that affected Russia more than Austria."[15] Dietrichstein was instructed to reply that because of a lack of naval power, Austria had no choice but to accede to French demands, and that Germany was more important.[16] Paul's dismay was increased by the realization that French troops and agents had been established on the Ottoman frontier for five months and by the belief that Russia was in the embarrassing position of lacking an ambassador in Constantinople who could take diplomatic countermeasures.[17] Even the

---

14. Lanin, p. 19; N. P. Panin to S. R. Vorontsov, 19 November 1797, in *Arkhiv Kn. Vorontsova*, 11: 6–7: Paul to Ushakov, 11 November 1797, in *Arkhiv grafov Mordvinovykh*, 1: 653–54.

15. Dietrichstein to Thugut, 14 November and 16 December 1797, HHSA, 86 Russland and II Berichte. The Austrian envoy was quite annoyed that he did not receive a copy of the treaty. Thugut did send one on 2 November, but for some reason (Was it intercepted by the Russians?) Dietrichstein was able to read the full text only late in January 1798. Thugut to Dietrichstein, 2 November 1797, HHSA, 181 Russland II Weisinger, and Dietrichstein to Thugut, 29 January 1798 (no. 6), HHSA 87 Russland II Berichte (Vermählung E.R.H. Josef u. Maria Pawlowna, 1797–1799).

16. Thugut to Dietrichstein, 25 January 1798, HHSA, 181 Russland II Weisinger.

17. This was not in fact the case. Kochubei had been recalled from Constantinople in June, and during October and November his arrival was expected in Saint Petersburg, but he remained in Constantinople until

"peace party" was afraid that the Sultan would be pressured into a French alliance or that the French would cause a serious internal crisis by support to the Balkan pashas. Kurakin told Dietrichstein in early December that French influence would inevitably mount in Constantinople and that Russia was prepared to take any action necessary to secure her interests.[18] Bezborodko wrote to Simon Vorontsov, "By the cession of the Venetian shores, France receives a better opportunity to command the Turks or to support them."[19]

The Russian court was also worried about a full-scale revolt against Sultan Selim III in Moldavia and Wallachia led by Pasha Pasvan-oglu. This spreading unrest just beyond the Russian frontier could be exploited by the French to tie down both Ottoman and Russian armies. When word was received that a Turkish fleet had entered the Black Sea, Paul sent orders, on 15 February 1798, to Admiral Mordvinov, commander of the Black Sea fleet, and to Vice Admiral Ushakov, celebrated hero of the last Turkish war, to outfit an observation fleet of twelve ships of the line to watch for the possibility that the French would enter the Black Sea.[20] In his ukaz to Mordinov, Paul stated that "although we do not see any intention on the part of the Ottoman Porte to break the peace and the present armament is directed solely for the pacification of the rebellious Pasvan-oglu and his accomplices," the present steps were being taken so that the French, "having occupied the islands of the Venetian Republic lying off the Turkish shores, . . . would not excite the Turks against us."[21] The orders caught the Black Sea fleet short of

after the end of the year. Tomara had been ordered on his way in October. See S. V. Arsen'ev, "Instruktsiia Imperatora Pavel I poslanniku v Konstantinopol V. Tamare," *Russkii Arkhiv* 55 (1917): 89–94.

18. Dietrichstein to Thugut, 16 December 1797, HHSA, 86 Russland II Berichte.

19. A. A. Bezborodko to S. R. Vorontsov, 13 December 1797, in *SIRIO* 29: 389–90.

20. In *Materialy dlia istorii russkago flota*, ed. S. Ogorodnikov, 16 (Saint Petersburg, 1902): 214–16.

21. Ibid., p. 215.

funds for supplies and with ships in a bad state of repair; it
over a month before the fleet could set sail.[22]

On 30 March 1789, Bezborodko wrote to Vorontsov that an
alliance of northern states against France was being sought; he
also reperated Russian fears of French activities in the Ottoman
Empire, stressing that France could stir up trouble in Poland.
He suggested that German problems being discussed at the congress in Rastadt might be solved by concessions to the French in
return for Austrian acquisition of the Ionian Islands.[23] Also in
March, Paul took the big step of inviting the count of Provence
(Louis XVIII) and the émigré corps of Prince Condé to take
shelter in Russia.[24] By the next month reports were being received
from Austria that a French fleet had arrived in the Straits on
the way to the Black Sea. Although Vienna often magnified
and circulated unverified rumors for her own benefit, in the
mood that prevailed in Saint Petersburg they were accepted as
genuine.

Except perhaps for the period from November 1797 to February 1798, when the Directory seriously considered direct invasion of England, the French threat to Russia was as great as
it was to England. Sir Mark Wood, a British member of parlia-
ment, predicted to Henry Dundas in April 1798 that the Toulon
fleet was headed east, and listed "Constantinople, the Black Sea,
and Caspian, and so to Persia" as the first possible route.[25] Paul,
meanwhile, was publicly using the Ionians as bait for the formation of an alliance in April, suggesting that they might become
Austrian or Neapolitan or even Turkish (he had apparently

22. Ushakov to Mordvinov, 27 February 1798, in *Admiral Ushakov*, ed.
R. N. Mordvinov, 2 (Moscow, 1952): 8. At this time Paul began to tempt
Suvorov out of retirement, where he had been since his frank and critical
assessment of Paul's army reforms. See Philip Longworth, *The Art of Vic-
tory: The Life and Achievements of Generalissimo Suvorov, 1729–1800*
(London, 1965).

23. In *SIRIO* 29: 394.

24. Lanin, p. 24.

25. J. Holland Rose, "The Political Reaction of Bonaparte's Eastern
Expedition," *English Historical Review* 44 (January 1929): 54.

pted the demise of Venice).[26] But he was also prepared to defend the Black Sea alone. On 20 April Paul ordered his Black Sea commanders to prepare to fight the French if they appeared in those waters, and directed his ambassador in Constantinople to offer the sultan aid of Russian troops to suppress internal revolts.[27] The Russian Empire was rapidly becoming committed to an outright struggle against France.

Hostile threats in the south promoted defensive alliance in the north as well. The British government, having pressed so long for Russia's active participation in the war, finally received a definite Russian response. On 8 May, Paul wrote to his ambassador in London that ten ships of the line with a number of frigates would be added to his naval forces in the North Sea, "in the conviction that Our real assistance will give to the king of Great Britain the ability to dispatch a considerable part of his fleet to the Mediterranean in order to destroy the French naval forces and frustrate their schemes in that quarter."[28] The Mediterranean loomed larger in the emperor's mind in 1798, for it was general knowledge that the fleet at Toulon was heading east despite British fears that it threatened an invasion of the British Isles.[29]

Paul's order to Ushakov, dated 24 May and based upon the assumed threat of a French fleet at the Straits or in the Black Sea, first committed Russia to direct military action.

> As soon as you receive the news that the French squadron has attempted to enter the Black Sea, immediately seek them out and give decisive battle, and We trust in your courage, bravery, and talent that the honor of Our fleet will be kept; in case [the French fleet] is greatly superior to

---

26. Dietrichstein to Thugut, 18 April 1798 (no. 18), HHSA, 88 Russland II Berichte.

27. Lanin, p. 26; Paul to Ushakov, 20 April 1798, in *Admiral Ushakov*, 2:̈ 21.

28. Paul to S. R. Vorontsov, 8 May 1798, in *Arkhiv Vorontsova*, 10: 239.

29. Pitt especially feared an invasion of Ireland, and Nelson was ordered to prevent above all the movement of the French fleet to the west. Local rebellions in both Ireland and the Balkans in 1798 magnified English and Russian fears, respectively, out of proportion to real direct danger.

Ours, do all that duty and necessity demands on all possible
occasions to do harm to Our enemy.[30]

But Russian preparations for war were far from complete.
The state of Russian finances and of the army and navy, the
cautious attitude of the "peace party," the lack of precedence
for a Turkish alliance, and Paul's aversion to war so early in his
reign all contributed in the spring of 1798 to slow negotiations
with Austria and Britain for the creation of a general coalition.
There was still no definite assurance that the Turks would accept
Russian assistance. French diplomacy, playing upon Ottoman
weakness and traditional fears of Russia, might easily succeed
in dominating the Porte. And could the traditional Russian hostility towards the Turks be overcome? Even the "peace party"
was prepared to accept this. Kochubei, the nephew of Bezborodko, returned from his embassy to the Ottoman Empire in
early May 1798 with pronounced pro-Turkish sympathies. He
led a small diplomatic revolution as head of the College of
Foreign Affairs and as interim chancellor during his uncle's
lengthy illnesses and trips to Moscow. But Kochubei believed that
Russia could secure its interests in the Ottoman Empire by diplomatic means alone, and opposed the use of the fleet. As Paul's
policy became more warlike in 1798, Rostopchin's influence
superseded Kochubei's.[31]

RUSSIAN PREPARATION IN THE BLACK SEA

Problems were still to be solved in preparing the Russian Black
Sea fleet for action. A personal feud between Vice Admiral Ushakov, in command of the fleet, and Admiral Mordvinov, the area
commander, developed in early 1798 over supply procedures and
the priorities of defense of coastal ports; the Admiralty College,
headed by Kushelev, found Mordvinov negligent of duty and

---

30. In *Admiral Ushakov*, 2: 42.
31. Stanislavskaia, p. 95; M. A. Taube, *Vostochnyi vopros i avstro-
russkaia politika v pervoi polovine XIX stoletiia* (Petrograd, 1916), pp.
11–12.

recalled him to Saint Petersburg.[32] Although Ushakov then got his way in organizing the fleet, he was still handicapped by the limited quantity of men and ships available in the Black Sea area.

News of the French capture of Malta reached Saint Petersburg on 23 July and prompted the emperor's resolution to take more decisive action. The territory of the Ottoman Empire, and perhaps that of Russia, was now definitely endangered by a large French expeditionary force. An imperial ukaz immediately set 16,000 infantrymen in motion to form an army of observation on the Dniester River frontier that would be ready to march into Ottoman territory.[33] Charles Whitworth wrote enthusiastically on 24 July of the "laudable Resolution manifested by His Imperial Majesty, of stepping forth decidedly, and I trust effectually, for the Defense of the Common Cause."[34] And Paul told the British ambassador in a private audience a few days later, "The contest . . . in which I am about to be engaged, requires not only Courage, but even in a great Degree, Patience and Perseverance. I have weighted well my own Means, and those of every Kind of of the Enemy, and have turned the Matter too much in my mind not to be fully prepared."[35] If Whitworth reported correctly, this is a remarkable statement in view of later events. At another conference, on 2 August, when Paul stressed the need for more forces in the Mediterranean, Whitworth suggested a reinforcement of the Russian North Sea squadron in order that British ships could be freed for the Mediterranean. Immediately Vice Admiral Kartsov was ordered with five ships of the line and two frigates to sail for the North Sea to augment the fleet of Admiral Makarov, a kind of relay action to aid the Mediterranean.[36]

---

32. G. G. Kushelev to Paul, 2 July 1798, in *Admiral Ushakov*, 2: 48–49. Mordvinov was reinstated two years later.

33. Whitworth to Grenville, 24 July 1798, PRO, FO 65/40; and Dietrichstein to Thugut, 27 July 1798 (no. 37), HHSA, 88 Russland II Berichte.

34. Whitworth to Grenville, 24 July 1798, PRO, FO 65/40. He spoke to the Austrian envoy privately in the same tone. Dietrichstein to Thugut, 27 July 1798, HHSA, 88 Russland II Berichte.

35. Whitworth to Grenville, 31 July 1798, PRO, FO 65/40.

36. Whitworth to Grenville, 3 August and 6 August 1798, ibid.

Paul had made it plain to the Turks that Russian aid could be secured upon request, to help police Ottoman territory against rebellious pashas. The sultan so far had preferred to have his own subjects in revolt than to have Russian soldiers on Turkish soil. But then, a dispatch from Constantinople, received in Saint Petersburg by 5 August, indicated the Porte was now somewhat concerned over the French fleet in the eastern Mediterranean, as it well might be.[37] Information was received by Ushakov on 28 July from a passing merchant ship out of the Turkish capital that a large French fleet had been sighted off the coast of Crete headed for Egypt.[38] His report, sent on 30 July, that the French expedition was not directly threatening Russia probably did not reach Saint Petersburg before the decisive action was taken by Paul on 5 August ordering Ushakov to cruise near the Dardanelles, to communicate with Tomara in Constantinople, and, if the Porte requested assistance, to combine his ships with the Turkish fleet to fight the French.[39]

Upon receipt of this order at sea on 16 August, Ushakov returned to Sevastopol to make final preparations for his departure. A reserve fleet under Rear Admiral Ovtsyn, commandant of Odessa, was formed to patrol the Black Sea. The fact that Ushakov loaded a six-month stock of provisions aboard his fleet indicates that he expected to sail some distance. The Russian fleet set sail for the Straits on 24 August with six ships of the line, seven frigates, and three smaller ships, and arrived at the entrance of the Bosporus on 4 September.[40] Paul's order of 5 August dispatching a fleet of this size to the Straits before the arrival of a definite request for aid and before subsidy arrangements were

---

37. Ibid.; Bezborodko to S. R. Vorontsov, 9 August 1798, and Bezborodko to Panin, 26 August 1798, in *SIRIO* 17: 403, 407. See also Lanin, p. 28, and D. A. Miliutin, *Istoriia voiny mezhdu Rossiei i Frantsiei v tsarstvovanie Imperatora Pavla I b 1799 g.* (Saint Petersburg, 1852), 3: 65.

38. Ushakov to Paul, 30 July 1798, in *Admiral Ushakov*, 2: 52–53.

39. Paul to Ushakov, 5 August 1798, in *Arkhiv Mordvinovykh*, 1: 670.

40. Ushakov to Kushelev, 16 August 1798, and Ushakov to Tomara, 5 September 1798, ibid., in *Admiral Ushakov*, 2: 55, 77. See also V. P. Il'inskii, "Admiral F. F. Ushakov, k 100 letiiu so dnia smerti," *Morskoi Sbornik* 408 (April 1919): 86 ff.

approved by Britain demonstrates the emperor's resolve to act independently if necessary.

In Britain, too, events in the Mediterranean were watched closely. On 16 August, before news of Bonaparte's landing in Egypt had reached England, and on the very day Ushakov obtained his orders to sail, Pitt announced his support of a subsidy plan based on the 1796 proposals to Catherine.[41] Sir Mark Wood, who steadfastly advocated British acquisition of Malta, on the same date admitted the following sentiment in a letter to Henry Dundas, the secretary of war:

> Russia is the only power that can check Bonaparte's career, and I am convinced, that could we hold out any temptation to that wary nation, so as to induce her to enter cordially into the war, we should not only destroy the French projects towards the East, but speedily restore peace to Europe. The force of the Russian empire is enormous, and the only difficulty is that of bringing this great power into action.[42]

The reluctance of Russia to fight was being disproved at that very moment.

On 2 September 1798, a whole month after Nelson had crippled the French fleet off Abukir, the Ottoman government escorted the French chargé d'affaires, Ruffin, to the Seven Towers. Not so coincidental perhaps was the arrival at Constantinople a few days before of Lieutenant Tizenghausen, Ushakov's advance scout, with the information that the Russian fleet was approaching the Bosporus;[43] there in fact appears to be a direct correlation between the Ottoman break with France and the appearance of Russian naval support. The grand vizir assured Tomara of the sultan's desire to conclude an alliance, but the

---

41. The English agreed to pay Russia 225,000 pounds sterling initially and 75,000 a month for an army of 45,000. Stanislavskaia, p. 97; and Rear-Admiral H. W. Richmond, ed., *Private Papers of George, second Earl of Spencer, First Lord of the Admiralty, 1794–1801* (London, 1924), 3: 110.

42. *The Importance of Malta Considered in the Years 1796 and 1798* (London, 1803), p. 22.

43. Ushakov to Tizenghausen, 24 August 1798, in *Admiral Ushakov*, 2: 72; Z. Arkaz, "Deistviia chernomorskago flota s 1798 po 1806 g.," *Zapiski Odesskago Obshchestva Istorii i Drevnosti* 5 (1863): 848.

cautious Ushakov refused to enter the Bosporus without a written guarantee from the Turkish government of safe return to the Black Sea. A document to that purpose, promising safe passage for military and transport vessels of the Russian Empire in either direction through the Straits for the duration of the military alliance, was signed promptly on 5 September by Atif Efendi, the Ottoman foreign minister.[44] The sultan formally declared war on France on 9 September, the day after the first conference was held with his new ally.

Paul followed up his sailing order of 5 August to Ushakov with more detailed instructions, sent on 18 August after learning of the French landing at Alexandria. In this ukaz, received at Constantinople on 9 September, Paul instructed the admiral to coordinate his actions with the Turkish and British fleets, limited his expedition to go no further than "Egypt, Candia, the Morea, and the Venetian Gulf," and warned him, unnecessarily, to enter the Straits only after obtaining assurances from the Porte of safe return passage.[45] Malta, in which Paul had shown so much interest, was not named as an objective, and in regard to the destination decided upon it is interesting that Paul listed Egypt first and the Venetian Gulf last.

The emperor's ukaz did not make it very clear what the Russian fleet was to do in the Mediterranean, but there it was, anchored peacefully before the walls of Constantinople for the first time in history, a remarkable achievement for which most of the credit belongs to a French general and his Eastern ambitions and a Russian emperor's surprisingly strong reactions.

THE RUSSO-TURKISH ALLIANCE

Diplomatic arrangements still had to be completed. The Russian ambassador at Constantinople chiefly responsible for the nego-

---

44. Declaration of the Turkish government, 5 September 1798, in *Admiral Ushakov*, 2: 78.

45. Paul to Ushakov, 18 August 1798, in *Admiral Ushakov*, 2: 63–64; R. Skalovskii, *Zhizn' Admirala Fedora Fedorovicha Ushakova* (Saint Petersburg, 1856), p. 359; Il'inskii, p. 86.

tiations was Vasili Tomara, a rich Greek merchant and state servant from the Russian Black Sea coastal region who had aided Catherine and Potemkin in the annexation of the Crimea in 1783 and as a special agent in the Mediterranean in the second Turkish war, gaining considerable wealth in the process. He claimed to know the Turks well and made up for a lack of diplomatic skill with a liberal distribution of bribes, for which he was generally despised by the rest of the diplomatic colony in Constantinople.[46] As the engineer of the Russo-Turkish alliance, Tomara was the most powerful foreign envoy in the Turkish capital.

A military conference was held on 8 September with Ushakov, Kadir Bey (the commander of the Turkish fleet), Sir Sidney Smith (representing the British), Tomara, Atif Efendi, and other Turkish officials in attendance. They quickly reached an agreement for the union of the Russian and Turkish fleets and for their joint action in the Mediterranean under the command of the Russian admiral.[47] The negotiators, except for Smith, had little difficulty agreeing on a destination—the Ionian Islands. According to Ottoman intelligence sources, the French were putting together a reinforcing expedition for Egypt, or possibly for invading the Balkans, at Ancona in the Adriatic. The object of the allied expedition then was to liberate the Ionians from the French, thereby eliminating an active threat to the mainland and providing bases for a blockade of the Adriatic. Smith endeavored unsuccessfully to get the combined fleet to sail to Egypt in order to release Nelson for other duties, but only a squadron of ten gunboats and four frigates under Captain Sorokin was promised for Egypt.[48]

---

46. Commodore Sir W. Sidney Smith to Grenville, 10 January 1799, and Spencer Smith to Grenville, 1 February 1799, in *Dropmore*, 5: 437, 463. The British representative found Tomara "extremely disagreeable . . . not compensated for by the useful cooperation and never-failing reciprocity I had been so long habituated to by the gentleman's predecessor Kochubei, whose polished manners, elegant hospitality, and friendly confidence, I must confess rather spoiled one for the contrast of a cold *enigmatical* politician." Ibid. (underlining in original).

47. Ushakov to Paul, 9 September 1798, in *Admiral Ushakov*, 2: 81.

48. Ushakov to Paul, 11 September 1798, in *Admiral Ushakov*, 2: 85; Ushakov to Sorokin, 24 September 1798, ibid., p. 103.

The decision to send the main part of the fleet to the Ionians was made in Constantinople, but both Tomara and Ushakov were certainly aware of the strong reaction in Saint Petersburg to the French occupation of the islands. Tomara's previous contacts in that area, the fact that he was Greek, and his sense of Ottoman concern with Balkan unrest and in particular with the pro-French tendencies of Ali Pasha—all provided a useful bond of common interest for launching the joint campaign of formerly bitter enemies. Close coordination with the British was abhorrent to Ushakov, especially after Abukir eliminated his concern about French superiority and increased his jealousy of the British, and the idea of a completely independent campaign fairly certain of succcess must have appealed to the proud Russian naval commander. It should also be pointed out that the negotiators in Constantinople were aware of Nelson's victory, which was unknown in Saint Petersburg when the instructions had been sent, but unaware of Paul's suddenly escalated interest in Malta. (The details of Hompesch's so-called treason and the possibility of Paul's becoming grand master were realized in Saint Petersburg only about 25 August.) Russia was committed by Tomara and Ushakov to naval action in the Mediterranean with no consideration of Malta. Ushakov had no idea of the diplomatic hornet's nest he was getting into.

As soon as Ushakov united his fleet with the Turkish squadron he encountered problems. During an inspection tour on 12 September, he found the Turkish ships to be of the latest design and well constructed but very poorly manned. And already the Russians were faced with a shortage of money for supplies and for paying their own crews; the problem of provisioning was eased by the Turkish agreement to supply the combined fleet for the duration of the expedition.[49] After being delayed by contrary winds, the expedition sailed on 1 October for the Greek islands.

Negotiations to complete the treaty of alliance continued in Constantinople after the departure of the fleet, but the matter

---

49. Ushakov to Paul, 17 September 1798, ibid., p. 95.

of a subsidy for the Russian forces delayed the signing for another two months. Russian involvement in a European war, without aggressive plans of aggrandizement of her own, customarily required the receipt of a subsidy, but the sultan refused to comply. Since the British had agreed to pay a subsidy and the Turks were furnishing supplies, Paul resolved the matter to the satisfaction of the Porte, and the treaty was signed on 3 January 1799. Besides the military arrangements already mentioned, Russia agreed to furnish an army of 75,000 to 80,000 on land if requested. No direct subsidy was to be paid, but the Turks agreed to provide all the necessary provisions and military supplies for the Russian forces.[50]

The stipulations regarding passage of the Straits in articles 2, 3, and 4 of the treaty occasioned little trouble at the time. The Turks were apparently satisfied that the permission granted Russian warships to sail both ways through the Straits was only for the duration of the hostilities,[51] and Russia was not likely to challenge the Porte's jurisdiction over the Dardanelles when she was chiefly interested in strengthening Turkish defense of that area. Some of the Russian naval officers remained concerned about the possibility that the Black Sea fleet would be cut off in the Mediterranean, but Tomara procured additional assurances from the Porte that the fleet could return safely. The chance remained that if Turkey broke the alliance, the ships would not be able to return to the Black Sea, and Russian naval power in that area would thereby be weakened—an idea that must have occurred to both Russians and Turks. Strangely enough, a Russian fleet in the Mediterranean this time meant security to the Turks against Russian hostility. Following, and clearly subordinate to, the Russo-Turkish treaty, a separate Anglo-Turkish accord

---

50. Miliutin, 3: 79–80; G. A. Kleinman, "Russko-turetskii soiuz 1799 g.," *Doklady i Soobshcheniia istoricheskogo fakul'teta MGU*, 3 (1945): 19.

51. The treaty stipulated that this passage "must not serve as a right or cause to maintain at a future time free passage for warships through the Straits." Kleinman, p. 20. The full Russian text of the treaty was published by Miliutin and by Kleinman but is not generally available in translation. For a recent discussion of the Straits Question, see J. C. Hurewitz, "Russia and the Turkish Straits: A Reevaluation of the Origins of the Problem," *World Politics* 14 (July 1962): 605–32.

was signed; the British envoy was deeply upset by the Russian dominance of the negotiations.

The Russo-Turkish alliance marked the beginning of the war of the Second Coalition against France, and Russia entered the Napoleonic wars through the Straits. But an alliance between Russia and the Ottoman Empire seemed to be a shaky foundation for a European coalition. Despite traditional Ottoman fears of the Russians and Russian hatred of the Turks, the bond of common interest proved stronger than many observers expected and lasted longer than the coalition.

THE SECOND COALITION

During the winter of 1798–99 the major powers of Europe combined in a general alliance against France. Russia had begun with overtures to the Ottoman Empire. England and Austria followed up with united efforts to broaden Russia's involvement and to bolster Paul's mood for action. Although the governments in London and Vienna were able to exercise some influence on the negotiations, their ambassadors were given wide discretion to adhere to Russian demands. This rather loose arrangement for diplomacy was necessary to bring the alliance into being soon enough to be effective, but it was also to be a cause of the collapse of the coalition.

Paul posed as leader of the Second Coalition, and negotiations were conducted in Russia by Alexander Bezborodko (the chancellor), Victor Kochubei, Fedor Rostopchin, and Alexander Kurakin. Although there is no evidence that any of these men exercised a decisive influence, they calmed Paul's initial ardor and arranged many of the details.[52] Bezborodko remained in

---

52. Boris Mouravieff has presented the argument that Russian foreign policy, which he considers very sensible during this period, succeeded on the whole because the "mad" and "foreign" Paul was restrained by Catherinian, or even Elizabethan, trained officials such as Bezborodko, Vorontsov, and Suvorov, who were true Russians acting in the best national interests. This interpretation cannot be supported by the evidence of the correspondence of Whitworth, Cobenzl, and Serracapriola. See Mouravieff's *L'Alliance Russo-Turque au milieu des guerres Napoléoniennes* (Neuchâtel, 1954), pp. 67–74.

favor throughout this period, but his earlier influence was diminished by ill health and his cautious attitude toward Russian commitments abroad. Kochubei rose to prominence in the autumn of 1798 through his uncle's support and his enthusiasm for Paul's policy of friendship with Turkey and England, but he was disinclined toward war, in favor of internal reforms, and, therefore, unsuited to be Paul's foreign adviser. Rostopchin was a master of intrigue, a francophobe, and an advocate of war. The competition for Paul's favor encouraged these men to carry out his wishes.

Bezborodko's illness and his departure for Moscow in December did not slow negotiations for the general coalition in Saint Petersburg. The chancellor reappeared at court at the end of February, 1799, but it was obvious that his illness had been aggravated by the long trip, and he died on 17 April. Already in a letter of 13 March, Paul requested Simon Vorontsov to assume the office of chancellor, but the ambassador refused to leave London and even turned down an insistent second invitation.[53] During March and April 1799, foreign affairs were in the hands of the vice-chancellor, Alexander Kurakin, an influential courtier who was known for his pro-French views; understandably he failed to hold the emperor's confidence and was replaced briefly by Kochubei, who halfheartedly attempted to solidify the Second Coalition.[54] Kochubei was replaced in August 1799, by Nikita Petrovich Panin who was, in contrast with his predecessor, devoted to the coalition. Because of his youth, connections (Vorontsovs and Orlovs), and anti-Austrian sentiments, and because of his abilities, Panin held office for over a year through the period of greatest strain and final rupture of the alliance. Ironically, when Paul pursued a warlike attitude, his top advisers were against war, and when he decided to withdraw, his advisers advocated continued involvement. This may be an overgeneralization but it helps explain why the government

---

53. *SIRIO* 29: 423.
54. V. Teplov, *Russkie predstaviteli v Tsar'grade*, 1496–1891 (Saint Petersburg, 1891), p. 49.

leader who was most consistently concerned with foreign policy was Rostopchin, the man who was to become the center of historical controversy for his role in 1812 (Who burned Moscow?). Demonstrating a remarkable talent for following Paul's twists and turns, Rostopchin acted as Paul's secretary for foreign affairs, but he possessed little ability to guide foreign policy and was disliked by the allied representatives in Saint Petersburg.

Whitworth had become worried about the fate of Malta as early as 4 October 1798. His concern was seconded by the Foreign Office in London, which still maintained, however, that Britain had no intention of taking possession of the island but wished to see it restored to the Order of Malta, strengthened by the addition of British and Austrian *langues*.[55] Whitworth jumped to the conclusion that the Russian expedition to the Mediterranean was sent "with a view to participate in the Reduction of Malta; ... and it is no less obvious, that the Restitution of the Order new modelled, and under new political Restrictions is the Principle on which the Emperor acts."[56] Paul tried to put the English at ease with assurances that he had no political interest in Malta. After his election as grand master, Paul drew up a "Mémoire pour Angleterre" hoping to give complete satisfaction to Britain regarding the island, and promising its use to English shipping.[57]

In London Vorontsov adjusted to the new pro-Turkish, anti-French attitude of the tsar; he wrote with a touch of sarcasm to Grenville on 7 October 1798: "I have always liked these good Turks, and I like them more and more since they are behaving themselves so well. They are behaving in a manner to cause their Apostolic and Catholic Majesties to blush. God bless these good 'Musselmans.' "[58] Wanting to keep more abreast of events than

---

55. Whitworth to Grenville, 4 October 1798, and Grenville to Whitworth, 5 October 1798, PRO, FO 65/41.
56. Whitworth to Grenville, 10 October 1798, PRO, FO 65/41.
57. Paul I, "Mémoire pour Angleterre," enclosure, Whitworth to Grenville, 13 December 1798, PRO, FO 65/41.
58. Vorontsov to Grenville, 7 October 1798, in *Dropmore*, 4: 338.

he could by his own communications from Saint Petersburg, Vorontsov begged Grenville for permission to read Grenville's correspondence from Constantinople.[59] Tomara was not keeping Vorontsov as well informed as Kochubei had done.

The major difficulty in forming the Second Coalition was reconciling Austria and Russia. Paul still held Austria responsible for the situation in the Mediterranean after Campoformio, and he was perhaps justified in his suspicion that Austria had intentionally turned France toward the Mediterranean in order to retain the Austrian Netherlands. But in the summer of 1798 Paul gave a warm reception to a special Habsburg envoy, Prince Ferdinand of Württemburg, whose mission was to influence Paul through his sister, the Empress Maria Fedorovna. Paul told Ferdinand at the end of July, "It seems to me that it is about time that I acted not only as an auxiliary but with all of my forces."[60]

The regular Austrian ambassador, Ludwig Cobenzl, returned to Saint Petersburg in August with the rather unsavory reputation as the co-architect of Campoformio, but he had special instructions to appease Paul. In late September the first attempts to coordinate supply of the Russian observation army on the frontier produced the first of a long series of frictions that were to plague Austro-Russian relations throughout Paul's reign. Cobenzl's offer on 5 October to furnish Austrian troops to the Russian fleet for the liberation of the Ionians seems to have flattered Paul, though the offer was turned down in favor of local troops.[61] Subsequent zig-zags of Austro-Russian relations are too complicated to follow here, but one of the first episodes concerned the Ionian Islands. According to a story originating in Trieste and circulating in Saint Petersburg in early November, Austria had authorized the inhabitants of Corfu and the other "islands

---

59. Vorontsov to Grenville, 6 October 1798, and 13 November 1798, ibid., 4: 338, 375, and Vorontsov to Tomara, 23 October 1798, ibid., 11: 311.

60. Prince Ferdinand to Dietrichstein, 31 July 1798, HHSA, 89 Russland II Berichte.

61. Cobenzl to Thugut, 3 and 5 October 1798, ibid.

of the Levant" to raise the Austrian flag and become Austrian subjects. Paul snubbed Cobenzl at court and remarked to Whitworth and Serracapriola, making certain that Cobenzl would hear, "Did you know that our neighbors would like to seize the Islands of the Levant?"[62]

One interesting effect of the Austrian flag affair was Paul's idea of a declaration to be signed by all members of the coalition promising that they would not retain any islands in the Mediterranean that were liberated from the French. Although ultimately forgotten, this "modern" suggestion was the embryo of the nonannexation provision of the Anglo-Russian protocol on Malta in December.

Other factors already in existence before Suvorov crossed the border prevented close relations—such as Tomara's complaints about the conduct of the Austrian representative at Constantinople and Paul's unhappiness with Razumovsky, his own ambassador at Vienna—but Austria repeatedly apologized and bowed to the tsar's wishes, and Cobenzl continued to warn Thugut, the Austrian chancellor, about Paul's special interest in the Order of Malta, the Ionian Islands, and Italy.[63]

Anglo-Russian cooperation reached a new peak in December, 1798, with the signing of the Convention of Saint Petersburg, which provided for a large British subsidy (£225,000 initially and £75,000 for each month) to offset the cost of two separate expeditionary armies, one of 45,000 for a joint invasion of Holland, another of 60,000 for an Austro-Russian campaign in northern Italy. A separate agreement stipulated that the island of Malta was to be occupied upon its capitulation by garrisons from three powers—Britain, Russia, and Naples—and that a

---

62. Cobenzl to Thugut, 6 November 1798, ibid.

63. An illustration of Austrian willingness to give way on Maltese questions is contained in Thugut to Cobenzl, 26 November 1798, HHSA, 89 Russland II Berichte. Cobenzl complained that other ambassadors, namely Whitworth, Serracapriola, and Litta, were more successful in taking advantage of Paul's predilections, and he even blamed Razumovsky's recall on them. He also believed, however, that their efforts would ultimately boomerang. Cobenzl to Thugut, 17 February 1799, HHSA, 90 Russland II Berichte.

formal joint protectorate was to be established over the island for the Order of Saint John.[64]

Paul's unselfishness in not asking for any direct territorial compensation for Russia impressed Whitworth, who, realizing the tenor of some contrary opinions in England, offered the following advice to Grenville:

> It is possible that in the opinion of many who are not conversant with the character of the Emperor of Russia, the assumption of the dignity of Grand Master may be construed into a desire of obtaining a preponderance on the Mediterranean. I think I can venture to assure Your Lordship that this is by no means the case. I believe most sincerely that if we were to offer Him the Sovereignty of the Island, he would refuse it without the least hesitation, indeed I am fully persuaded of it. It is simply to His high flown notion of Chivalry, a subject on which His ideas go sometimes beyond enthusiasm that His conduct is to be imputed.[65]

Paul even pressed Vorontsov on 30 December to demand that Britain fulfill her part of the agreement by sending to Malta a force equal to the Russian division of three battalions of grenadiers and several artillery batteries destined for that island.[66]

The Anglo-Russian treaty of 29 December 1798 formed the basis of the military cooperation against France in 1799. Joint military arrangements were already in existence in the Mediterranean—Anglo-Turkish forces (with nominal Russian naval support) in Egypt and Russo-Turkish in the Ionians. Encouraged by these combinations and by British military successes and diplomatic influence, the kingdom of Naples prematurely began action on the continent with General Mack's occupation of Rome

---

64. George Frederic de Martens, ed., *Recueil des principaux traités d'alliance,* . . . vol. 6: 1795–1799 (Göttingen, 1829), pp. 556–61. The first official treaty of the coalition was that between Russia and the Kingdom of the Two Sicilies, signed on 10 December 1798, but the terms of the treaty with the Ottoman Porte had been negotiated in September and October and ratified by Paul before 10 December. Ibid., pp. 524, 532.

65. Whitworth to Grenville, 25 January 1799, PRO, FO 65/42.

66. Paul to S. R. Vorontsov, 30 December 1798, in *Arkhiv Vorontsova,* 10: 249.

on 29 November 1798. A French counterattack under General Championnet recaptured the city on 15 December and went on to overrun the mainland part of the kingdom, forcing the Neapolitan court to flee to Sicily. The immediate adherence by Naples to the Anglo-Russian convention saddled the coalition with a badly crippled ally.

On the positive side, however, British and Neapolitan policy makers endeavored both in Vienna and Saint Petersburg to achieve a reconciliation between Russia and Austria. Grenville suspected that Whitworth was adhering to Paul's anti-Austrian feelings and delivered a reprimand to that effect.[67] These efforts convinced Paul that in order to deal an immediate blow to France, Austrian cooperation was essential, especially since Prussia insisted on remaining neutral. In Vienna the possibility of using Russia's military might to recoup Austrian loss of prestige and territory in the wars appeared attractive. The vulnerability of France, caused by overextension in the Near East, and the defeat of Naples, which brought all of Italy under French control, were the primary factors in the successful completion of arrangements for the sending of a Russian expeditionary army to Italy. The appointment of the venerable Suvorov as commander added prestige to the campaign and raised the morale of Austria's field armies. Though Austria participated in military planning and adhered to the coalition from the beginning of January 1799, she did not formally break with France until the rupture of the Rastadt Congress in April, by which time Suvorov had already passed through Vienna on his way to command the Austro-Russian armies in northern Italy. The coalition, now including Russia, Britain, the Ottoman Empire, the kingdom of Naples, and Austria, prepared for war on three fronts—in the eastern Mediterranean, in Italy, and in the Netherlands.[68]

The affairs of the Order of Malta provided a colorful, shifting backdrop to the negotiations in Saint Petersburg. Since the

---

67. Grenville to Whitworth, 25 January 1799, PRO, FO 65/42.
68. For the Anglo-Russian expedition to North Holland consult A. B. Rodger, *The War of the Second Coalition, 1789–1801: A Strategic Commentary* (London, 1964), pp. 176–94.

ratification of the original convention with the order had been received in November 1797, Paul often wore the Maltese regalia at court ceremonies. At the end of March 1798, Bezborodko announced that Paul had taken the order under his special protection,[69] and during the summer the sumptuous Vorontsov palace in Saint Petersburg was presented to the Russian priory for its home. Contrary to the view presented in most general histories, however, it was the French occupation of the Ionian Islands and the directing of a large French expedition to the eastern Mediterranean, not the French capture of Malta, that brought the Russian fleet into action and Emperor Paul into the Second Coalition.

Arrangements for the coalition went hand in hand with Paul's involvement with the Order of Malta. In September and October, Litta and a few other knights, under the auspices of the Russian priory, engineered the election of Paul as grand master, officially proclaimed on 7 November. Paul accepted on 24 November and was formally invested on 10 December. At the ceremony the new grand master issued a manifesto creating ninety-eight new commanderies for Russian Orthodox nobles with Russian state funds; these were constituted a separate Russian Orthodox priory on 8 January 1799, and four days later, on New Year's Day by the old calendar, the Maltese flag was raised above the Admiralty and given a thirty-three-gun salute. On the same day Paul created an honor guard of sixty knights under command of "Vice Admiral" Litta.[70]

In order to speed the formation of the coalition, Austria relented on matters concerning the knights. Hompesch, who had sought refuge on Austrian territory, was held in a virtual state of arrest; the remaining treasures of the order, mostly religious relics rescued by Hompesch, were transferred to Saint Petersburg in token recognition of Paul's status as grand master.[71] Paul was

---

69. Dietrichstein to Thugut, 30 March 1798, 88 Russland II Berichte.
70. Maisonneuve, p. 213; Antoshevskii, pp. 47–48.
71. The Maltese relics, including a finger of John the Baptist and a piece of the cross, remained in Russia until 1917. They were saved by Empress Marie and bequeathed by her to the Yugoslavian royal family. They dis-

so satisfied with the Austrian response that he deferred to
request of Archduke Joseph to retain Razumovsky as ambassade
after he had already been recalled. The disgrace of Litta was
then completed by Razumovsky's disclosure to Rostopchin of
the contents of papal dispatches forwarded through Vienna in
March 1799. Whitworth, who had tried to win Litta—probably
with money as he had tried with others—but had failed, was
happy to see him go.[72] Ironically, the man who had done so much
to introduce Paul to the Knights of Malta was now removed.

Paul, in addition to the religious projects he may have harbored
for the future, was using his position in the order to implicate
himself permanently in the affairs of the Mediterranean. In case
any knights felt doubts (and even those in Saint Petersburg must
have wondered) about the alliance of their grand master with
the Ottoman Empire, the age-old enemy of the order, they were
put at ease by Maisonneuve in his official history published by
the Imperial Press in 1799: "We believe it would be useful at
the beginning of our work to destroy the error too often accred-
ited that the Religion of Malta by its principles must be in a
perpetual state of war with the Turks and cannot conclude
peace with them."[73]

---

appeared completely during World War II. Michel de Taube, *L'Empereur
Paul Ier de Russie, Grand Maître de l'Ordre de Malte*, pp. 66–67.

72. Whitworth to Grenville, 29 March 1799, PRO, FO 65/42.

73. Maisonneuve, p. 8.

4

A Mediterranean Protectorate

The honor of commanding the Russo-Turkish expedition which sailed west from Constantinople toward the Aegean on 1 October fell to Vice Admiral Fedor Fedorovich Ushakov, a shy, roughly-educated Russian who had achieved fame as a scourge of the Turks in Catherine's second Turkish war. But now he had dined in the sultan's palace and was endearingly hailed by his new friends as "Pasha-Ushak."

Ushakov spoke only Russian, but there were a few young Russian officers in the fleet like Captain Dmitri Seniavin who were conversant with foreign tongues. In addition, several non-Russian officers such as Klopakis, Alexiano, and Metaxa (Greek), and Messer and Baillie (British) were to be of considerable value serving in liaison capacities between the Russians and their allies and the local populations.[1] Although the fleet was not adequately prepared for the scope of the foreign enterprises in which it was soon to be involved, Ushakov was fortunate in having experienced officers and crews, who were probably among the best seamen Russia had yet produced. Most of the Russian ships were veterans of the last Turkish war, but a few like Ushakov's eighty-four-gun flagship the *St. Paul* were quite new. All of the capital Russian

---

1. Z. Arkaz, "Deistviia Chernomorskago flota s 1798 po 1806 g.," *Zapiski Odesskago Obshchestva Istoriia i Drevnostei*, V (Odessa, 1863), 848.

ships—six ships of the line, seven frigates, and three brigs suffered from hasty construction, because the construction of warships for the Black Sea was a recent development and a regular naval program had not been established. Ships had been built when needed, but since their use was more or less temporary, they were not kept fit for immediate service. For example, copper sheathing for the lower portion of the hulls, necessary for extended sailing in warm waters, had been applied, hastily and crudely, to only a few of Ushakov's ships.[2]

On the other hand, the Turkish ships in the united fleet, approximately equal in number and size to the Russian ships, were of the most recent French design and construction.[3] Kadir Bey, the commander of the Turkish fleet and second in command of the expedition, lived in regal splendor aboard his flagship and stayed out of action as much as possible. He was generally disliked by his officers, some of whom were Greeks who needed interpreters to relay orders to the Turkish seamen. Although the crews by most accounts consisted of poorly trained, undisciplined sailors, they could fight well when there were spoils to gain.[4]

Since Nelson's victory had disposed of most of the French fleet, the Russians and Turks under Ushakov's command were expecting easy progress and were glad to see the mouth of the Dardanelles disappear behind them and to rendezvous a few days later at the picturesque island of Hydra. From there a squadron sailed to Egypt by way of Rhodes, as arranged in Constantinople, while the main fleet set off for the Ionians. Ushakov sent ahead to the islands proclamations calling upon the people to overthrow the French garrisons. One proclamation in Paul's name flattered the Greek inhabitants with concern for their own

2. V. L. Snegirev, *Admiral Ushakov (ocherk zhizni i deiatel'nostei velikogo russkogo flotovodtsa)* (Moscow, 1945), pp. 105–8; Al. Sorokin, "Morskiia kampanii 1798 i 1799 gg.," *Zapiski Gidrograficheskago Departamenta Morskago Ministerstva* 8 (1850): 280.

3. R. Skalovskii, *Zhizn' Admirala Feodora Feodorovicha Ushakova* (Saint Petersburg, 1856), pp. 239–40.

4. B. V. Modzalevskii, ed., *Pis'ma morskogo ofitsera P. I. Panafidena* (Petrograd, 1916), pp. 71–72.

are and promised them a government of their own choosing, ...nting strongly that the Ragusan Republic might be used as a model. A second proclamation on behalf of the other ally was in the form of a bull from the patriarch of Constantinople calculated to stir up religious sentiment against the French.[5] It was indeed a sign of the unusual times that the absolutist tsar of Russia advocated a republic and the Turkish sultan backed a call for renewed Christian fervor!

THE IONIAN ISLANDS

The Ionian Islands form a long chain of seven large islands— Corfu, Cephalonia, Zante, Santa Maura (Leucas), Ithaca, Paxo, and Cerigo (Cythera)—and a number of smaller ones off the western and southern coast of the Greek peninsula, with a total population in 1798, of just over 200,000, about the same number as in the mid-twentieth century.[6] For many years before

---

5. Emmanuel Rodocanachi, *Bonaparte et les îles Ioniennes: un épisode des conquêtes de la République et du Premier Empire (1797–1816)* (Paris, 1899), p. 120; Giorgio Paulini, *Memorie Storiche sulla fondazione della repubblica Ionica ossia della sette isole unite* (Italia, 1802), p. 13; Nicolas Bulgari, *Les Sept-Iles Ioniennes et les 'traités qui les concernent* (Leipzig, 1859), pp. 5–6; and Ermano Lunzi, *Storia della Isole Ionie sotto il reggimento dei repubblicani francesi* (Venice, 1860), pp. 163–65. Ragusa (present-day Dubrovnik) was an independent commercial republic along the Dalmatian coast which acknowledged the suzerainty of the Porte. Because of the time involved in communications between Saint Petersburg and Constantinople, it would seem unlikely that the idea of the Ragusan Republic could be credited to Paul, but the emperor was familiar with the government and history of Ragusa; in July he had expressed concern over the fate of the republic, but the first recorded indication that he considered using it as a model for the Ionians was in early November. Cobenzl to Thugut, 6 November 1798, HHSA, 89 Russland II Berichte. Tomara should be credited with the responsibility for the proclamations, though it is quite possible that Peter Fonton, an ex-French diplomat in Constantinople who had just joined Russian service, had a hand in it.

6. A questionable French census of 1798 lists 242,300, a figure probably inflated for home consumption. Other contemporary estimates range from 200,000 to 220,000. The population in 1960 was 212,573, not counting the mainland enclaves. The area, population, and dates of Venetian occupation of the largest islands are as follows: Corfu—229 square miles, 97,412 and 1368; Cephalonia—300 square miles, 39,790, and 1479; Zante—157

1797 these islands had been ruled by Venice. Widely scat
along the coast, the islands developed along separate lines, rela
in racial, linguistic, and economic characteristics to the adjacen
mainland, yet distinct and separate from it and from each other.
While poor and neglected Cerigo, farthest south, was more
isolated and more sparsely settled than the others and used
chiefly as a refuge by pirates raiding the commerce of the eastern
Mediterranean, Zante, off the Morea, had an especially rich and
well-developed economy based on the export of dried currants,
mainly to England. Corfu, the most populous and the northern-
most of the islands, was dominated by olive plantations established by the Venetians, and exported large quantities of oil to
central Europe.[7] Economically, the Ionians represented one of
the few territories of the Mediterranean which could realize an
immediate profit to the controlling authority, providing there was
little interference in the established pattern of trade. Strategically,
the Ionians were also much more important than today; a fleet
based there could control the entrance to the Adriatic and cruise
over much of the Mediterranean. The Ionians' potential as a
base for political activity in the Balkans had been realized by
Bonaparte, then by the Turks and Russians. Under Venice the
Ionians were quiet and harmless, but occupied by a great power,
the islands could affect the stability of the whole Balkan Peninsula and the eastern Mediterranean. Today in the quiet, haunt-
ingly beautiful countryside, in the bustling towns, or along the
rocky coasts of these islands one can easily discover historical
evidence—a Venetian palazzo, a French esplanade, a rusting
Russian cannon—of the drama of change and continuity. Beginning in 1797 the Ionians were subjected to a series of shocks
which were to be surpassed only by the destruction wrought by
the Second World War and the 1953 earthquake.

---

square miles, 35,499, and 1470; and Santa Maura (Leucas)—114 square
miles, 26,970 and 1699. *Columbia Encyclopedia*, 3d. ed. (1963). The
largest town by far was Corfu with about 19,000 inhabitants in 1798 (24,-
000 in 1960). Raymond Matton, *Corfou* (Villes et paysages de Grèce:
collection de l'Institut français d'Athènes) (Athens, 1960), pp. 115–16.
For atmosphere, see Lawrence Durell, *Prospero's Cell.*

7. Matton, pp. 116–25.

ʌst came the French, in June 1797. The Treaty of Campo-ʌmio sanctioned the division of the Venetian Republic between Austria and France, with Bonaparte gaining his much-desired beachhead in the Ionian Islands and their continental enclaves. From there he could launch an attack on the Middle East, influence the neighboring areas of unrest in the Balkans, or cover a flank while the main effort went in a different direction. Bonaparte attached much value to the possession of these eastern outposts for France, as we have seen, but the French appearance in this area caused considerable alarm in distant Saint Petersburg.

The islanders, who had been economically exploited as inhabitants of the richest colony of the declining Venetian Republic, at first welcomed the French as liberators. A mood of anticipation prevailed on the islands in advance of the young Jacobin officers and administrators, who came, they claimed, to bestow the benefits of French culture and administrative efficiency upon the "backward" islanders. The leading church official presented the French commander with a copy of Homer, trees of liberty were planted, delegations were sent to Paris, token public improvements were made, and new schools were started.[8] But the territory was incorporated into the French Republic, irrespective of the wishes of the inhabitants, and taxes were raised, so that after more than a year of "enlightened" French government, the Greek residents almost unanimously welcomed a chance of liberation by the Russo-Turkish fleet.

The French occupation of the Ionians provided an early example of the difficulty of exporting revolution. French expectations of finding a solid base of pro-French sentiment in the towns proved premature. The former Venetian aristocracy, originally Italian but by this time predominantly of Greek blood, controlled the economic life of the islands. The nobles were divided into rival factions or families, while the peasants, still largely ignorant of social movements, were devoted to family and church life in their poor but neat villages. The peasants usually supported

---

8. Lunzi, pp. 48–50.

different aristocratic factions as much for their own l rivalries as for the interests of the landlords. The French r propaganda found a receptive audience only among the siza number of Jews, who earned meager livings as artisans and small traders in the larger towns.[9] Perhaps because they were too confident of the superiority of their own progressive culture, the classically-minded French underestimated the Greek religious intensity and were unable to gain general support among the population. The "trees of liberty" planted by the French withered and died in the rocky Ionian soil.

When the expedition to Egypt was launched from Toulon in 1798, the French garrison at once tightened its control over the islands. Restrictions on trade were increased to prevent any ships under Russian or British flags from trading or using the islands as bases. The British and Russian consuls-general were arrested in July 1798, detained briefly, and then deported to Venice.[10] The small French garrisons on the less important islands had little hope of defending themselves against a sizable naval force; some were evacuated to assist in the defense of the larger islands. For the defense of the large, rambling fortresses at Corfu there was a garrison of about 2,000 militia, augmented by a naval squadron consisting of the *Généreux*—one of the few major warships to escape Nelson off the coast of Egypt—a battered, captured English frigate, the *Leander*, and a small brig, the *Brune*.[11] The French were assisted by about 300 local inhab-

---

9. J. B. Bellaire, *Précis des opérations générales de la division française du Levant chargée, pendant les années V, VI, et VII, de la défense des îles et possessions ex-vénitiennes de la mer Ionienne, formant aujourd'hui la République des Sept-Iles* (Paris, an XIII (1805)), p. 370. There were about 2,000 Jews in the town of Corfu (10 percent of the population).

10. Foresti to Grenville, 24 August 1798, PRO, FO 42/3.

11. The number of French defenders varies widely in the sources. Most Western accounts based on French records place the number just under 2,000, while Russian works, from firsthand accounts to later reports, both imperial and Soviet, based on those same accounts, claim that the garrison was about 3,000. A more complete examination of this and other Ionian problems has been made by James L. McKnight, "Admiral Ushakov and the Ionian Republic; the Genesis of Russia's First Balkan Satellite" (University of Wisconsin Ph.D. Thesis, 1965).

mostly Jews, in serving the 600 old, rusty, Venetian ᴐn.

Relying on information obtained at Constantinople, Ushakov believed that the French garrison was much larger and that a large land assault force would be required to capture the main islands. He did not press his attack on Corfu at once, thus giving the French more time to improve their defenses and to stock supplies for a lengthy siege. On 5 October the French commander on the island of Cerigo was attending a ball when he received the news of the approach of the Russo-Turkish fleet. The small garrison of approximately one hundred, only half of whom were French, put up a token resistance to a small squadron dispatched in advance by Ushakov and then surrendered on the twelfth to the magnanimous terms offered by the Russian commander over Turkish objections: the French soldiers were allowed to sail to Toulon promising only never to fight the Russians or Turks again.[12] The first action of Russian arms in the Napoleonic wars turned out to be a very polite and simple affair.

The strategy employed at Cerigo was followed for the other islands; squadrons were sent from the main fleet to engage the enemy and, if possible, to complete the occupation. On Zante the inhabitants, having been disappointed that their chief crop, currants, could no longer be sold to Britain because of French trade restrictions, rose to arms upon learning of the approach of the Russian fleet and forced the small garrison to surrender. The Turks took charge of these unfortunate prisoners, of whom many died on the cruel overland journey to Constantinople.

Cephalonia, the largest of the islands in area, fell easily since most of the fortresses had been abandoned by the French. A smaller island close to the mainland, Santa Maura, was better fortified, and its garrison, reinforced from Cephalonia and the mainland town of Prevesa, was at first able to hold out against the uncoordinated attacks of Captain Seniavin's squadron and Ali Pasha's irregular Greek and Albanian forces. Russian rein-

---

12. Paul Pisani, "L'Expédition russo-turque aux îles ionniennes en 1798–1799," *Revue d'histoire diplomatique* 2 (1888): 209.

forcements soon brought about a capitulation that was undoubtedly abetted by the desire of both the French and the inhabitants to avoid falling into the hands of the Albanians.

ALI PASHA

While virtually ruling a large portion of western Greece and Albania, Ali Pasha had already achieved fame for his daring and bloody military exploits.[13] Confined to the mountainous interior, where he maintained a court at Janina and launched plundering expeditions against the Suliot villages, Ali developed quite a talent for intrigue and double-dealing. With the collapse of Venice the pasha's interest was drawn toward the west and the possibility of realizing his ambition of annexing a commercial outlet on the coast. This augmentation would give Ali a greater degree of independence and possibly recognition by the great powers. He was at first receptive to French overtures, but when the French would not meet his price immediately, he remained loyal to the sultan, and in the summer of 1798 Ali was fighting in the northeast against the rebellious Pasvan-oglu, missing by his absence a special emissary from General Bonaparte who came to Janina to treat for Ali's support.[14]

With the rebels thrown back, Ali rushed back to his home territories with a firman from the sultan to assist the Russo-Turkish expedition. After dallying for a while with a French

---

13. See F. C. H. L. Pouqueville, M.D., *Travels through the Morea, Albania, and several other parts of the Ottoman Empire to Constantinople during the years 1798, 1799, 1800, and 1801 . . .* (London, 1806), pp. 28–36 *et passim,* for an excellent contemporary survey of the domains of Ali and the other pashas. Tarle (pp. 67–76) sums up the Russian attitude toward Ali Pasha and recounts the events of the Battle of Santa Maura. See also Ushakov to Paul, 1 November 1798, in *Admiral Ushakov,* 2: 141.

14. Pouqueville describes Janina as the most industrious town in Greece with a population of 40,000. A good biography of the amazing pasha has not been published in English. An old and popular description based mainly on Bellaire and Pouqueville is A. de Beauchamp, *The Life of Ali Pacha of Jannina, late Vizier of Epirus surnamed Aslan, or the Lion,* 2d ed. (London, 1823). The best and most recent treatment is by G. L. Arsh, *Albaniia i Epir v kontse XVIII-nachale XIX v.* (Moscow, 1963).

agent from Corfu, Ali sent him in irons to Constantinople. He then sought to take advantage of both French and Russian weakness on land to seize the disputed towns of Prevesa and Butrinto along the coast, and some of the islands if possible, for his own ends. The continental enclaves, belonging originally to the Venetian Ionian colony but ceded to the French at Campoformio, were particularly vulnerable. Prevesa was taken by Ali with brutal consequences to the French defenders and inhabitants. During a friendly reception at Ali's capital in November the Russian emissary, Lieutenant Metaxa, received a promise of troops to participate in the siege of Corfu.[15] But the scheming pasha was looking to his own interest first, a fact that the Russians were soon to realize.

THE SIEGE OF CORFU

The main Russo-Turkish fleet arrived in the channel separating Corfu from the mainland on 20 November to await a promised army of 12,000 sailing from the Black Sea and to begin the first attack on the fortresses of Corfu since the celebrated but unsuccessful Turkish siege of 1716. A blockade of the island was first established to prevent reinforcements from reaching the French garrison. Contacts were at once made with leading nobles to provide local support for the siege—and soon only the fortresses of the town were still in French hands.

The Russian military venture in the Mediterranean had now achieved a scope of some international complexity. Besides the

---

15. Ali had hurried back to negotiate with General Rose at Janina, but he dragged out the discussions until he was certain that Corfu would fall to the expedition. General Guillaume de Vaudoncourt, *Memoirs of the Ionian Islands . . . including the Life and Character of Ali Pacha*, trans. William Walton (London, 1816), p. 243. The Russian emissary reported that Ali respected Ushakov for his earlier victories over the Turks but did not understand his meddling in "internal affairs" concerning the mainland towns of Prevesa, Parga, Vonitsa, and Butrinto. The Albanian pasha had a fond memory of Potemkin: "There was a man! He valued me." Ali emphasized that Ushakov should send rich presents as Potemkin did. Egor Metaksa, "Ali Pasha," *Syn Otechestva*, no. 42 (12 October 1820), pp. 63–66, and no. 43 (19 October 1820), pp. 101–3.

main antagonists—Russians, Albanians, Turks, French, and Greeks—British, Austrian, and Neapolitan envoys were on hand as observers. All were interested in the fate of the islands, and occupation plans materialized from every quarter. Ushakov's diplomatic talents, later to be praised by Soviet historians, were put severely to test by the presence of allied representatives, who had never been a problem in the admiral's previous naval experience in the Black Sea. Now he simply ignored them as much as possible.

The British naval command viewed the Russians with disdain from the beginning. Nelson had wanted to keep them out of the Mediterranean altogether: "Malta, Corfu, and those Islands are my object after Egypt, and therefore I hope that the Russian fleet will be kept in the East; for if they establish themselves in the Mediterranean, it will be a bad thorn in the side of the Porte."[16] On 9 October, the day that Cerigo fell to the Russians, Nelson drafted a proclamation, to be distributed to all of the islands, calling upon the inhabitants to drive out the French and to raise the British flag, thereby coming under the protection of his fleet, and promising that "no contribution or any thing like a Tax will be asked."[17] Lieutenant Woodhouse was sent with an armed transport to gather intelligence and to negotiate with the French for the release of the crew of the *Leander*. Arriving at Corfu several days before Ushakov, Woodhouse was forced to wait to confer with the Russian admiral before successfully completing his mission. In the meantime Nelson ordered Captain Troubridge, his most trusted lieutenant, to occupy the islands, but before he could sail, a report was received that the Russians were already there.[18] On 12 December Nelson, obvi-

---

16. Nelson to J. Spencer Smith, 7 October 1798, in *The Dispatches and Letters of Vice Admiral Lord Viscount Nelson*, ed. Sir Nicholas Harris Nicholas (London, 1845), 3: 145–46. See also A. E. Sokol, "Nelson and the Russian Navy," *Military Affairs* 13 (1949): 130–32.

17. "Admiral Nelson to the Inhabitants of Corfu, Cephalonia, Zante, and Serrigo," BM, Add. MSS. 34,907, f. 396.

18. Woodhouse's report to Troubridge, BM, Add. MSS. 34,908, ff. 413–18; Nelson to Troubridge, 11 November 1798, in *Dispatches and Letters of Nelson*, 3: 169.

ously piqued that the Russians had beaten him to the Ionians, greeted the Russian admiral by vainly requesting his assistance on the Egyptian coast: "Egypt is the first object—Corfu the second." He repeated this view in a letter to Kadir Bey on the seventeenth: "I was in hopes, Sir, that a part of the united Turkish and Russian Squadron would have gone to Egypt— the first object of the Ottoman arms: Corfu is a secondary consideration."[19] Nelson was now busy evacuating the Neapolitan court to Palermo, but Spiridion Foresti, the British consul-general at Corfu, stayed aboard the Turkish flagship during the siege and did everything in his power to make it appear a joint Anglo-Russo-Turkish operation.[20]

Cooperation between the Russians and Turks was difficult, and effective coordination of the siege weathered increasing friction only thanks to the good humor of the Turkish admiral and the patience of Ushakov. Kadir Bey, though blaming Ushakov for lack of action, anchored his ship to the rear far out of range of gunfire and kept his own polished guns quiet in order to avoid breaking the extensive collection of priceless crystal that decorated his luxurious cabin; there he lavishly entertained various visiting dignitaries, much to the exasperation of the Russians.[21] The Russian command also experienced long delays in securing the promised supplies and troops from the mainland. It was not an easy task for Ushakov to maintain friendly relations with a traditionally hostile power at such close working quarters.

Militarily, the Russian fleet was at its best in such a siege. The ships were equipped with the best Russian cannon, heavier and

---

19. Nelson to Ushakov, 12 December 1798, and Nelson to Kadir Bey, 17 December 1798, in *Dispatches and Letters of Nelson*, 3: 198, 204.

20. Foresti to Grenville, 14 January 1799, PRO, FO 42/3. The English consul-general was unimpressed with the Russian admiral's diplomatic talents: "I lament that I have to mention another circumstance contributory to the firmness of the French. This is the temper of Vice Admiral Ushakov. With many truly estimable qualities such as courage and zeal in the service of His Sovereign, he cannot be said to possess much conciliatory talent, nor much of that species of policy so necessary to the attainment of the good will of the islanders."

21. Pouqueville, p. 107; Bellaire, pp. 349–51, 356–58.

more powerful than those normally used in Western ships. Already the floating-fortress theory of naval strategy, as later defined at A. T. Mahan, was employed in the Russian Black Sea fleet. There were handicaps, however. The heavy guns tended to make the ships top-heavy and harder to handle in the storms that swept along the Greek coast in winter, and the recoil of the guns, especially when fired in salvos, tended to loosen the ships' timbers.[22] Moreover, the practice of Russian gunnery in firing regular barrages allowed the French to take cover during each barrage.

While conducting a haphazard siege and waiting for land reinforcements, Ushakov received orders to send patrolling squadrons along the Adriatic coast and this caused further interference with siege plans. Ushakov lacked the means and the will to coordinate from Corfu with allied agents and parties, and in these circumstances was forced to use more of his time and equipment than necessary to investigate reports of a French build-up at Ancona that might be intended to relieve either Corfu or Egypt. A half-hearted French attempt to reinforce the garrison of Corfu was cut off successfully, but the *Généreux* succeeded in escaping the harbor of Corfu on the night of 5–6 February.[23] The prodding of the Neapolitan minister of war, Micheroux, who had arrived at Corfu from Italy on 19 February to request urgent Russian assistance for Naples, finally succeeded in getting Ushakov to mount a more sustained attack.[24] The long delay usually blamed on Ushakov's lack of initiative or intelligence was actually caused by his belief that the fortresses of the city could most successfully be assaulted from the land side. By mid-February the Russian reinforcements had still failed to appear, but about 2,000 Albanian mercenaries were secured by Turkish di-

---

22. Bellaire, pp. 353–55. For the "fortress fleet" concept see A. T. Mahan, *Naval Strategy: Compared and Contrasted with the Principles of Military Operations on Land* (London, 1911), pp. 385, 391–93.

23. Foresti to Grenville, 8 February 1798, PRO, FO 42/3.

24. Benedetto Maresca, *Il Cavaliere Antonio Micheroux nella Reazione Napoletana del 1799* (Naples, 1895), pp. 8, 27, 29–33; Foresti to Grenville, 3 March 1798, PRO, FO 42/3.

rective and Ali Pasha's cooperation; these new allies proved to be more interested in sacking the town and peasant villagers than in attacking the French. Since the presence of Albanians on the Greek islands posed yet another problem, and since Ushakov was reluctant to use his own marines on costly charges, another alternative—using untrained peasants from the countryside— was tried. Though the Greeks were willing and spirited enough, their assault became a bloody fiasco. Even here war was a professional business.

On 1 March 1799, a major attack was finally launched from the sea on the fortified island of Vido, which held a commanding position in the bay in front of the city. Some sources, based on accounts by French observers, credited Captain Stuart, a British officer who was visiting the Russian fleet at the time, with directing Russian attention to this key point, but observers with the fleet are silent on the matter.[25] Vido was obviously of strategic importance to any plan of attack from the sea, but Ushakov, thinking the defenders were more numerous, had wisely tried to conserve Russian naval strength by planning a land effort. His determination to proceed with a sea approach was no doubt strengthened by the anxiety of the British and Neapolitan visitors. Captain Messer led the attack on Vido for the Russians, although Turkish troops composed most of the landing party— to the misfortune of the defenders. The Russian officers were barely able to restrain the Turks from dispatching all the French captives. With Vido in Russian hands, the main fortresses of Corfu were directly vulnerable. The French, exhausted by the strain of the siege and faced with a shortage of food and wood,

---

25. Lunzi, p. 229, and Henry Jervis-White Jervis, *History of the Island of Corfu and the Republic of the Ionian Islands* (London, 1852), p. 174, mention Stuart's role. Maresca and Foresti are silent except to say that Captain Stuart offered his services but they were declined. Tarle emphatically declares that Ushakov saw Vido as "the key to Corfu" immediately upon his arrival in November. Tarle, p. 91. The French observers may have been confused by the fact that Ushakov invited Stuart and Foresti to witness the attack from aboard his flagship. Foresti to Grenville, 3 March 1798, PRO, FO 42/3.

agreed to the allied terms of surrender. In hazy remembrance of the Russian siege of 1799 an area of ruined fortifications on Vido is today referred to as "Russia" by the local inhabitants.[26]

On 3 March, the gallant French garrison marched out with all honors to participate in the surrender ceremonies. By the terms of the capitulation, the French were to be disarmed and escorted at allied expense to a French port. Most of the garrison arrived in due course at Toulon, but those on a borrowed Cephalonian ship were captured by Barbary pirates and languished for a while in North Africa.[27] The Russian and Turkish flags now flew over all of the Ionian Islands.

Reports of the capture of the Ionians soon reached the allied capitals. In Saint Petersburg a number of decorations were awarded; Ushakov was promoted to full admiral and made a knight of Malta. On 10 May, the Saint Petersburg *Vedomosti* announced "a book for sale at the Imperial Academy of Sciences, *Ode to His Imperial Highness Paul Petrovich on the occasion of the capture of Corfu*—ten kopecks."[28] After examining the Imperial and Soviet glorifications of the military feat of liberating the Ionian Islands, it must be admitted that this accomplishment deserves its important place in the military history of Russia, since a comparable instance of the independent use of the Russian navy to seize an important land objective cannot be found. Fedor Ushakov should not be given sole credit for the achievement, as he is according to most of the Russian sources. Without the use of Turkish auxiliaries, especially the marines, the capture of Corfu would have been considerably delayed if not impossible. The diplomatic arrangements that made the campaign feasible must not be forgotten. The role of the Russian ambassador in Constantinople in cementing the Russo-Turkish alliance and

---

26. Little remains of the fortifications since they were blown up by the British in 1864 before the islands were handed over to Greece, an action that created much bitterness at the time.

27. Lunzi, p. 237.

28. "Petersburgskaia Starina," *Russkaia Starina* 41 (1884): 364.

probably in designating the initial target has been generally neglected in the historical literature.[29]

The capture of Corfu initiated another phase in Russia's involvement in the Mediterranean. Ushakov, as commander of the liberating fleet, was now faced with the responsibility of organizing a government for the islands. Given only vague instructions from distant Saint Petersburg, Ushakov was forced to tackle some difficult problems on his own. First, there was harmony to maintain with the allies, and neither the uneasy Turks nor the British made this a very simple matter. Second, the problem of administering the newly-conquered islands raised difficulties that taxed the limited political experience of Ushakov and his small staff. Third, Ushakov was hampered by a fleet that was literally rotting away, and Corfu was not adequately equipped for repairing it. Finally, the infrequent and long-delayed communications from Saint Petersburg and Constantinople resulted in confused and contradictory instructions regarding areas of responsibility.

THE ALLIES

Admiral Nelson and Sir Sidney Smith, having been forced to stand by while the Russo-Turkish expedition conquered the Ionian Islands, still tried to secure Russian and Turkish assistance for guarding the Egyptian coast and for besieging Malta. Lord Nelson, who was paying court to Lady Hamilton at Palermo during the summer of 1799, was now willing to have Russian help in the Mediterranean as long as it advanced British and not only Russian interests and did not limit his own supreme authority. Ushakov had become acutely aware, however, of the expansion of British ambitions in the Mediterranean after the Battle of the Nile and wrote to Tomara in March that he saw no reason to assist the British directly since the French naval threat in the area had vanished.[30] Russia had acquired additional military

---

29. From Tomara's subsequent actions, there is a strong indication that Venetian interests may have played a part in his policies. He was certainly operating on his own initiative in a manner quite rare for a Russian diplomat.

30. Ushakov to Tomara, 16 March 1799, in *Admiral Ushakov*, 2: 409.

obligations in the Adriatic by her alliance with Naples, and now that a base had been secured, prospects for more positive action in that quarter were improved.

The Turks remained skeptical about the aims of their new "friends," but as far as the expedition was concerned, Kadir Bey continued to cooperate with the letter of the alliance if not with its spirit. He had little choice, since the sultan in Constantinople was convinced of the necessity of Russian aid, and the Turkish fleet, weakened by low morale and desertions of many seamen to the Greek and Albanian mainland, was in no position to reject Russian leadership. The second-in-command of the Turkish fleet, Patron Bey, represented the anti-Russian side of Ottoman officialdom, and since he and his position were popular among the Turkish crewmen, dissension grew within the fleet. Under pressure of Patron Bey and in order to counterbalance Russian influence and create a three-power union of action, Kadir Bey corresponded with both Smith and Nelson in hopes of securing British naval participation; he also proved his friendship by serving as host to visiting Englishmen aboard his palatial flagship.[31] The Turkish admiral could not accede, however, to British requests to put his fleet at their disposal. Ushakov, on his part, was lenient toward the Turks and allowed crimes committed by them against the local population to go lightly punished—perhaps, as Tomara advised and an English observer guessed, to make the Turks, continuing their misbehavior, appear more odious in the eyes of the local population.[32]

Turkish marines were needed initially to help garrison the islands. Ushakov was reluctant to employ any additional troops of Ali Pasha after the troubles they had created on Corfu during the siege, and even levied a special tax on the islanders to pay off the Albanians that were left.[33] A message informed Ushakov in June that Major General Borozdin was being sent from

31. Foresti to Grenville, 14 January 1799, PRO, FO 42/3.

32. Tomara to Ushakov, 24 November 1798, in *Admiral Ushakov*, 2: 198–99; Danish to Wyndham, 20 September 1799, Windham Papers, vol. 11, BM, Add. MSS., 37,852, f. 299.

33. Foresti to Grenville, 26 March 1799, PRO, FO 42/3.

the Black Sea with three thousand soldiers, but the departure was again delayed by transport and supply problems.[34] The larger army of 12,000, originally destined for the Adriatic, was rerouted to augment Suvorov's army in northern Italy. To send the Russian divisions to southern Italy after liberating the North rather than to bring them around by sea was considered easier and less expensive. Since the passage of Borozdin's battalions suffered additional delays, Ushakov was forced for the time being to establish and maintain order on the islands with small units of mixed Russian and Turkish marines and to make greater efforts than he probably would otherwise have done to conciliate local authorities.

Although the Russians decided against recruiting an Albanian army, other powers were still interested. In Constantinople, Sidney Smith, as hard-pressed as the Russians for troops in the Mediterranean, pursued the possibility of employing Albanian infantry under command of English officers. On 8 March, Smith wrote Spencer at the Admiralty, "The Albanians are the Swiss of this part of Europe, and he [Windham of the War Office] may have two regiments of a thousand men to serve in this country [Egypt] if he likes it, on writing me a single line."[35] After the Porte approved, and Ali had warmed to the idea of international publicity and financial gains, General Villettes was sent to the Ionians to supervise the recruiting and training of the proposed Albanian regiments for Britain.

Other governments were also interested in Albanian mercenaries. The Kingdom of the Two Sicilies, always short of loyal and willing troops, and the Ionian Islands, lacking a trained militia of their own, considered their use. The Queen of Naples even wrote of throwing 20,000 Albanians into the heart of

---

34. Paul to Ushakov, 27 May 1799, in *Admiral Ushakov*, 2: 513; and M. Polivanov, *M. M. Borozdin, nachalnik okhrany neapolitanskago korolia, 1800–1802 gg.* (Saint Petersburg, 1912), pp. 12–13. The original plan called for the use of the Black Sea flotilla that Ribas had organized in 1790 to carry the Russian reinforcements, but it was found to be completely unseaworthy.

35. Sir Sidney Smith to Spencer, 8 March 1799, in *Dropmore*, 5: 45.

France.[36] The Russians, however, were opposed to their allies' obtaining soldiers from a source they deemed unreliable, and proceeded to hamper recruiting activities from Ionian bases. The British and the Neapolitans, after encountering expenses, difficulty of transport, the unpredictability of Ali, and, above all, Russian opposition, eventually gave up their plans. Ali, in the meantime, cruelly oppressed the continental enclaves that he had conquered from the French. Refugees from these territories took shelter on the islands, and, through their tales of Ali's barbarity, fomented a strong anti-Albanian sentiment among the Greek population. This was at least part of the reason for Russian opposition to Ali.

But Russia found another ally in the Balkans—Montenegro. Previous Montenegrin contacts with Russia, even the visits by the prince-bishop Peter I (Petrovich) Negosh in 1778 and 1784, brought no results. Negosh won an impressive victory over the Turks in 1796, but, with the appearance of the French and Austrians in the Adriatic in 1797, he feared that a combination of one of these powers, or both, with Ali Pasha would result in the end of Montenegro's hard won independence. Using every channel of approach that he could think of—including letters carried by a personal envoy to Paul, letters to Russian ministers in Vienna, Naples, and Ragusa, and direct contacts with Ushakov at Corfu—Negosh succeeded in gaining Paul's attention.[37] A ukaz, published on 12 May 1798, conferred upon Peter the Order of Alexander Nevsky. On 22 January 1799, after the Second Coalition had been formed and while Corfu was being besieged, Paul sent a *gramota* to the people of Montenegro, promising that the Russian fleet in the Mediterranean would preserve law and order and protect Christianity, and granting a subsidy of 1,000 chervons (approximately 3,000 rubles) annually

---

36. Maria Carolina to Gallo, 1 May 1799, in *Correspondance inédite de Marie-Carolina, reine de Naples et de Sicile, avec le marquis de Gallo,* ed. Commander M. H. Weil and Marquis C. di Somma Circello (Paris, 1911), 1: 76.

37. V. Zhmakin, "Rossiia i Chernogoriia v nachale XIX veka," *Drevniaia i Novaia Rossiia* 19 (1881): 409–10.

to the country.[38] This marked the beginning of direct Russian involvement in the fate of the Balkan slavs, but Russia's first "Balkan protectorate" was worth very little economically or strategically for the time being. The country was so isolated that Lieutenant Klopakis, a special emissary from Ushakov, had great difficulty reaching it.

THE IONIAN CONSTITUTION

Although it is not exactly clear where the idea originated, Paul told Cobenzl in November 1798 that the Ionian Islands should govern themselves under the protection of the Turks, like Ragusa.[39] The problem was introduced in the negotiations at Constantinople, and Tomara forwarded in December a Turkish proposal that offered three possible alternatives: (1) give them to Naples in exchange for Malta or as an inducement to enter the coalition; (2) set up a republic like Ragusa; or (3) incorporate them into the Ottoman Empire as a principality like Moldavia and Wallachia. Tomara added that both he and the sultan preferred the latter, and suggested that Ypsilanti would be appointed as hospodar. Kochubei feared that Paul would accept the Ottoman preference and that a principality would ruin the commerce of the islands and deny the British "raisins for their plum puddings."[40] Perhaps influenced by Kochubei, the emperor decided

38. Zhivko Dragovich, "Chernogoriia i eia otnosheniia k Rossii v tsarstvovanie Imperatora Pavla, 1797–1801 gg.," *Russkaia Starina* 35 (1882): 368–69.

39. Cobenzl to Thugut, 6 November 1798, HHSA, 89 Russland II Berichte. There was an excellent memoir on Ragusa, written by the Russian consul there in 1792, available on Saint Petersburg at the time. S. V. Arsen'ev, "Raguzskaia respublika v XVIII veke (is donesenii Rossiiskago general'nago konsula Grafa Dzhiki)," *Russkii Arkhiv* 55 (1917): 124–28.

40. Kochubei to S. R. Vorontsov, 14 December 1798, and 15 June 1799, in *Arkhiv Vorontsova*, 18: 183–86, 210–11. Tomara's support of the Turkish position was apparently only an effort to strengthen the alliance. After the fall of Corfu he wrote, "Now I begin the business of establishing a government for the former Venetian islands according to the will of the tsar which is very much against the goals of the Turks and Greeks [Phanariots?] to set up these islands as a third 'milk cow' like Moldavia and Wallachia." Tomara to Alexander Vorontsov, 27 June 1799, in *Arkhiv Vorontsova*, 20: 250.

on the Ragusan form by February 1799, but because of Russian and Turkish military responsibilities in the area, the government that actually existed for the duration of the republic was a compromise between that of Moldavia and that of Ragusa.

Soon after the capture of the last Corfiot fortresses, Ushakov set about organizing a government with the help of three leading nobles of the islands, Spiridion Theotokis, Angelo Orio, and Antonio Capodistrias. On 23 April, a joint proclamation of the Russian and Turkish admirals declared the Ionian Islands a united republic and created a constiutional assembly of eighty-three members, most of whom were selected by Ushakov.[41]

Under guidelines furnished by Ushakov, the assembly drafted within two weeks a provisional constitution that provided for the election of a republican senate and defined its powers. The franchise was limited to a small number of inhabitants of a certain net income per year with the amount varying from island to island in recognition of the disparity of wealth among them. The *consiglio* (electorate) of each island chose the deputies for the central senate in Corfu. The first senate began its session in June with fourteen members. Angelo Orio, an ex-Venetian naval commander who had married into a wealthy family of Santa Maura, was selected by Ushakov as its first president in remembrance of his assistance during the siege. Theotokis was elected vice-president.[42] The "May" or "Ushakov" consitution, as it was variously called, provided in general for an extension of the electorate and office holding rights, in comparison with the old Venetian system, to include more of the commercial class or bourgeoisie. Another distinguishing feature was the assignment of predominate power to the senate, thus centralizing the government at Corfu, an arrangement that would be convenient for the Russian admiral.[43]

The first major difficulty that the senate faced was in the selection of deputations to go to Constantinople and Saint

---

41. Lunzi, *Della Repubblica Settinsulare*, 2 (Bologna, 1863): 5–6.
42. *Admiral Ushakov*, 2: 520–26; Lunzi, 2: 6; Il'inskii, 103.
43. McKnight, pp. 168–71.

Petersburg at the invitation of the sultan and the tsar. The elected senate was far from unanimous in its support of Ushakov, and several senators, led by Capodistrias, seized this opportunity to carry their grievances to higher authority. This faction favored the old aristocracy, a weak central government, and less Russian interference, and its adherents were prepared to court the Turks to achieve their aims. Ushakov, embarrassed by a development that posed a potential danger to his authority, favored a small delegation to be headed by his friends, Orio and Gerassimo Cladan. The senate, however, in a tumultuous session approved the more popular demand for a larger number representing all of the islands. Twelve were finally chosen.[44] By October the delegates had reached Constantinople, but, since the Porte refused to treat with more than two, Tomara selected Capodistrias and Securo Silla to negotiate with the sultan, and sent two others, Orio and Cladan, on to Saint Petersburg. The rest returned home disgusted with the high-handed Russian treatment.[45]

Orio and Cladan, after a grand reception at Odessa, arrived at Saint Petersburg in February 1800, suffering a long winter journey across the Black Sea and Russia. They presented a folio from Tomara to Rostopchin and held initial conferences with Panin, the vice-chancellor. But then the delegates had a falling out. Cladan wrote back to the senate complaining of the dictatorial attitude of Orio, "this Venetian Cromwell in Greece" who was more concerned with a proper uniform than with the negotiations.[46] A shortage of funds and the hostility of the senate in Corfu brought them back together in early 1801, but by that time their cause was damaged and Russia had withdrawn from the Second Coalition. Orio's insistence on the restitution of the mainland enclaves taken by Ali Pasha and his long diatribes

---

44. Lunzi, *Della Repubblica*, 2: 12.
45. Ibid., 16–17; Tomara to Theotokis, 8 October 1799, and 21 October 1799, Senato Settinsulare, Dipartmento degli Affari Esteri, Corfu, Box 22, f. 1, nos. 1, 4–5. Cited hereafter as SS, DAE.
46. Orio to the Ionian Senate, 19 February 1800, and 25 February 1800, SS, DAE, Box 1, f. 6, nos. 3–4; Cladan to the Ionian Senate, 19 April 1800, ibid., no. 4.

against the Turks were of little avail, and most of the deputies' communications back to Corfu pertained to the payment of their mounting debts in Russia.[47]

From August 1799, the most important consultations regarding the new Republic were held at Constantinople under the aegis of Tomara. The Ionian delegates there had little influence on the negotiations for the Russo-Turkish Convention that was signed on 2 April 1800 laying the formal foundation for the Republic. In article 1 of this agreement the Ragusan Republic, as approved earlier by Paul, was named as the model for the new "Republic of the Seven United Islands," which was to be ruled by "the principal and notable men of the country."[48] Like Ragusa, an old commercial city-state on the Adriatic Sea, the Republic was declared a "suzerainty" of the Ottoman Empire, but uniquely under the "protection" of the Russian Empire.

By article 2 the two powers guaranteed that "the said republic and its subjects shall enjoy in their political affairs, in their internal constitution, and in their commerce, all the privileges enjoyed by the Republic of Ragusa and its subjects." The Ottoman Porte agreed to protect Ionian merchant shipping from the Barbary pirates in the same manner as Ragusan ships (article 3). The next article stipulated that the Republic was to pay a tribute of 75,000 piastres every three years by a "solemn embassy," again following the tradition of Ragusa. By article 5, Russia and the Ottoman Empire agreed to garrison jointly the fortresses of the islands for the duration of the war and to evacuate them upon its conclusion. By article 6, Ionian merchant ships were

47. Orio to the Ionian Senate, 6 July 1800, ibid., no. 8 and following letters. See also *Documents Illustrative of the Character and Public Conduct of Signor Gerasimo Cladan commonly called Count Cladan of the Island of Cephalonia one of the United Ionian States* (London, 1819), pp. 23–27, and Lunzi, *Della Repubblica*, 2: 41.

48. Rodocanachi, p. 178. The full text of the convention can be found in Stefanos Xenos, *East and West: A Diplomatic History of the Annexation of the Ionian Islands to the Kingdom of Greece . . . between 1799 and 1864* (London, 1865), pp. 219–22. The Russian edition is "Konventsiia mezhdu Imperieiu Vserossiiskoiu i Portoiu Ottomanskoiu o Respublike sed'mi Soedinennykh Ostrovov zakliuchenaia v Konstantinopole 21 marta 1800 goda" (Saint Petersburg, 1801).

given an important commercial privilege—free access to the Black Sea.

Hostility was engendered in the islands by the provision that the four towns on the mainland were to be given to the Porte and not become part of the Republic. They would thus come under Ali's "protection," constituting his reward for remaining faithful to the sultan.[49] At Russian insistence liberal religious privileges were guaranteed in these towns on the same basis as in Moldavia and Wallachia, including Russian right to present petitions on behalf of the Christian population. Their tribute to the Porte, collected by Ali, was to be moderate. The last articles of the convention provided for general ratification arrangements and for the use of Russian diplomatic influence to secure the adherence of the other allies.[50]

The Ionian deputies at Constantinople under the guidance of Tomara drew up a constitution to be included in the convention that revised Ushakov's provisional arrangements. A federated, more aristocratic republic was the result, although the chief governing body remained the senate in Corfu. A faction in the senate continued to favor a more democratic plan and accused Capodistrias and Silla of acting independently in Constantinople, surpassing their vaguely designated powers.[51] The new "Byzantine" constitution was more advantageous to the established aristocracy of Venetian origin, while the powers of the lower nobility and merchants were more restricted than the original Ushakov plan. Venetian tradition carried over into the new republic in other ways; even the flag adopted in Constantinople for the new republic featured the lion of Saint Mark's. On 1 November 1800, after receipt of the ratifications of the convention, the flag was saluted in the harbor of Constantinople.[52] The "Republic of the Seven United Islands" was launched.

---

49. Ibid. Tomara to the Ionian Senate, 22 June 1800, SS, DAE, Box 22, f. 1, no. 13.

50. Xenos, p. 221.

51. Tomara to the Ionian Senate, 8 April 1800, SS, DAE, Box 22, f. 1, no. 10.

52. Lunzi, *Della Repubblica*, 2: 43–46.

RUSSIAN OCCUPATION PROBLEMS

The islands remained in a state of flux and were plagued by disorders of various kinds between 1 March 1799, when Corfu fell to the allied forces, and 1 November 1800, when the Republic officially came into existence. Old and new rivalries rose up among individuals, families, towns, and islands, and friction increased between the allied garrisons and the local population. While some groups of nobles and individual towns tried to secure the favor of their liberators and were quick to accuse, often unjustly, those who had been partisan to the French, others tried independently to gain local support in areas that were dissatisfied with the central authorities. Some aristocrats who had been leaders under both Venetian and French rule remained in key positions, while Venetian diplomats, out of jobs since 1797, were employed in the consular posts of the Republic and of Russia through the patronage of Tomara.[53]

Rivalries and intrigues continued unabated throughout the period of transition. Zante retained its pro-British orientation based upon commercial ties, sent impressive gifts to Admiral Nelson, and in February 1801, after the departure of most of the Russian force, raised the British flag over the main fortress. Only strong pressure from the central government at Corfu and the cooperation of a British brig were able to restore Ionian authority there.[54] On Cephalonia the unrest was centered on the rivalry between the towns of Lixuri and Argostoli, each vying for the honor of serving as the capital and for the control of the island's government.[55] Much blood was lost and energy spent upon this animosity. Claims and counterclaims of the rivals belabored the senate in Corfu throughout its existence. French and English observers blamed the Russians for the disorders, but

---

53. Several examples of Tomara's influence are found in the ambassador's letters to Theotokis, the president of the Ionian Senate, in the archives at Corfu; for example, a letter of 16 November 1800, on behalf of Mr. George Paul, SS, DAE, Box 22, f. 1, no. 21.

54. Foresti to Grenville, 28 February and 14 March 1801, PRO, FO 42/4; Lunzi, *Della Repubblica*, 2: 30–31.

55. Lunzi, *Della Repubblica*, 2: 32.

while it is true that Russian administration was careless and inconstant, most of the blame must fall upon the proud and ambitious islanders who could not put aside old animosities and new quarrels in order to cooperate in strengthening the central government against Russian and Turkish interference.

Illustrative of the difficulties faced by the "protecting" power during the first year were the complications involved in the selection of a metropolitan, the leading church official. Upon restitution of the metropolitanate by the patriarch of Constantinople, a popular local priest, Calichiopoulo Manzaro, was elected by the clergy of the islands in June 1799.[56] But his death in October left the position vacant again. Attempts by the Metropolitan of Janina, acting perhaps as Ali's agent, to subordinate the post to his own authority, brought the Russians into the squabbles. Two rival candidates from widely respected and influential families were brought forth: Pietro Bulgari of an illustrious family which besides extensive estates also owned title to the relics of the patron saint of Corfu, Saint Spiridion;[57] and Niceforo Theotokis, a noted church scholar who happened to be in Astrakhan at the time. Ushakov, who returned to Corfu early in 1800, first supported Bulgari, who was elected, but when popular opposition arose, the admiral ordered a new election to be held on 9 February at which a compromise candidate, Ciyala, was finally chosen.[58] Negotiations still had to be conducted through Tomara at Constantinople for full recognition of the title.

Difficult as these problems were to the Russian officials, they were not insurmountable. Ushakov and his lieutenants on the whole performed their duties in fairness to those concerned, and Tomara, although tending to dictate constitutional arrangements, resisted Turkish pressure for application of a stricter suzerainty. The islanders' resentment of the Russian occupation was sharply increased by the practice of exacting taxes from the already hard-pressed islands in order to pay for the garrisoning of the Russians and the transporting of the surrendered French

---

56. Ibid., pp. 19–22.
57. The four annual processions in honor of the saint attest to the reverence still paid to him by the Corfiots.
58. Lunzi, *Della Repubblica*, 2: 25–27.

troops. If the Russian military campaign in the Mediterranean had been accompanied by experienced diplomatic personnel and ample financial resources, many of the difficulties would have been alleviated.

The Russians tried to leave local problems to the solution of the governing authorities. Tomara even bypassed Ushakov to order Captain Alexiano, the officer left in charge of the Ionian garrison in 1799, to stay out of local squabbles as much as possible.[59] But Tomara effectively controlled the foreign affairs of the new republic by selecting personal acquaintances to serve in the strategically most important posts of chargés d'affaires at Constantinople and at Saint Petersburg.[60] He also prevented the republic from establishing diplomatic relations with Britain. Additional problems were encountered in rebuilding the destitute Ionian economy. Liberan Benachi, the Russian consul-general at Corfu, found himself involved in a long series of disputes regarding the improper use of the Russian flag by Ionian and Greek shippers who sought better protection against piracy and favored commercial privileges in the Black Sea afforded by the Russian flag while avoiding the customs of the new republic.[61]

Even before the fall of Corfu the lines of military and diplomatic commands were becoming confused. While Ushakov was besieging Corfu, he was already receiving orders directly from Paul to extend his operations to the coast of Italy in concert with the Russian army that was being prepared to operate in that area. The Russian admiral decided that the extended nature of his mission placed him directly under the tsar and the Admiralty College in Saint Petersburg, and in the period from March to July 1799 he addressed practically all of his communications directly to Saint Petersburg rather than through Constantinople.[62] The practical matter of a faster route from Austrian Istria

---

59. Tomara to Captain Alexiano, 11 October 1799, SS, DAE, Box 22, f. 1, nos. 2–3.

60. Tomara to the Ionian Senate, 8 December 1800, SS, DAE, Box 22, f. 1, no. 19.

61. Benachi to the Ionian Senate, 5 July 1800, SS, DAE, Box 30, no. 20.

62. See Ushakov's reports to Paul during this period in *Admiral Ushakov*, 3 (Moscow, 1956): 4–46.

(Trieste) overland to Russia and the admiral's personal desire to be independent of Tomara's interference were influential in this course of action.

Ushakov quite naturally blamed Tomara for changing the constitution without his approval or that of the original constituent assembly, and he considered the ambassador's patronage and diplomatic scheming to be interfering with his quest for a stable government independent of Turkish domination. The Russian ambassador in Constantinople, on the other hand, believed that, since the occupation of the Ionian Islands was a joint Russo-Turkish project, he should have a part in the decision making, and he was willing to make compromises with the Turks to maintain harmonious relations. Tomara's personal ambition to play the dominant role in Ionian affairs and the technical obligation to coordinate the arrangements in the islands with the Ottoman government caused him to complain persuasively to Saint Petersburg of Ushakov's independent actions. There it was apparently decided that, since it was impossible to govern Ushakov's activities directly from Saint Petersburg, Tomara should be given a greater role (at least as far as the Ionian Islands were concerned) than would normally in wartime have been the case for a Russian ambassador.[63] Ushakov was ordered in July 1799 to cooperate with Tomara and the Ottoman government in the establishment of order in the Ionian Republic.[64] As the result of these instructions and of Ushakov's departure for the Italian area of operations, Tomara's authority and the role of his agent in Corfu, the Russian consul Benachi, increased considerably. The problem of military and diplomatic coordination was by no means solved by the departure of the main Russo-Turkish forces. Ushakov was still dependent upon Corfu for a base for his fleet, and civil authorities on the islands were dependent upon Ushakov's small garrison for maintaining order and for defense.

---

63. Examination of the full correspondence between Saint Petersburg and Tomara, if it survives, would be necessary for a complete analysis of the delegation of authority.

64. Ushakov to Tomara, 12 July 1799, in *Admiral Ushakov*, 3: 49–50.

5

The Italian Campaign

On the heights of Kanoni on Corfu a rusting cannon embossed with the double-headed eagle overlooks the Corfu Channel and the picturesque monastery of Pontikonissi, the legendary island of Ulysses' ship turned to stone. After defenses had been erected on Kanoni in 1799, Russian activities in the Mediterranean expanded to another, even more complicated area—the Italian peninsula. Russian interest in Italy had increased rapidly during the eighteenth century; Russian technical and artistic needs had brought waves of Italian architects, artists, musicians, singers, and tutors to the Russian cities. Many Russians, even Emperor Paul, had toured Italy and carried back fond memories of the warm climate and hospitality that they had enjoyed. Paul, with his ideas of an autocratic and religious crusade against revolution, was especially attracted to a land of imperial tradition, which was also the seat of a great church.[1] The sharp increase in direct trade between Italy and Russia after the opening of the Black Sea helped spread mutual awareness.

At the time of the French Revolution, Italy was divided into

---

1. Paul's summer palace at Pavlovsk has a markedly Italinate character. The semicircular wings, recalling Saint Peter's in Rome, are decorated with busts of Roman emperors. The Roman motif carries over in the interior designs, completely and carefully restored by Soviet craftsmen after heavy war damage, especially in Paul's study, in the rooms of "war" and "peace" flanking the main reception hall, and in the "hall of the knights."

a number of small, weak states. In the middle of the peninsula were a number of territories under the jurisdiction of the pope. They were flanked in the south by the kingdom of the Two Sicilies—ruled by a branch of the Spanish Bourbons—and in the north and west by the independent duchies of Tuscany, Modena, and Parma. The kingdom of Sardinia-Piedmont under the House of Savoy was the major state of the north, while Lombardy was practically an Austrian province. On the fringes—in Genoa and Venice—aristocratic commercial republics lived on past glories and diminishing wealth.

So divided, Italy was natural prey for the great land and sea powers. France especially watched for opportunities to dominate Mediterranean trade by expanding her influence in the peninsula. Austria and England were interested too: Austria in order to annex the rich Po Valley in the north and to obtain a valuable access to the sea (Venice); England to secure commercial advantages and naval bases along the coasts and to erect a barrier against French expansion eastward .

In the campaigns of 1796–97, General Bonaparte swept northern Italy and put most of it under a single occupational command. The subsequent partition of Venice at Campoformio, according to Ferrero, upset the balance of power in Italy and was the major cause of the Napoleonic Wars.

> The Directory started it all with the Italian adventure. Carried away by its initial successes, it became more and more involved. But war without rules, though guaranteeing unhoped-for successes to the French army, provoked a rapid dissolution of the Old Regime in Italy, a general anarchy that threatened to engulf the invaders. . . . Until the peace of Campoformio the only effect of the Revolution on the rest of Europe had been the increased watchfulness of the police, charged with the surveillance of the malcontents and hotheads. . . . But after 1797 all the great courts were beginning to feel great anxiety and to be affected by the spirit of adventure. France had brought the Revolution to Italy; why, she might spread her subversive doctrine over all Europe![2]

---

2. Guglielmo Ferrero, *The Reconstruction of Europe: Talleyrand and the Congress of Vienna, 1814–1815,* tr. Theodore R. Jaeckel (New York,

Evidence already presented from the Russian side shows that the French occupation of the Ionian Islands was the chief factor in Russia's entry into the war.

The kingdom of Naples, encouraged by reports from Saint Petersburg and the entry of the Russian fleet into the Mediterranean, began the offensive on the continent. After the surprise capture of Rome, in December 1798, the Neapolitan army was quickly defeated by a French counterattack which left all of the peninsula under French control by January 1799. The "kingdoms" were still in being, however, with their island refuges on Sicily and Sardinia still inaccessible to the French armies. Although revolutionary ideas had penetrated the whole peninsula, their force varied considerably from region to region, and Italian revolutionary nationalism was already leaning toward an anti-French attitude. In the South, for example, the Parthenopean Republic, established under French auspices in Naples on 4 January 1799, faced opposition from the lower classes who remained faithful to the expelled monarch and the church. Many of the republican rebels were well-intentioned Neapolitan aristocrats who had been disgusted with the fumbling Bourbon court and its foreign influences but now were alienated by the dictatorial and vengeful French generals, whose armies were quartered on the already impoverished countryside of southern Italy.[3] In the spring of 1799, after reverses in the East, the French decided that they were overextended in Italy and began withdrawing their forces to meet the Austro-Russian threat in northern Italy.

Austria had wielded a dominant influence in the kingdom of Naples through the Vienna-bred Queen Maria Carolina of the House of Hapsburg, who virtually ruled the country and her weak-willed husband, King Ferdinand IV. But French armies had

---

1963), pp. 9–10. See also his first volume on the Napoleonic period: *The Gamble: Bonaparte in Italy, 1796–1797*, tr. Bertha Pritchard and Lily C. Freeman (London, 1961). "Preserving the balance of power" is a game any number can play: one could start with the partitions of Poland or of the Ottoman Empire.

3. Harold Acton, *The Bourbons of Naples, 1734–1825* (London, 1957), pp. 320–55.

temporarily ended Austrian ascendancy on the mainland, and it was supplanted at the exile court in Sicily by English. With the forming of the Second Coalition under the active leadership of Tsar Paul, Austria saw an opportunity to regain lost prestige and to establish a more formidable position in Italy by using the anti-French zeal of the Russian emperor for advancing her own goals of recovering a dominant position in northern Italy and, if possible, annexing territory to compensate for gains made by France, Russia, Prussia, and England since 1792. In January and February 1799, an Austro-Russian expeditionary army was organized under Field Marshal (Prince) Alexander Suvorov, the renowned military genius of Catherine's Turkish wars. Ushakov, whose fleet was already in the Adriatic Sea, was ordered to assist the Russian land force along the coasts.[4] Concerned with defeating the French, Paul discounted the fact that victories in Italy would result in Austrian expansion.

Britain, with a fleet in the Mediterranean, intended to preserve and increase her diplomatic and military influence in the kingdom of Naples. John Acton, the first minister, was of English ancestry; Lady Hamilton, the young, flirtatious wife of the elderly British ambassador, was a close friend of the queen; and the celebrated, battle-scarred Horatio Nelson was a visible symbol of British power. The temporary capital at Palermo was virtually occupied by the English.

The anti-Russian sentiment openly voiced by Nelson did not deter the kingdom, however, from accepting overtures of assistance from Russia. Since neither Austria nor Britain had military forces to spare for a campaign in southern Italy, the idea of gaining a "disinterested" Russian ally with what seemed to be unlimited manpower to offer was quite appealing to the anti-Austrian party at the Neapolitan court headed by the marquis di Gallo and Cardinal Ruffo. Paul's friendly attitude, especially after the signing of the treaty of alliance in December 1798,

---

4. Ushakov to Suvorov, 9 May 1799, in *Admiral Ushakov*, 3: 3. See also L. M. Leshchinskii, "Ital'ianskii i shveitsarskii pokhody—vershina polkovodcheskogo izkusstva A. V. Suvorova," *Suvorovskii sbornik*, ed. A. V. Sukhomlin (Moscow, 1951), pp. 89–131.

raised the hopes of the destitute Sicilian court. Even the queen in her private correspondence wrote joyfully of the prospect of 15,000 Russian soldiers liberating the mainland.[5]

Before the fall of Corfu, orders were sent from Saint Petersburg to the Ionians to prepare Russian assistance for Naples, and Neapolitan envoys on their part tried to spur the Russian siege. At the end of March, Ushakov dispatched two squadrons to patrol the Adriatic, blockade the important French-held ports along the coast, and cooperate with anti-French irregulars in the interior. Rear Admiral Pustoshkin, second in command to Ushakov, went north along the Italian coast to Ancona with one squadron, and Captain Sorokin inspected the coast around Brindisi and Bari. Both disembarked small detachments of marines to take advantage of the French withdrawal and capture a few strategic points with the help of local Italian insurgents. Cardinal Ruffo landed in Calabria with a commission from the king, and, much to the surprise of the professional generals in Sicily, gathered a large body of untrained peasants whose religious fanaticism was fired by the cardinal and his priest-lieutenants, and set out to deliver the kingdom from the French. The Parthenopean Republic, established only in January, had not long to live.

In May, Captain Henry Baillie, an Englishman serving in the Russian fleet, landed at Brindisi with a detachment of about 600 Russian marines. He occupied several important cities with little opposition, united with Ruffo's Neapolitan militia, and entered Naples on June 14.[6] There the experienced Russian soldiers were instrumental in helping to maintain discipline in Ruffo's army during the siege of the city's fortresses, which were defended by French and Parthenopean units. An armistice was granted by the allied assault troops, and negotiations were being conducted for the surrender of the garrisons on liberal terms when Nelson

---

5. Maria Carolima to Gallo, 19 March 1799, in Weil and Circello (see chap. 4, n. 36), p. 64.

6. B. Maresca, *Il cavaliere Antonio Micheroux nella reazione Napoletana del 1799* (Naples, 1895), p. 59; Z. Arkas, "Deistviia Chernomorskago flota," pp. 860–62.

arrived with a British squadron on June 24. During the dispute that ensued between Ruffo and the British admiral over the terms of amnesty to be granted the Parthenopean leaders, the Russians supported Ruffo, but Nelson prevailed, with the approval of the court in Palermo and the Hamiltons who accompanied him. A bloody repression of the Neapolitan rebels resulted.[7]

By engaging his forces in Italy, Ushakov had entered a second zone of the Mediterranean. When the plans for the Ionian campaign had been made in Constantinople the year before, it was not anticipated that the fleet would be required to go beyond Ottoman waters. Ushakov was now acting independently of his Turkish ally, using only Russian ships and marines in Italy. Readjustments also had to be made to provide for coordination with another diplomatic center in Palermo. Ushakov's mission was complicated even more by his orders to cooperate with Suvorov in northern Italy, who relied upon communications through Vienna.

From the beginning of Russian participation in Italian affairs, an independent Russian course of action can be observed. Russia took both military and diplomatic steps to support and strengthen weak states against Austrian and British influences as well as to remove French domination. This pattern, which was developing in the Baltic area also, was caused not only by a reaction against the self-interested policies of Britain and Austria but also by deliberate planning in Saint Petersburg. The spectacular successes of Russian arms so far from home contributed to the growth of Russian prestige and influence throughout

---

7 . A controversy developed over Nelson's actions at Naples in 1900, with the eminent American naval historian A. T. Mahan defending Nelson. See the following pamphlets: A. T. Mahan, *Nelson at Naples*, (London, 1900) reprinted from the *English Historical Review* of October 1900, and F. P. Badham, *Nelson at Naples: A Journal for June 10–30, 1799, Refuting Recent Misstatements of Captain Mahan and Professor J. K. Laughton*, [Mahan's copy with notes in British Museum] (London, 1900). Harold Acton, Guiseppe Berti, and most Russian historians are critical of Nelson's activities in Italy.

Europe but especially in the Italian states that benefited from them.

GALLO'S MISSION TO SAINT PETERSBURG

While the fleet under Ushakov's command was becoming engaged in Italy, diplomatic measures were taken by a Neapolitan leader to increase the Russian commitment in that quarter. The marquis di Gallo, special ambassador to Vienna, became convinced that only Russia could save the kingdom of Naples from being a pawn in the hands of Austria:

> Russia is the only power that can exercise an influence on this court [Austria] and use all possible resources in order to force its hand. . . . It would surely raise the prestige of our prince and secure his position to join with a state possessing vast territory and with more of a grasp of His Majesty's interests; Russia, by a policy directly opposed to the one of Austria, could protect these interests if Austria, by jealousy, indifference, pride, or any other plausible motives, happened to neglect them.[8]

The king approved Gallo's suggestion that he proceed directly to Saint Petersburg to appeal to the tsar.[9]

Immediately upon reaching the Russian capital in early July 1799, Gallo entered into negotiations with Rostopchin and Paul. He presented a memoir to the tsar outlining a plan for the ultimate settlement of Italian affairs, a plan that included a large indemnity to be paid by France to the kingdom of Naples. In a private audience at the end of July, Gallo explained that an advance arrangement was necessary to secure the future stability of Italy. Paul was at first alarmed by Gallo's expansionist aims ("You would take Rome!"), but later appeared convinced of the merit of the project and admitted that his sympathies lay

---

8. Gallo to Acton, 20 May 1799, in Carlo di Somma (Marquis di Circello), *Une mission diplomatique du Marquis de Gallo à Saint Petersbourg en 1799* (Naples, 1910), p. 45.
9. Ibid., pp. 57–60.

with Naples but that Austria had the position of power and remarked, "Well! What can one do for the King?"[10] Gallo's plan would have given Naples the "Three Legations," or Tuscany plus Ancona, to balance expected Austrian gains in northern Italy. A second memoir to Rostopchin outlined the details of the plan. In an unusual man-to-man debate with the emperor, Gallo convinced Paul that it was not practical to insist on a complete restoration, that some Italian states (not the pope's) would have to be sacrificed to strengthen Naples. Gallo even managed to win the backing of Whitworth for his program.[11]

According to the marquis di Circello, Rostopchin revealed the Neapolitan envoy's proposals in a letter to Vorontsov in London with the satirical comment: "The marquis di Gallo has come here with some ideas of partitioning the world like Caesar."[12] Since Vorontsov was not a person to keep confidences, he passed on this news in a tone of dissatisfaction to Circello, the Neapolitan ambassador in London, and the plan quickly became common knowledge.[13] Austria was outraged and made remonstrances to Naples. The result was a long letter from Ferdinand to Paul, written on 24 September and probably dictated by Acton at the instigation of the queen, denouncing the "unauthorized" action of Gallo. Believing that Paul would be upset by Gallo's schemes, the Neapolitan monarch apologized profusely for the

---

10. Ibid., pp. 74, 79. Gallo even expanded possible Neapolitan gains to include the Ionian Islands; Paul felt that the argument that the Ionians were too weak to remain independent had merit.

11. Ibid., pp. 310–38; Whitworth to Grenville, 13 November 1799, PRO, FO 65/42.

12. As quoted in Somma, p. 139. In the Vorontsov Archives a milder expression is found: "The marquis di Gallo, who believes himself to be in the time of tsars and regards himself perhaps as Adam Olearius or Tavernier, has presented a memoir on the indemnification at the peace accompanied by a bad map of Italy." Rostopchin to S. R. Vorontsov, 21 July 1799, in *Arkhiv Vorontsova* 8 (Moscow, 1879): 229–30. Later the chancellor found Gallo's ideas "not unreasonable." Rostopchin to S. R. Vorontsov, 5 September 1799, ibid., p. 239. Apparently Gallo made a bad initial impression, which was amended.

13. Somma, p. 141. Gallo blamed Rostopchin for the debacle, but it would appear that Vorontsov was more at fault. Rostopchin to S. R. Vorontsov, 26 November 1799, *Arkhiv Vorontsova* 8: 266.

arrogance of his envoy and disclaimed any interest in annexing territory.[14]

Austrian influence had again proved its dominance, and the kingdom of Naples was the ultimate loser, despite the fact that Paul's approval and British support had virtually been obtained by Gallo. Ferdinand's letter recalling Gallo and Paul's dissatisfaction with the Second Coalition hampered further negotiations to enlarge the kingdom of Naples. But Paul had again demonstrated a desire to strengthen a small power as a counterbalance to a larger one, in this case Austria. A modern historian of the Risorgimento, Giuseppe Berti, claims that Italy might have been united from the South instead of from the North, and sixty years earlier, had Gallo's plan been followed.[15]

RUSSIA AND THE KINGDOM OF SARDINIA

When Gallo left Saint Petersburg at the end of November, 1799, dejected and upset that his plan had been so unceremoniously disowned, another special envoy from Italy was just arriving. Gaetano Balbo, brother of the Sardinian envoy to France, had been dispatched by Charles Emmanuel IV at Suvorov's suggestion in order to renew diplomatic contacts and, like Gallo, to gain Russian support against Austria. "One must bridle Austria by Russia," Balbo wrote, although he was not as anti-Austrian as Gallo.[16] Balbo had ample justification for his attempts to prevent Russian troops from evacuating northern Italy: the Sardinian territories there were overrun by Austrian administrators; the king was shut out of his capital at Turin by the Austrians despite Suvorov's invitation—prompted by Paul—

---

14. Somma, pp. 219–24.

15. Giuseppe Berti, *Russia e stati italiani nel Risorgimento* (Turin, 1957), pp. 181–92. See also Somma, pp. 217–18.

16. M. A. Polievktov, *Proekt soiuza Rossii s Sardinskim korolevstvom v tsarstvovanie Imperatora Pavla I* (Saint Petersburg, 1902), p. 8. Balbo's predecessor, Bossi, had insulted Paul by a careless remark and had been asked to leave the country in early 1799. During the important campaign of 1799 in northern Italy, Sardinian affairs in Saint Petersburg were handled

for him to return; and a Piedmontese army was not allowed to form. Chalembert, the Sardinian prime minister, favored reaching an agreement with Austria, however, and Balbo's powers were thus limited. Although Balbo was able to secure an extension of the token subsidy first granted by Russia in 1799 (and continued until 1814), he was unable to sign a treaty of alliance.

In February 1800, when Balbo received instructions from Chalembert on treaty terms, Sardinia was no longer threatened by France, and held out for recognition as a nearly equal partner in a simple reciprocal defense arrangement. Russia was to furnish 12,000 troops if Sardinia were attacked; Sardinia would provide 10,000 soldiers to serve under Russian command in case of an attack on Russia. The expenses concerned were to be paid by the country requiring assistance. An alternative of paying 500,000 rubles in place of the military force was provided. Sardinian ports would be open to all Russian ships.[17] According to Greppi, Paul was still interested in organizing a league of small, southern European states under his leadership (as he was soon to do in the Baltic) and might have signed a treaty on these terms. But in April, the Sardinian terms were raised to include a Russian guarantee for the return of Nice and Savoy and a commitment to increase the number of Russian troops to 20,000. As must have been expected by Chalembert, who had been repeatedly warned by Balbo of the estrangement of Russia and Austria, these new provisions were unacceptable to Russia.[18]

USHAKOV AND NELSON

Meanwhile, on the seas around Italy, Russian activity was increasing in the spring of 1799. The persistence of Micheroux, who went to Corfu again in April to hurry the Russians on, and reports from the British in May that the French Atlantic fleet was at large in the Mediterranean, brought the Russian admiral

---

by Austria. Giuseppi Greppi, *Sardaigne, Autriche, Russie pendant la première et la deuxième coalition* (1796–1802), 2d ed. (Rome, 1910), p. 39.

17. Polievktov, pp. 11–13.

18. Ibid., pp. 17–18; Greppi, pp. 110, 151.

to action.[19] The blockading squadrons of Sorokin and Pustoshkin were hastily summoned from Brindisi and Ancona. A new squadron of three frigates under Captain Voinovich was dispatched to Ancona on 10 July to renew the siege so suddenly interrupted.[20] Ushakov finally set sail, on 3 August, with the combined fleet.

Ushakov arrived in the Straits of Messina on 14 August with six ships of the line, three frigates, and four dispatch vessels of the Russian fleet, and four ships of the line, three frigates, one corvette, and one dispatch vessel under Kadir Bey.[21] At Messina the fleet stopped to take on supplies and establish communications with Palermo. Happily for Ushakov, the Russian consul-general, Manzo, hurried to meet him with 100,000 rubles, with which he bought needed supplies and paid part of the back salary owed to the Russian officers and sailors.[22] Dispatches were sent to the Russian and allied officials advising them of the arrival of the Russian fleet; Musin-Pushkin-Bruce, the Russian ambassador at the Neapolitan court, and Italinsky, who was then serving as Russian military coordinator in Italy, arranged for consultations between Nelson and Ushakov at Palermo. After receiving news of the arrival at Palermo of a squadron of the Baltic fleet under Vice Admiral Kartsov, but before leaving Messina, Ushakov sent two squadrons along the Italian coast. On 20 August, three Russian frigates under Sorokin were sent to Naples, where Baillie's troops, having recently taken part in the capture of Naples, were serving as part of the garrison. Pustoshkin was sent to Genoa with two seventy-four-gun ships of the line and two dispatch vessels from the Russian fleet; one large Turkish ship and two frigates were ordered to accompany him.[23] In his order to Sorokin, Ushakov promised to send Vice Admiral Kartsov from Palermo as reinforcement. Having committed a large portion of his fleet to action along the Italian coasts, Ushakov then sailed on to his historic meeting with Nelson.

---

19. Maresca, *Il cavaliere Antonio Micheroux*, p. 59.
20. Ushakov to Voinovich, 10 July 1799, in *Admiral Ushakov*, 3: 44–45.
21. Ibid., 3: 88.
22. "Istoricheskii Zhurnal," 14 August 1799, in ibid., 3: 102.
23. Ushakov to Suvorov, 20 August 1799, in ibid., 3: 93.

There was more than a difference in nationalities separating the two admirals. Ushakov, who represented an older generation of Russian naval commanders, had been confined to the Black Sea, fighting the Turks; Nelson, though considerably younger, represented the glory and fame-seeking traditions of the British naval officer who had been all over the world. The time of their meeting could not have been more inopportune. While Ushakov was worried about leaking ships and hostile Turks, Nelson, as several of his biographers have noted, was deeply affected by a lethargic and pessimistic mood, conditioned by the environment of the Sicilian court and especially the presence there of Emma Hamilton, who had lost at Sicilian gambling tables a considerable part of his fortune gained in the Nile victory. He had recently received orders from Earl St. Vincent, head of the Admiralty, to sail to Gibraltar and Minorca with all of his ships to meet a French-Spanish naval threat in those waters. These new instructions disturbed his dreamy reveries and were forcing him to part from his beloved Emma.[24]

When Nelson learned of the arrival of the Russian fleet, he expressed the hope that they would relieve his own ships off the coast of Italy, and, confident that the Russian admiral would accept his suggestions, sent orders in advance to his commanders there not to leave for Minorca until the Russian ships had been sighted. With his first message of welcome to Ushakov on 18 August, Nelson dispatched a ship with an extra crew to take over the *Leander*, to which Nelson was particularly attached for its meritorious duty at the Battle of the Nile and which had been captured from the French at Corfu. Authority for the transfer had come to Nelson from London. As he reported to Ushakov, "I presume the Courts of Petersburg and London have decided the matter respecting the restoration of the *Leander*, otherwise the Admiralty would not have sent such an order to the Commander-in-Chief, and appointed Officer to that Ship."[25]

---

24. Fletcher Pratt, *Empire and the Sea* (New York, 1946), pp. 270–72, 277.

25. Nelson to Ushakov, 18 August 1799, in *Dispatches and Letters of Nelson*, 3: 448.

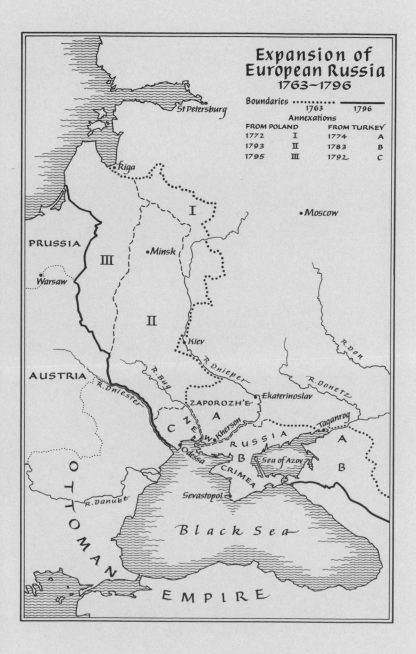

Expansion of
European Russia
1763–1796

Boundaries ·········· ——————
　　　　　　　　1763　　　　1796
Annexations
FROM POLAND　　　FROM TURKEY
1772　　I　　　1774　　A
1793　　II　　　1783　　B
1795　　III　　　1792　　C

• St Petersburg

• Riga

• Moscow

I

PRUSSIA

III　　• Minsk

• Warsaw

II

Kiev

R. Don

R. Dnieper

AUSTRIA

R. Bug

R. Dniester

R. Donetz

ZAPOROZH'E

Ekaterinoslav

C

A

N. Kherson

Taganrog

RUSSIA

A

O

Odessa

B

Sea of Azov

CRIMEA

B

T

Sevastopol

T

R. Danube

O

Black Sea

M

A

N

EMPIRE

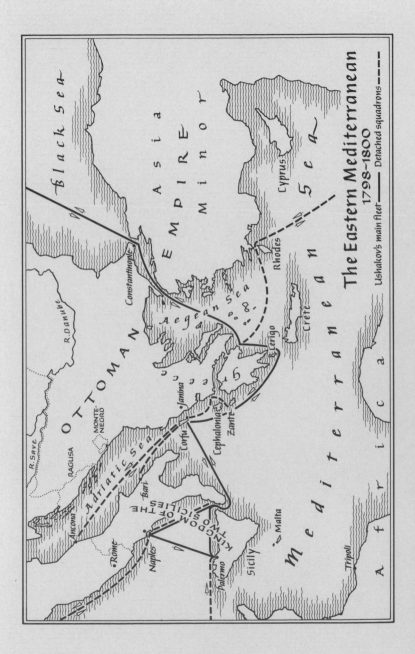

The Eastern Mediterranean
1798–1800

Ushakov's main fleet ——— Detached squadrons ---------

Black Sea

R. Danube

Constantinople

OTTOMAN EMPIRE

Asia Minor

Aegean Sea

Cyprus

Rhodes

Crete

Cerigo

Greece

Janina

Cephalonia
Zante

Corfu

MONTE-
NEGRO

RAGUSA

R. Save

Adriatic Sea

Ancona

Bari

Rome

Naples

KINGDOM OF THE TWO SICILIES

Palermo

Sicily

Malta

Mediterranean Sea

Tripoli

Africa

The return of the *Leander* to Britain for a payment had been readily approved by Paul and reported back to London by Whitworth already in April, but either the emperor had neglected to inform his commander in the Mediterranean or the communication had gone astray.[26] Ushakov received Nelson's letter on 22 August and was taken by surprise at the request for which he had no authorization; the *Leander* was the only prize ship captured by the Russians, and the largest active ship still on duty in the Ionians. In his reply to Nelson, Ushakov curtly refused to comply, and he immediately complained to Tomara at Constantinople, "I am surprised by such a shameless demand contrary to the laws of the whole world. . . . I would be better satisfied by another payment, to give instead, if it were possible, any Turkish frigate that I would choose."[27]

Nelson was irritated by Ushakov's stubbornness, and to Italinsky, with whom he was socially acquainted, he complained,

> Herewith I have the honour of sending you a copy of my letter to Admiral Ouschakoff, and of his answer, in order that you may transmit them to your Court. Whenever the Admiral chooses to send the *Leander* to Mahon, she will be received but after even my word not being taken by his Excellency, I cannot again subject myself to a refusal of giving up the *Leander*, agreeable to the intentions of the Emperor, although the form of the order on this occasion is not arrived.[28]

In a letter to his friend Troubridge on 31 August, he despondently wrote that he had given up hope of Russian help arriving and was considering resigning his command.[29] The affair of the

---

26. Whitworth to Grenville, 30 April 1799, PRO, FO 65/42.

27. Ushakov to Tomara, 22 August 1799, in *Admiral Ushakov*, 3: 98–99; Ushakov to Nelson, 22 August 1799, ibid., 3: 96.

28. Nelson to Italinsky, 28 August 1799, in *Dispatches and Letters of Nelson*, 3: 467. Nelson, above all, should have understood the vicissitudes of communications at sea. Ushakov eventually received proper orders and transferred the vessel to Nelson. Ushakov to Nelson, 6 September 1799, in *Admiral Ushakov*, 3: 111.

29. Nelson to Troubridge, 31 August 1799, in *Dispatches and Letters of Nelson*, 3: 472.

Leander had certainly not eased the way for the meeting between the allied commanders.

On 1 September 1799, the Russian fleet sailed into the harbor of Palermo to be met by an impressive reception committee of Musin-Pushkin-Bruce, Italinsky, Vice Admiral Kartsov, who had just arrived with a squadron from the North Sea, Nelson's flag captain, and various Neapolitan officers. On 2 September, Nelson visited the Russian admiral and reported, "The object of the Russian Admiral is Malta solely; as to the idea of going to Naples to land troops, in order to go into the Roman State, or to prevent anarchy in the Kingdom, those are secondary operations."[30]

According to Ushakov's logbook, the Russian admiral was indeed desirous of going to Malta, and he had good reasons.[31] Squadrons had already been dispatched along the Italian coast; Paul, it was known, was quite partial to restoring the island to the order of Malta; and the Turkish allies were uninterested in any other object. At a return meeting on 3 September aboard the *Foudroyant*, Nelson's flagship, Ushakov remained obstinate, but in the exchanges of official visits that followed, diplomatic pressure was brought to bear by Nelson and especially by the king upon Italinsky and Ushakov, and on 5 September the admiral agreed to go to Naples. He realized that with Nelson's squadron gone and (according to a report) the Portuguese fleet at Malta withdrawing, and without sufficient soldiers of his own, he could do little at Malta. Ushakov reported to Saint Petersburg that he had deferred to the request of the king of the Two Sicilies.[32]

Ushakov's reluctance to change destination was soon to be strengthened by a serious conflict that occurred between Turkish sailors on shore leave and the local Sicilians. Dissatisfied by the change of orders, and perhaps drunk on Sicilian wine, the Turks

---

30. Nelson to Spencer, 4 September 1799, ibid., 4: 3. "The Russians are anxious to get to Malta, and care for nothing else—therefore I hope you get it before their arrival." Nelson to Ball, 5 September 1799, in ibid., 4: 5.

31. "Istoricheskii Zhurnal," 27 August 1799, in *Admiral Ushakov*, 3: 106.

32. "Istoricheskii Zhurnal," 6 September 1799, in *Admiral Ushakov*, 3: 108; Nelson to Spencer, 6 September 1799, in *Dispatches and Letters of Nelson*, 4: 5.

created incidents that stirred up the traditional feelings of the Sicilians. In the riot that followed Ushakov reported there were 14 killed, 53 wounded and 40 missing from the Turkish crew.[33] The officers had great difficulty restraining the other Turkish sailors from turning the guns of their ships upon the city. The persistent opposition of Patron Bey, the second-in-command of the Turkish fleet, who had troubled both Kadir Bey and Ushakov since they had left Constantinople, was now supported by more officers and seamen of the Turkish fleet. Kadir Bey explained to Ushakov that the Turks were not accustomed to such long campaigns away from a home base, and now that the Maltese destination had been postponed and there appeared little prospect of any capture of booty, morale had collapsed.[34] Ushakov and Nelson did agree on one thing—they sympathized with Kadir Bey's problems, but neither regretted the sailing of the Turkish fleet back to Constantinople on 12 September.[35] As far as Ushakov's naval strength was concerned the addition of the squadron of Vice Admiral Kartsov offset the loss of the Turkish fleet.

The arrival of the Russian fleet in Palermo had one important and beneficial effect—it brought Nelson to action and out of a long period of despondency. On the *Foudroyant*, the writing desks were cleared for action, and flurries of paper missiles were sent flying about the Mediterranean. To the marquis de Niza, Prince of Brazil and commander of the Portuguese squadron that was united with the British at Malta, Nelson wrote, on 5 September: "I send you the *Strombolo*, and a large mortar; and I hope, from the number of people you will be able to land, that La

---

33. Ushakov to Tomara, 13 September 1799, in *Admiral Ushakov*, 3: 121. The Russian commander may have belittled the incident. Acton reports 120 Turks killed and 80 wounded including the Turkish admiral's nephew. Acton. p. 414. See also Danish to Windham, 20 September 1799, in Windham Papers, XI, Add. MSS., BM, 37,852, f. 301.

34. Kadir Bey to Ushakov, 10 September 1799, in *Admiral Ushakov*, 3: 119–20.

35. Nelson to Spencer, 6 September 1799, and Nelson to Smith, 10 September 1799, in *Dispatches and Letters of Nelson*, 4: 5, 7. Ushakov to Tomara, 13 September 1799, in *Admiral Ushakov*, 3: 122.

Valetta will fall to your efforts. The Russians are very anxious to go there—therefore I am doubly interested for your success."[36]

He was at the same time convincing Ushakov that the Maltese siege must be temporarily abandoned. Nelson appealed to every quarter for able ships that could keep the sea in winter, "for the Russian Admiral has already told me that his ships cannot."[37] On 6 September, Nelson wrote to Spencer,

> The King has prevailed on the Russian Admiral to go to Naples, but the more I see, the more I am satisfied they can do no good for active operations, and that they will be a dead weight on their Sicilian Majesties. The Russian Admiral has a polished outside, but the bear is close to the skin. He is jealous of our influence, and thinks whatever is imposed, that we are at the bottom. The Turk, who is by no means a fool— on the contrary has more natural sense than the other—is our brother, and I am sure there is not a thing that we could desire him to do that he would not instantly comply with.[38]

Troubridge was ordered not to go to Minorca as ordered a few days before but to "go direct to Civita Vecchia, and try what can be done; and if you can get possession, then to land not only your Marines, but such other force as you can spare . . . but this must be kept secret, or we shall give jealousy to the Russians."[39] Nelson apparently aimed at beating the Russians to Rome. From his letter of 13 September to the marquis de Niza it is clear that there was little coordination between the British and the Russians at Palermo: "The Russian Squadron is still here, nor can I guess when they sail."[40] Ushakov left that very day for Naples.

That Ushakov's visit had left Nelson in an angry and anti-Russian mood is shown by all his letters of those two weeks and

---

36. Nelson to Marquis de Niza, 5 September 1799, in *Dispatches and Letters of Nelson*, 4: 5. Portugal had been allied with England for many years; the Portuguese contribution in the Mediterranean was small but allowed Nelson a degree of flexibility with his own fleet.

37. Nelson to Duckworth, 5 September 1799, in ibid., p. 6.

38. Ibid.

39. Nelson to Troubridge, 7 September 1799, in ibid., p. 7.

40. Ibid.

most clearly, perhaps, by his important and consequential order to Ball, the English commander at Malta:

> As far as relates to myself, I wish to strain every nerve to get Malta before the bad weather sets in, therefore land guns and use what the Ships afford for taking it. . . . The Russians are very much disposed to pay you a visit. If so, you will, I am sure, heartily co-operate with them, but in that case none but his Sicilian Majesty's colours are to fly in the *whole* island. *All* the ships are to remain without colors, in the care of the Governor, and to be disposed of as the Allied Courts shall agree, but I hope you and Niza will take them, which will save me much trouble.[41]

Nelson had succeeded in getting Ushakov detoured to Naples and was pressing the attack on Rome and Malta to secure their capture before Russian forces got into action.

USHAKOV AT NAPLES

While Nelson was laying these plans at Palermo, the Russian fleet with Italinsky aboard arrived in the Bay of Naples on 18 September. The presence of the fleet and of Captain Baillie's marines in the city helped maintain order and increased Cardinal Ruffo's authority.[42] On 29 September, Ushakov ordered a contingent of 818 men under Colonel Skipor to unite with a Neapolitan force organized by the cardinal to march against Rome and attack the French garrisons in the strongholds of Civita Vecchia and Sant-Angelo.[43] Before these units could march, however, word was received from the Neapolitan force already there that Commodore Troubridge, Nelson's faithful lieutenant, had opened negotiations with the French garrisons under General

---

41. 14 September 1799, in ibid., p. 18. One of the main reasons that the siege of Malta lasted so long was Nelson's reluctance to dismantle ships' guns for use on land, as Ushakov had done at Corfu.

42. Berti, pp. 137–39.

43. Ushakov to Skipor, 29 September 1799, in *Admiral Ushakov*, 3: 128–29.

Bouchard offering rather favorable terms in return for their capitulation to his squadron.[44]

When he heard this, Ushakov was outraged, especially because Troubridge, who had been at Naples when the Russian fleet arrived, had explicitly refused to cooperate with the Russians following the tenor of Nelson's instructions and was obviously acting in a manner detrimental to the allied effort by allowing trapped French garrisons to sail out to Toulon with all arms and ammunition, which probably would soon be reemployed against Suvorov in the north. Despite Ushakov's remonstrances, the surrender of Rome was signed on 27 September.[45] The detachment of Russian marines and Neapolitan soldiers reached Rome on 11 October, marching into the city by the Appian Way, which, according to Russian reports, was lined with Romans shouting "Viva Paulo Primo."[46]

Back at Palermo, new orders that had arrived from London on 20 September helped cool Nelson's temper. The long overdue packets from the Admiralty contained a memorandum of July stating the official British policy regarding Malta, disclaiming any intentions of keeping it, and ordering that it be restored to the Order of Saint John.[47] Another order of 20 August instructed Nelson to cooperate fully with the Russian forces and to concentrate his efforts on capturing Malta. These letters also rebuked Nelson for disobeying Admiral Keith's orders in June (when he had refused to join him at Minorca).[48]

The recent French threat to the western Mediterranean had now passed, with a British fleet sailing into the Atlantic in chase.

---

44. Ushakov to Paul, 1 October 1799, in ibid., 134–35; Nelson to the Admiralty, 1 October 1799, in *Dispatches and Letters of Nelson*, 4: 32.

45. Ushakov to Ruffo, 3 October 1799, and Ushakov to Suvorov, 6 October 1799, in *Admiral Ushakov*, 3: 141–42; Nelson to Troubridge, 7 September 1799, in *Dispatches and Letters of Nelson*, 4: 6.

46. Il'inskii, p. 152; Mouravieff, p. 42.

47. Nelson to Evan Nepean, Esq. (Admiralty), 21 September 1799, in *Dispatches and Letters of Nelson*, 4: 25.

48. Rear Admiral H. W. Richmond, eds., *Private Papers of George, Second Earl of Spencer, First Lord of the Admiralty, 1794–1801*, vol. 3 (London, 1924), p. 98.

Nelson was left in charge of the whole Mediterranean and, in view of the tone of the dispatches he was receiving from London, apparently had second thoughts about the employment of Russian forces. He turned his attention to Malta and was now prepared to cooperate with Ushakov. Since Nelson's personal resources had been exhausted, he may have looked ahead to the probability of receiving rich presents from a grateful grand master, who had already given him an expensive snuff box for his victory at Abukir.[49] At any rate, his tone toward the Russians changed, as can be seen by his letter of 25 September to Ushakov:

> I am more at liberty to act from myself; therefore I again take the opportunity of assuring your Excellency that it is my wish and desire that we should cooperate and join most cordially together for the benefit of the common Cause, and, as is my duty, I shall be as open to you as our two Sovereigns are to each other. I shall rejoice most cordially when we can go against Malta; for I am satisfied it is not to be taken without more force against it.[50]

Russian prospects in the Mediterranean never looked more promising than in October 1799. Russian squadrons were blockading most of the Italian coast, Ushakov was maintaining order at Naples, and the path had been cleared to Malta and for its restoration, upon capture, to the order. Major General Michael Borozdin was on the way from Odessa with two battalions of Imperial Guards for duty as Ferdinand's personal bodyguard; and on 15 October, Ushakov received the important news that Major General Volkonsky was marching from Turin toward Livorno with three battalions of crack grenadiers destined for action against Malta. Volkonsky, however, was delayed by lack of transport and then went to the aid of General Klenau's Aus-

---

49. Acton, p. 355; Nelson to Ball, 6 March 1799, in *Dispatches and Letters of Nelson*, 3: 281. Through the Neapolitan envoy, Nelson had requested honorary Maltese crosses for Hamilton and Captain Ball. Serracapriola to Acton, 8 January 1800, ASN (Archivio di Stati di Napoli), Russi diversi (1800–1802), f. 1681. Nelson could also have been apprehensive about the extended Russian stay in Naples.

50. Nelson to Ushakov, 25 September 1799, in *Dispatches and Letters of Nelson*, 4: 29.

trian army, which was having trouble with the French at Genoa.[51]

While Ushakov dallied in Naples gathering his forces, Nelson sailed to Minorca and back looking for British troops; those that he found could not be obtained because the army was not under his jurisdiction. He repeatedly begged the marquis de Niza to wait at Malta until Russian forces arrived and daily throughout November and December he expected Russian sails to appear on the horizon.[52] Anticipating Russian arrival, but, significantly more than a month after receiving instructions from London, Nelson sent the following order to Ball at Malta:

> I am sure you will co-operate cordially with both Admiral and General; at the same time, you will take care of the honour of our King and Country, and also of His Sicilian Majesty, and recollect that Russia, England, and Naples, are the Allies of the Great Master, that although one Power may have a few men more in the Island than the other, yet they are not to have a preponderance. The moment the French flag is struck, the colours of the Order must be hoisted and no other, when it was settled otherwise the orders from England were not so strong.[53]

On 4 November Ushakov informed Nelson that he would sail by the seventeenth of that month, but no Russians appeared, and Nelson waited impatiently for some word.[54] Although both commanders had long realized that the Russian ships were barely able to keep to the sea, one continued to promise, and the other to expect, their arrival. By the end of December, Nelson had finally given up hope of securing Russian aid and was asking the British army for more land forces. General Graham had already arrived at Malta with 1,500 men, but this was still too few to storm the Maltese castles.

---

51. Ushakov to Volkonsky, 5 November 1799, in *Admiral Ushakov*, 3: 176.

52. Nelson to marquis de Niza, 17 November 1799, in *Dispatches and Letters of Nelson*, 4: 103.

53. Nelson to Ball, 28 October 1799, ibid., p. 72.

54. Ushakov to Nelson, 4 November 1799, in *Admiral Ushakov*, 3: 175; Nelson to Spencer, 18 December 1799, in *Dispatches and Letters of Nelson*, 4: 145.

Ushakov had decided, meanwhile, that his own Black Sea squadron could not effectively participate in the blackade and must go to Corfu for wintering and repairing. The squadron of Vice Admiral Kartsov from the better-constructed Baltic fleet was ordered to proceed to Malta with the grenadiers under Volkonsky.[55] The whole fleet, with the exception of Sorokin's frigates, left the Bay of Naples on 20 December. Before Ushakov and Kartsov separated at Messina, packets were received from the Russian embassy at Palermo on 3 January containing an imperial ukaz, dated 3 November, which ordered Ushakov to return to the Black Sea with all of his forces; no further explanations were given.[56]

---

55. Ushakov to Paul, 24 December 1799, in *Admiral Ushakov*, 3: 223–26; Ushakov to Admiralty College, 31 December 1799, in *Materialy dlia istorii russkago flota*, 17: 410.

56. Paul to Ushakov, 3 November 1799, in *Admiral Ushakov*, 3: 174; Polivanov, p. 17.

6

"Scylla and Charybdis"

A political reason for the orders withdrawing the Russian fleet from the Mediterranean is not difficult to find. Ushakov's sudden recall was probably the result of the deterioration in Austro-Russian relations. Paul, who had never been particularly friendly with the neighboring European power, was angered by what he considered Austria's shameless expansionist policy in Italy. In the wake of Suvorov's liberating army Austrian administrators had established themselves so thoroughly in northern Italy that restitution of the territory to the former sovereigns, particularly to the king of Sardinia, appeared more and more remote. Finally, Suvorov's army, having outlived its usefulness to the Austrians in Italy, was lured into the famous tactical feat of marching over the Alps into Switzerland, where it retreated before the superior French army of Massena.[1] This last reverse was also blamed on lack of proper Austrian support.

The Austrian prime minister, Thugut, whose recalcitrance may have been enough to anger Paul into withdrawing from the coalition, had become the main opponent of the Russian activities in the Mediterranean. Thugut believed that Russian

---

1. Vasil'chikov, *Semeistvo Razumovskykh*, 3: 310–21; Miliutin, *Istoriia voiny*, 3:620–23; Greppi, *Sardaigne, Autriche, Russie*, p. 89. For a discussion of Suvorov's tactics, see the articles of L. M. Leshchinskii and M. L. Al't-govzen in *Suvorovskii Sbornik*, pp. 89–155.

influence in Italy posed a real threat that would always be detrimental to Austria, which he believed must expand and rebuild in Italy in order to balance the advances of France and Russia. As a result of the last two partitions of Poland, Thugut believed that Russia was now firmly entrenched in Central Europe.[2] Austria should be compensated in Italy.

Throughout the summer of 1799, Suvorov had complained to Paul of his treatment by Austria. After the first, tentative recall in August, negotiations were successful in bolstering the weakening alliance, but again the handicap of uncertain control of both diplomatic and military operations hindered the coordination of the war effort.[3] Austria was proceeding on her own course despite her repeated promises of cooperation, and harmony could not be achieved either by British mediation or by Russian diplomacy when the respective ambassadors in Vienna—Minto and Razumovsky—supported the Austrian chancellor.[4] London was

---

2. Greppi, p. 86; Vasil'chikov, 3: 331–34. Thugut had originally looked with favor on Russian arms in the Mediterranean and agreed with Ferdinand of Württemburg's remark, "When the Russian flag passes through the Dardanelles, our affairs in Italy can only improve." Ferdinand to Thugut, 11 September 1798, HHSA, 217 Russland II Corresp.; Thugut to Cobenzl, 10 March 1799, HHSA, 183 Russland II Weisinger. In September, Thugut offered the opinion "that the partitions of Poland were motivated principally only by the necessity to furnish the Powers compensation for the expenses and sacrifices made in the war against France." Russia and Prussia received what they did in anticipation that their sacrifices would be as great as Austria's; now Austria needed more territory in compensation. Thugut to Cobenzl, 12 September 1799, HHSA, 184 Russland II Weisinger.

3. For examples, see Suvorov's letters to his sovereign of 27 May 1799, and 30 August 1799, in Greppi, pp. 72–75. Paul stuck it out gamely: "I charge you to occupy Malta and punish wickedness, envy, and ingratitude by new triumphs." Paul to Suvorov, 20 August 1799, in Greppi, p. 85. Thugut, on the other hand, complained of the "incoherences of Marshal Suvorov" and "the alienation of the inhabitants by the unbelievable ravages of the Russians." Thugut to Cobenzl, 12 September 1799, HHSA, 184 Russland II Weisinger. Suvorov went to Italy with an elite, hard-striking army that was unencumbered by the usual quartermaster, foraging and ordinance units. His success rested on an ability to move fast and to achieve surprise by not letting anyone know where he was going. And he expected the Austrian quartermaster to keep up with him!

4. F. Martens, *Sobranie traktatov i konventsii, zakliuchennykh Rossieiu s inostrannymi derzhavami* (Saint Petersburg, 1874–1909) 11: 2–3.

on a tightrope trying to offend neither power and retain both as continental allies. By September the break had been temporarily mended, and it seemed quite possible that the coalition would survive the winter and that in the spring another Russian army could be brought to fight on the battlefields of Western Europe.

Paul himself had taken a major step toward solving the differences between the allies by proposing, in September 1799, a congress to be held at Saint Petersburg in October to solve the problem of indemnities and compensations, future borders, and military strategy. Britain agreed to such a meeting to satisfy the tsar, but Austria refused to attend.[5]

Paul even offered tentative territorial arrangements as a basis for negotiations at the congress. A copy of his suggestions, which Whitworth believed were inspired by Rostopchin, Gallo, and Serracapriola, was forwarded to London by the British ambassador on 23 September. Paul gave Austria the choice of Venice or the Low Countries but not both. Russia would received only Malta, "as the property of the Order, of which H. I. M. the Emperor is the Grand Master." Naples would get the Three Legations, as Gallo proposed, and Genoa would go to Sardinia. "The Venetian Islands would be established as a republic under an aristocratic government protected by Russia and the Porte."[6] The refusal of Austria to allow him the possibility of arbitrating peace for Europe increased Paul's hostility. An anti-Austrian mood was also reflected by several important diplomats in the Russian capital, notably Whitworth, Gallo, and Serracapriola.[7]

---

5. Whitworth to Grenville, 6 October 1799, PRO, FO 65/44; Gallo to Acton, 23 September 1799, in Somma, *Une mission diplomatique*, p. 213; Rostopchin to S. R. Vorontsov, 5 September 1799, in *Arkhiv Vorontsova*, 8: 239. Thugut objected that a congress would be subject "to the hostile insinuations of the smallest prince in Italy" and that Austria could not "defer to Russia the right to dispose of the fruit of our blood and our efforts. . . . We have a right to obtain following the present war what will be considered perfectly equal to the acquisitions made by Russia in the last two partitions of Poland." Thugut to Cobenzl, 12 September 1799, HHSA, 184 Russland II Weisinger.

6. Whitworth to Grenville, 23 September 1799, PRO, FO 65/44.

7. Whitworth to Grenville, 22 August 1799, PRO, FO 65/44.

THE RECALL OF USHAKOV

In early October 1799, Paul received news of the defeat of the Russian army in Switzerland, due, it seemed to him and his advisors, to Austrian inertia or duplicity. When this was confirmed he wrote on 22 October to the Austrian emperor announcing forthwith his withdrawal from the coalition, "seeing my troops abandoned and sacrificed to the enemy."[8] A few days later the emperor announced his decision to a court assemblage at Gatchina.[9] Suvorov's army was immediately called back to the Russian frontier for the winter. And one week later, on 3 November, the order was issued recalling the Russian fleet to the Black Sea:

> LORD ADMIRAL USHAKOV:
> Because of circumstances revealed we find that it is necessary to bring the squadrons under your command to the Black Sea. Therefore, we order you to reunite all detached squadrons with yours, i.e., those of Vice Admirals Pustoshkin and Kartsov also located in the Venetian Gulf [sic]; and, taking into consideration orders already given to you, if Malta has still not been captured, the Maltese garrison and our troops located in the Neapolitan Kingdom are to be transported to our ports. On Corfu and other islands Turkish garrisons should be introduced upon your departure. This gesture of ours should be accepted by the Porte as a sign of our friendly disposition so that, in exchange, objections should not be raised to the passage of Vice Admiral Kartsov's squadron [which was originally from the Baltic] into the Black Sea for repairs. On the other hand all other countries' ships will be forbidden entrance there—we have written our minister Tomara on this subject. Our best wishes are extended to you.
>
> PAUL[10]

But it could also be argued that the Suvorov episode had little to do with the withdrawal of the fleet. The Russian fleet in the Mediterranean was never wholly involved in Austria's advances

---

8. Paul to Francis II, 22 October 1799, in Greppi, p. 92.
9. Whitworth to Grenville, 24 and 27 October 1799, PRO, FO 65/44.
10. In *Admiral Ushakov*, 3: 174–75.

in Italy, and most of it was in the process of disengaging from that area to assist in the siege of Malta, the apple of the grand master's eye. Dissatisfaction with Austria set the mood of the court at Saint Petersburg for the recall, but additional factors can be cited that contributed to the withdrawal. Ushakov had complained numerous times directly to Paul and to the Admiralty College about the condition of his ships. Even before reaching Constantinople they had shown signs of weakness; by December 1799, the ships could barely be kept in service. And the admiral had already decided to withdraw the main fleet from action before receiving his orders of recall.[11] He planned to send the worst ships back to the Black Sea, repair the others at Corfu, and hope for arrival of reinforcements from Russia.[12]

Taking into account the delays in communications, but not the slowness of Ushakov, Paul could have expected that Malta would be captured by Russian forces and garrisoned by Volkonsky's troops by the time the order arrived at its destination. But if the island had not fallen by December, there would be little likelihood of its capture before the next summer.[13] The recall of Ushakov's fleet, coming at this moment in the Mediterranean campaign, could thus be interpreted as only routine in nature. The Russian fleet was of little value to anyone without extensive renovation and reinforcement, and Ushakov probably delayed his departure from Naples in December in the hope of receiving orders relieving him from further action that winter.

This step, therefore, does not prove that Paul's interest in the Mediterranean had dramatically changed. The passage of a Baltic Sea squadron into the Black Sea "for repairs" and the increased ship building activity in the Black Sea ports indicate that the tsar was looking forward to another campaign in 1800.[14] But Paul's orders of October and November 1799, however justified they might appear, left Europe in an extremely dan-

11. Ushakov to Paul, 24 December 1799, ibid., p. 225.

12. Ushakov to Tomara, 24 December 1799, ibid., pp. 227–28, and Ushakov to Kushelev, 31 December 1799, ibid., pp. 231–32.

13. *Materialy dlia istorii russkago flota*, 17: 307–14.

14. Ibid.

gerous situation and set the stage for Bonaparte's triumph over the Austrians at Marengo in June 1800.

When the order for recall arrived, Ushakov complied with unusual vigor, but he found some matters to be beyond his control. The fleet simply needed major repairs before it could make passage to the Black Sea. Facilities for repair of large ships were practically nonexistent in the Ionians, and Ushakov lacked the necessary funds to build them.[15] The main fleet did not leave Corfu until July 1800, and even then ships that were under restoration had to be left behind under Captain Voinovich through the winter of 1800–1801.[16]

A complete withdrawal of Russian forces simply could not materialize because of the nature of Russia's commitments in this theater. Borozdin, refusing to be considered under Ushakov's command, insisted that his own instructions had not been canceled and eventually went on to Naples in March 1800, without receiving further orders from Saint Petersburg.[17] There he found a Russian garrison under Captain Baillie and Captain Sorokin still performing guard duties. He also encountered acute supply problems. Moreover, there was no king at Naples to guard. Russian efforts to bring Ferdinand to Naples or to transfer the troops to Palermo were frustrated, and the curbs placed upon Borozdin's authority brought about conflicts not only with the Neapolitan ministers but also with Sorokin and Italinsky. But still the presence of these Russians was considered essential by the Neapolitan court, and Ferdinand prevailed upon Paul to leave

---

15. The Russian commanders made several attempts to obtain masts and other materials from Sicily. Acton to Serracapriola, 14 and 30 April 1800, ASN, 2699.

16. Ushakov to Paul, 14 June 1800, in *Admiral Ushakov*, 3: 373–74; Foresti to Grenville, 18 March 1801, PRO, FO 42/4.

17. Borozdin had been an aide-de-camp to the tsar and may have felt that his mission was a personal matter of Paul. One order named him commandant of Malta; so this may have been intended as his ultimate destination. M. Polivanov, *M. M. Borozdin, nachalnik okhrany Neapolitanskago korolia, 1800–1802 gg.* (Saint Petersburg, 1912), pp. 20–23. Foresti claimed that Borozdin's stay of five months on the Ionian Islands with 1,800 men cost the inhabitants 20,000 imperial dollars. Foresti to Grenville, 20 March 1800, PRO, FO 42/4.

them in Italy after the abandonment by Russia of the coalition.[18]

Before Ushakov sailed from Corfu on 18 July he was more active than ever, sending squadrons across the Mediterranean as far as the north coast of Africa and using the elite corps of General Volkonsky to police the islands and to bring the "Ushakov Constitution" into full force. He even ordered Vice Admiral Kartsov to join his squadron to the English fleet under Admiral Keith, but more explicit instructions, sent after it became clear in Saint Petersburg that the Russians were not about to take Malta, forced Ushakov to call in all of his remaining forces in the Mediterranean for departure to the Black Sea.[19] The Ionians were cleared of Russian forces in July, but Captain Voinovich arrived in September with the limping remnants of the Russian fleet. He and Lieutenant Tisenghausen were left in charge of preserving order in the Ionians until reinforcements arrived in the summer of 1801.[20]

ANGLO-RUSSIAN RELATIONS

British diplomats still hoped in November 1799 that the deepening rift between Russia and Austria might be patched. Whitworth continued to warn Grenville of Paul's special concern with the island of Malta; from Berlin, Thomas Grenville, brother of the English minister, wrote sympathetically of Russian policy.[21] Arthur Paget in Naples consoled Italinsky over the shallow vicissitudes of the Neapolitan court, and Lord Elgin entertained Tomara with after-dinner soliloquies on classical

---

18. Polivanov, p. 29 ff. Rostopchin confirmed that Borozdin was under separate orders in a note to Serracapriola, 5 January 1800, ASN, 1681. After a series of exchanges in which the Neapolitans tried to retain the Russian guards, Paul decided to recall them at the beginning of 1801. Paul to Ferdinand, 2 January 1801, ASN, 2699.

19. Foresti to Grenville, 9 April, and 26 May 1800, PRO, FO 42/4.

20. Foresti to Grenville, 7 October 1800, PRO, FO 42/4. On his way to Corfu, Voinovich delivered some cannon to the Montenegrins at Budva.

21. Whitworth to Grenville, 1 November 1799, PRO, FO 65/45; T. Grenville to Lord Grenville, 12 July 1799, and to Lord Minto, 15 August 1799, in *Dropmore*, 5: 137, 302.

marbles.[22] On the gray November evenings in Londo, abnormal supply of candles and ink were devoted to arbitrat the differences between the two allies; one dispatch from Gren ville to Whitworth ran to sixty-four pages.[23]

Although many high officials in London believed that the winter storm would blow itself out and spring would again find Russian armies backed by substantial subsidies on the march, there was a growing body of opinion supporting Thugut's view that Russian power had expanded too rapidly in central and southern Europe and that Austria and Britain could take care of things themselves. William Pitt looked forward to the possibility of Russia and Britain acting without Austria in the next campaign, if necessary, but he believed in September that the coalition could be saved if certain steps were taken immediately, such as to replace Whitworth by Thomas Grenville and to secure Razumovsky's replacement by Panin.[24] Lord Grenville sympathized with Vorontsov's violently anti-Austrian mood in September and October but in November began to bow to the opinion of Henry Dundas, the India minister, who, after reading the reports of Colonel Wickham on the Russian performance in Switzerland, wrote,

> I am impressed with a perfect conviction that it is in vain to look for any effectual aid from the armies of Russia in the course of the next campaign. They are brave men, and are, I suppose, as good materials as can be for the formation of a powerful army; and, even in their present state, are in Russia itself, or in Turkey, as irresistable troops as can be supposed. But on the other hand if they are to act either in Italy or in Switzerland, they must be totally new modelled.[25]

22. Paget to Grenville, 13 May 1800, in *Paget Papers*, 1: 206–17. On Tomara's relations with Elgin see P. Coquelle, "La Mission de Sebastiani à Constantinople," *Revue d'histoire diplomatique* 17 (1903): 444; and Pouqueville, *Travels Through the Morea*, pp. 148–50.

23. Grenville to Whitworth, 19 November 1799, PRO, FO 65/44.

24. "I think the chief difficulty remaining will be to bring the Emperor Paul to go as far as we may think right, towards satisfying the avidity of Austria." Pitt to Grenville, 10 September 1799, in *Dropmore*, 5: 379.

25. 5 November 1799, in *Dropmore*, 6: 12–13.

more anti-Russian feelings of the military commanders, ecially now that they had time to resent the publicity gained y Suvorov and the presence of the Russian navy outside of the Baltic and Black Seas, influenced British policy. Influenced by Whitworth's hostile opinions of Paul and troubled by complaints from the Russians wintering on Jersey and Guernsey, Grenville gave in to the Austrian loan demands and considered offering Austria a free hand in Italy in return for acquiescence to a united and independent Netherlands.[26]

PROBLEMS OF RUSSIAN LEADERSHIP

The last months of 1799 were busy ones in Saint Petersburg too. As expected, the vacancy left by the death of Bezborodko in the spring presented difficulties for Russian administration. S. R. Vorontsov, Paul's first choice for the post of chancellor, declined to leave London for the "chilly" atmosphere of Saint Petersburg, and the emperor personally disliked his capable brother, A. R. Vorontsov.[27] But a new generation of diplomats was rising and filling positions in the foreign departments. Serving in minor posts were two newcomers, Czartoryski and Nesselrode, who steered Russian foreign policy for most of the first half of the nineteenth century. Occupying the highest positions were three outstanding young men whose energy and dedication left little to be desired—Victor Kochubei, Fedor Rostopchin, and Nikita Panin. It was Russia's misfortune that these men lacked experience in leadership and could not get along with each other.

---

26. Whitworth wrote on 13 November: "We are in a dreadful crisis, and I scarcely see how we shall be able to calm the Emperor's mind. His indignation against the Court of Vienna is carried beyond all bounds; and indeed so much so, that one would be tempted to suspect it was affected; or at least fomented and made use of as a pretext for withdrawing his troops, and returning to that passive system which we so long lamented. It is a dreadful consideration to reflect that all these misfortunes are to be attributed entirely to the character of the sovereign, in whom, I am sorry to say, vigour of mind, and patience under adversity are so much wanting as they are necessary." *Dropmore*, 6: 19–20.

27. S. R. Vorontsov to Paul, 9 October 1798, and to A. R. Vorontsov, 14 June 1799, in *Arkhiv Vorontsova*, 10: 326, 49.

Kochubei, as vice-chancellor, first tried to fill the breach left by his uncle's death but was unable to surmount the opposition of the emperor's favorites, especially Kutaisov. He disliked the war and would have preferred to work on internal reforms. A long absence while serving as ambassador to Constantinople deprived Kochubei of solid social connections in the Russian capital. In addition, his kinship to the former chancellor made him a target of Bezborodko's enemies.[28] One of them, Fedor Rostopchin, emerged in August 1799 with the duties of chancellor.

Rostopchin's character and role in Russian history have remained controversial. A skillful manipulator, he rose from the lower nobility to the first rank in the empire by catering to the tsar's whims. Rostopchin's views, in general, represented the spirit of Moscow, a dislike for foreign involvement in Russian affairs and for Russian involvement in foreign affairs. He supported a return to the "sit and march" theory of Russian expansion—to sit on the border and wait for the opportunity to march; later, in 1800, he was involved in some vague proposals for the dismemberment of the Ottoman Empire.[29] He was also partial toward France, despite the prevailing sentiment in Saint Petersburg in 1799. Although Rostopchin's career lacked distinction because of his inability to gain the complete confidence of the emperor or to win public support, his ascendancy came at an opportune time to lend support to the tsar's resolution to withdraw from the coalition.[30]

Nikita Petrovich Panin was one of those who opposed Paul's

---

28. Rostopchin to S. R. Vorontsov, 23 June 1799, in *Arkhiv Vorontsova*, 8: 219.

29. The partition plan is contained in Rostopchin's memoir of 14 October 1800. For a discussion of this see Duc de Broglie, "Politique de la Russia en 1800 d'après un document inédit," *Revue d'histoire diplomatique* 3 (1889): 1–12, and Trachevsky, "L'Empereur Paul et Bonaparte, Premier Consul," *Revue d'histoire diplomatique* 3 (1889): 281–86.

30. Rostopchin followed Bonaparte's rise very closely. See his letter to S. R. Vorontsov, 3 December 1799, *Arkhiv Vorontsova*, 8: 270. See also A. L. Narochnitskii, *Mezhdunarodnye otnosheniia evropeiskikh gosudarstv s 1794 do 1830 g.* (Moscow, 1946), p. 18.

policies most severely. As the nephew of the Russian statesman Nikita Ivanovich Panin, Catherine's foreign advisor in the 1770s, he rose rapidly in state service, serving with a great deal of responsibility for his twenty-eight years as special ambassador to Berlin in 1797. Though nothing came of his negotiations with a special French emissary, Paul remembered his services and recalled him to Russia in September 1799 as a special adviser on foreign affairs and to replace Kochubei with the rank of vice-chancellor.[31] The emperor may have wished to muster the best available talent in the capital at a critical time, to counterbalance the powers of Rostopchin, or to suit his purpose of isolating himself from foreign influences. Panin's support of the coalition and his pro-British sentiments obviously conflicted with the views of Rostopchin.

The technical supervision of Russian foreign affairs from November 1799 to November 1800 rested with the three "members" of the college—Rostopchin, Panin, and Dmitri Tatishchev. Rostopchin was the only one who had regular access to Paul; foreign diplomats could confer regularly only with Panin, and Tatishchev, befitting his lower rank, handled routine business. Thus, the influence of Panin and foreign diplomats on Russian policy was severely limited. At the end of November, however, Panin made strong remonstrances to Rostopchin about the recall of Suvorov's army and even threatened to resign. Paul, to his surprise, agreed to modify the orders to allow Suvorov to winter in Austria.[32]

The two leaders of the government and the more experienced diplomats abroad, such as Razumovsky, Vorontsov, Krudener, Kolychev, Italinsky, Mordvinov, and Tomara, were often engaged in mutual recriminations, seldom acted in harmony, and

---

31. Rostopchin to S. R. Vorontsov, 5 September 1799, in *Arkhiv Vorontsova*, 8: 235; Panin to S. R. Vorontsov, 19 September 1799, *Arkhiv Vorontsova*, 11: 92.

32. *Materialy dlia zhizneopisaniia Grafa Nikity Petrovicha Panina* (1770–1837), ed. A. Brikner, 5 (Saint Petersburg, 1891): 33–37; Whitworth to Grenville, 5 December 1799, PRO, FO 65/45.

generally failed to secure loyalty among subordinates. Russian administration at this time might best be described as government by intrigue. Is it any wonder that few Russian officials were able to gain the confidence of the emperor? Or was this situation due to the emperor's own inconstant leadership? The machinations of the ministers certainly improved neither the temperament of the tsar nor the atmosphere of the court; but this picture was not unique to Russia.

It was not the best season for working in Saint Petersburg, London, or Vienna—dark and cold, with rain and snow. Diversions were found in gambling salons and theaters and at private parties—to brighten the spirits and to lighten the diplomatic purse; while in drafty rooms beside sputtering lamps the secretaries scribbled the long, wordy dispatches that provided the unsteady connection between remote capitals. In these conditions so much could depend on daily moods or illnesses, the speed of a courier, the interception of dispatches, a social faux pas, a gambling loss, or the weather, which was especially bad in the winter of 1799–1800.

Panin tried to negotiate with Cobenzl, the Austrian ambassador, through Abbé Georgel, a Maltese official who offered to mediate, but Cobenzl soon returned to Vienna for both private and official reasons, and discussions with Dietrichstein, Cobenzl's replacement, were unsuccessful.[33] Whitworth gradually became estranged from the Russian court, and for this he blamed Rostopchin, although he really had himself to blame.[34] The allied cause was not entirely lost, however. In December Paul showed signs of forgiving Austria and made arrangements to reverse his army's retreat across that country. In addition, a French émigré general in Russian service, Viomesnil, was summoned to take charge of the Russian troops wintering on Jersey and Guernsey in the English Channel and to command an ambitious project

---

33. Georgel, *Mémoires*, pp. 178–80; Vasil'chikov, 3: 351.
34. Grenville to Whitworth, 19 November 1799, PRO, FO 65/45; Whitworth to Grenville, 28 November 1799, PRO, FO 65/45; and Whitworth to Grenville, 2 April 1800, PRO, FO 65/46.

drawn up by Paul, on earlier suggestions of General Dumouriez, for invading the Southwest of France, a plan that counted heavily on a pro-Bourbon revolt within France.[35]

But at the end of December 1799, dispatches arrived in Saint Petersburg relating the circumstances of the fall of Ancona, a strategic port on the upper Adriatic coast of Italy. According to Ushakov's reports, Captain Voinovich had fought diligently to secure the surrender of this French Adriatic base, but an Austrian army under General Fröhlich arriving in support began separate negotiations with the French defenders.[36] Not only were the Russians prevented from participating in the surrender, but the Russian flags that had been raised on several captured ships in the habor were unceremoniously removed by Austrian detachments.[37] Ushakov complained in detailed letters to the tsar, who demanded immediately that Vienna apologize and punish the general involved, and, although Austria eventually complied, Paul's anger had become implacable; the Austro-Russian alliance was at an end.

Even after the Ancona affair, allied diplomats hoped that Russia would in some degree continue her support of the coalition in the spring campaign. Paul, they thought, would still be interested in gaining more glory through the feats of the Russian army. Surprisingly, his animosity toward Austria was again waning at the beginning of the new year. Paul's recall of the army and the fleet appeared to optimists as a normal withdrawal of forces for the winter; he had expressed his anger at Austria

---

35. Georgel, p. 155–57; Whitworth to Grenville, 5 December 1799, PRO, FO 65/45; Grenville to Whitworth, 17 December 1799, PRO, FO 65/45. See also Robert Meynadier, "Un Plan de l'Empereur Paul de Russie," *La Revue de Paris* 17 (1920): 185–97.

36. Voinovich to Ushakov, 23 November 1799, in *Admiral Ushakov*, 3: 191–93, and three reports of Ushakov to Paul, 27 November 1799, and Voinovich to Kushelev, 12 December 1799, in ibid., pp. 201–3, 212–19. For Paul's reaction see Whitworth to Grenville, 27 December 1799, PRO, FO 65/45; Serracapriola to Acton, 5 January 1800, ASN, 2699; and Dietrichstein to Thugut, 27 December 1799, HHSA, 93 Russland II Berichte.

37. Voinovich to Fröhlich, 19 November 1799, in *Admiral Ushakov*, 3: 190; Sorokin, "Morskiia kampanii 1798 i 1799 gg.," *Zapiski Gidrograficheskogo Departamenta*, 8: 316–18.

only in the form of a strong rebuff intended to bring Austria into line by the time of the next campaign.[38] There was always time for this sort of maneuver in the winter.

Maltese affairs still influenced Russian policy. In December, Paul ordered four squadrons to be prepared to sail under the flag of the Order of Saint John to Malta. Admiral Kushelev, a Maltese knight and president of the Admiralty College, was given command.[39] It began to appear that the cause of the Order of Malta might dominate that of the Russian empire. Good news from Ushakov was expected at any moment; as late as 9 February 1800, Rostopchin wrote, "We expect at any moment news of the expedition against Malta, and if Ushakov has concerted well with Nelson, success must not fail."[40] The eventual arrival of dispatches announcing the withdrawal of Ushakov from the campaign and the inability of Nelson to press the attack discouraged the emperor.

THE ANGLO-RUSSIAN HIATUS

The British ambassador was another cog in the imperial machine that failed to turn according to Paul's wishes. Dejected and separated from diplomatic society during the winter, Whitworth found solace in the company of his young and vivacious mistress, Madam Zherebtsova, who entertained regularly a group of the "outs" of Saint Petersburg—consisting of her brothers, the Zubovs, and their friends—until March 1800, when she was expelled from the city.[41] This was not suitable society for the English ambassador, and his dispatches that winter show its influence in his careless, unflattering references to the emperor. These messages were sent in cipher but sometimes by Russian courier, and

38. Whitworth to Grenville, 7 and 14 January 1800, PRO, FO 65/46.
39. Ukaz of Paul, 25 December 1799, in *Materialy*, 16: 483.
40. Rostopchin to S. R. Vorontsov, 9 February 1800, in *Arkhiv Vorontsova*, 8: 272.
41. S. R. Vorontsov to A. R. Vorontsov, 12 August 1801, *Arkhiv Vorontsova*, 10: 113; Cobenzl to Thugut, 10 February 1800, HHSA, 94 Russland II Berichte.

it soon became apparent, even to Whitworth, that the Russians had the key to his cipher and that Rostopchin was using his indiscretions to alienate the emperor from him. Paul officially requested Whitworth's replacement in a letter to Vorontsov on 11 February,[42] but the ambassador was not aware of this until March, when his private couriers were refused passports.[43] He was forced to resort to the public mail, but he still insulted the intelligence of the Russian chancellor by diatribes against Russia written in invisible ink. Paul's anger increased with Whitworth's growing desire to be relieved of such an uncomfortable post.

The expulsion in May of the British ambassador was the result of a personal feud between the emperor and Whitworth, brought about by the latter's lack of discretion and propriety at the Russian court and Rostopchin's animosity.[44] The crisis in Anglo-Russian relations that followed might not have developed if England had been respresented in Saint Petersburg by an ambassador of sounder diplomatic bearing like Thomas Grenville, who had been offered (but refused) a special mission to Russia in August 1799.[45]

The lapse of diplomatic communications between Britain and Russia effactually ended the prospects of Russia's further participation in the war. The troubles involving the supply of Russian troops quartered for the winter on Jersey and Guernsey, and Nelson's high-handed attitude in the Mediterranean, aggravated the estrangement.[46] In February Vorontsov was ordered to take a rest on the continent; he chose to resign his commission and, with Paul's permission, stayed in England.[47] Panin, the Vorontsovs, and other Anglophiles were saddened by the emper-

---

42. Martens, 11: 5; Rostopchin to Vorontsov, 11 February 1800, in *Dropmore*, 16: 113.

43. Whitworth to Grenville, 2 April 1800, PRO, FO 65/46.

44. Cobenzl, the Austrian ambassador, was equally isolated and left soon after Whitworth. Cobenzl to Thugut, 17 May 1800, 94 Russland II Berichte.

45. T. Grenville to Lord Grenville, 3 September 1799, in *Dropmore*, 5: 352.

46. S. R. Vorontsov to A. R. Vorontsov, 14 December 1799, in *Arkhiv Vorontsova*, 10: 71.

47. S. R. Vorontsov to Rostopchin, 9 March 1800, in ibid., 8: 515; S. R. Vorontsov to Paul, 8 May 1800, and 26 June 1800, ibid., 10: 335, 352.

or's abandonment of the coalition, but Paul was firmly convinced that Russian arms had simply been used by Austria and England during the last campaign to advance their own ends, and he saw no reason for this to continue.

Russia's growing estrangement from the coalition coincided with changes in France. On 9 November 1799 (18 Brumaire) the Consulate had been established with General Bonaparte as First Consul and, in effect, ruler of France. Paul, who had always admired the military feats of the French general, was probably one of the first to suspect that the rise of Bonaparte signaled the slackening of the revolutionary fervor in France.[48] A country ruled by a strong general now seemed more to his taste than those headed by weak monarchs. Paul compromised his monarchical principles but did not intend to abandon his role as the great crusader.

Bonaparte saw the golden opportunity presented by Paul's alienation from the Second Coalition. Fortunately for him the ablest diplomat in Europe, Talleyrand, was at his disposal. The first French overture for opening talks was made in Hamburg, where the Russian minister, Muraviev, responded in a cool and noncommital manner. A clever act of diplomacy was then initiated. Since the British had refused to exchange French captives for Russian soldiers captured in Switzerland and Holland, and the Russians had no French prisoners to barter, Bonaparte shrewdly decided to return them to Russia simply as a goodwill gesture. This offer was bound to impress the knightly inclinations of the emperor. More pleasing to Paul personally were the gift of a historic Maltese sword and an offer to restore the island of Malta to the possession of the Order of Saint John. Bonaparte released one of the captured Russian officers in August 1800 to carry his offers to the emperor.[49]

---

48. Rostopchin to S. R. Vorontsov, 4 December 1799, in *Arkhiv Vorontsova*, 8: 270. Just after receiving this news on 4 December, Paul wrote to his agent in England, "It is extremely important to know just what turn the new revolution in the French Government will take." Paul to Viomesnil, 4 December 1799, in Meynadier, p. 193.

49. Emile Bourgeois, "L'Alliance de Bonaparte et de Paul Ier (1800–1801)," *Séances et travaux de l'Académie des sciences morales et politiques: Compte Rendu*, 82, (1922): 278; K. Voenskii, *Bonapart i russkie plennye*

Late in 1799, Bonaparte had sent peace feelers to Britain partly in the hope of retaining Malta as a stepping stone in the Mediterranean, but the British stalled, and by the summer of 1800 the capture of the island by the British besiegers seemed inevitable, unless through Russian pressure Britain could be forced to give up the siege and agree to transfer the island to the order of Saint John, as indeed was still the announced policy in London. As the most active supporter of the interests of the knights, Paul would be pleased to accomplish the restoration. This would have been awkward for Paul, however, for he could not leave his empire to reside at Malta as grand master of the order; Malta would become an advance post of the order, but the Grand Council would probably have remained safely at the grand master's doorstep in Saint Petersburg. Because of the destruction of papers by his successors, evidence of the emperor's designs at this time is quite fragmentary: Paul may have envisaged a grand pilgrimage through western Europe to receive the homage of grateful monarchs, the embrace of Bonaparte, and the blessings of the pope, and to sit for a few days on the grand master's throne in Valetta.

But how could the territory of the order really be separated from that of the Russian Empire? The specter of the Russian threat to British interests in the South was rising even before the rumors of the restoration of relations between France and Russia added weight to British apprehensions. It was not necessary to raise a parliamentary outcry, as Pitt had done in 1791, to create public concern over the danger to British interests in the Mediterranean. Although Paul's repeated disavowals of territorial acquisition for Russia and the sacrifices of Suvorov in Italy had been noted and appreciated in Britain, they did not erase the fear of a new Russian expansion into the Mediterranean, going far beyond Catherine's moves in that direction in 1770. This sentiment is well summed up in Lord Elgin's dispatch to Arthur Paget from Constantinople: "Its [sic] probable that the Emperor

---

vo Frantsii (1799–1801): *epizod iz istorii franko-russkikh otnoshenii v kontse XVIII e nachale XIX veka* (Saint Petersburg, 1906), pp. 16–17.

himself may disclaim all views of conquest on Turkey, but I defy a Russian agent to divest himself of the idea that by working for that object he is performing the most essential service to his sovereign."[50] And regarding Malta, Dundas explained to Grenville,

> I have not the treaty with Russia by me as to Malta, but, if my recollection is right, neither the Grand Master of the Order of Malta or his deputy, *as such*, under the agreement have any thing to do with it, until the island is restored to the Order *at a general peace*, or *at such earlier period as may be agreed upon by mutual consent*. So that I am sure we are acting accurately within both the words and the spirit of the treaty. I hope in God you will be able to make such an arrangement with Russia as may secure to us, *as a naval power*, all the advantages which the island of Malta possesses.[51]

If some English diplomats and officials did not trust Russian motives, the quasi-independent military authorities in the Mediterranean were even more suspicious of them. After the departure of Nelson (aboard a Russian frigate) for a continental tour and home rest in 1800, Viscount Keith became the naval commander in the Mediterranean. He expressed his annoyance with the northern ally in picturesque terms: "I wish you would tell me how the Pulse of the Russians beats, I hardly know how to write them there are so many reports from various quarters." Later, when referring to the Russians, he wrote, "When will England become wise and have no Continental connections?"[52] In another letter Keith guessed, "I do not believe the Russians have any intentions of sending a Man to Malta."[53]

Pitt still favored efforts to placate Russia, but a rift between him and the king weakened his influence, and various domestic problems were overshadowing foreign policy making in London.

---

50. Elgin to Paget, 8 March 1800, in *Paget Papers*, 1: 187.
51. Dundas to Grenville, 20 April 1800, in *Dropmore*, 6: 199. Italics represent underlining in original.
52. Keith to Paget, 20 June and 24 July 1800, in *Paget Papers*, 1: 233, 259.
53. Keith to Paget, 25 July 1800, in ibid., p. 259.

Although the break between Britain and Russia, further aggravated by personality feuds and a misunderstanding over the treatment of Russian soldiers still quartered on Jersey and Guernsey, could have been patched with a little give and take on both sides, the split continued to widen in the summer of 1800, and Bonaparte and Talleyrand were busily pounding in the wedge. On 1 August definite instructions were sent from London to army authorities at Malta to act independently of the Russians.

It was one thing for France to encourage a rupture between Russia and Britain and quite another to achieve for herself a rapprochement with Russia. It is surprising that the French did not move more quickly in restoring relations with Russia, but at the beginning of the nineteenth century, power relationships were in an unusual state of imbalance, and both sides seemed to be waiting for the other to move. Paul finally pounced and created a stir of confusion, which was not even ended by his murder. General Sprengporten, a Hanoverian adventurer in Russian service, was dispatched to take charge of the returning Russian prisoners and to make certain discreet overtures to Bonaparte.[54] This led to the resumption of diplomatic relations between the French Republic and the Russian Empire. In the balancing equation, agreement with England became more remote as relations with France improved, but the possibilities of peace grew also as the chances of continental military activities by the Second Coalition dimmed.

The affairs in the Baltic must be briefly mentioned because of their close connection with the Mediterranean. The leading neutrals of the north, Denmark and Sweden, had been offended by British naval practices during the war; they took advantage of the Anglo-Russian breach to appeal to Paul's acute, though sometimes unbalanced, sense of justice. These northern powers, especially Sweden, possessed first-class diplomats in Saint Petersburg.[55] The British seizure of the Danish ship *La Freya* on 25 July resulted in the Russian step, in early September, of issuing

---

54. Voenskii, pp. 19–20.
55. Count Stedingk represented Sweden from 1792 to 1812.

a strong protest and placing a temporary embargo on British shipping in Russian ports.[56] But when Britain made a conciliatory move toward Denmark, the embargo was immediately lifted.[57] This apparent success brought the northern countries into even closer cooperation.

In early November 1800, Paul received the details of the fall of Malta (in September) to the British.[58] Instead of complying with the two-year old Convention of Saint Petersburg, which provided for a joint Anglo-Russian-Neapolitan occupation in the name of the Maltese Order, the British army in charge of the siege raised only the British flag over the fortress. This action was contrary to the announced policy of the Foreign Office in London. British diplomatic and naval authorities in the Mediterranean were informed of the change in policy only after the event had occurred.[59] Paget had learned of the army orders in August and had immediately complained to General Pigot, who was in charge of the siege:

> It is in direct opposition to the spirit both of Lord Keith's and my own Instructions upon the subject of Malta—which are that the fortresses of Malta shall be garrisoned by the

---

56. The declaration of the embargo was signed by Rostopchin and Panin on 28 August 1800, but was not put into effect until 4 September. A copy was found in ASN, 1681. For an excellent survey of Paul's inauguration of the armed neutrality, see Alexander I's long letter to Baron Krudener, 17 July 1801, in *Vneshniaia politika Rossii XIX i nachale XX veka*, ed. A. L. Narochnitskii, A. A. Gromyko, et al. (Seriia pervaia: "1801–1815 gg."; Vol. 1: mart 1801 g.-aprel' 1804 g.) (Moscow, 1960), pp. 42–49.

57. M. D. Khmyrov, ed., "Imperator Pavel Petrovich, 1800–1801: Vysochaishiia poveleniia i ukazy s-peterburgskim voennym gubernatoram," *Russkaia Starina* 33 (1882): 196–97.

58. Paul to Pahlen, 2 November 1800, in ibid., p. 201.

59. Grenville to Paget, 17 October 1800, in *Paget Papers*, 1: 274–75. The army instructions provided that (1) if the enemy surrendered before the arrival of Russian forces, British troops alone were to garrison the island, but refusal of the Russians was to be given with the greatest tact, or (2) if the Russian troops arrived before the surrender, they might have to be admitted to occupancy, but all measures were to be taken to limit their authority, and they were to be discouraged as much as possible from landing. Dundas to Abercromby, 1 August 1800, in *The Keith Papers, Selected from the Papers of Admiral Viscount Keith*, ed. Christopher Lloyd (London, 1950), 2: 135–38.

combined forces, and kept as a deposit for the Order of St.
John of Jerusalem, of which order the Emperor of Russia
is acknowledged Grand Master. If between the Three Powers, it seems a little hard that La Vallette should be occupied
by the British to the Exclusion of the Neapolitans, without
any previous declaration or assignement of reason for such
an exclusion. . . , My idea would be, in the event of either
the surrender or reduction of La Vallette, and the other
fortresses to hoist English and Neapolitan Colours, and also
those of the Order of St. John of Jerusalem.[60]

And when the island actually fell and Paget's advice was ignored,
he again wrote the general,

I still maintain that to hoist the British flag exclusively, is
a direct and open breach of existing treaties, and between
ourselves I am convinced within my own mind, that such
was never the intention of Government. . . . How matters
will be made up with the Grand Master for excluding His
flag, remains to be seen. I am upon the whole extremely
sorry to observe the conduct we have adopted on this
occasion.[61]

Paget also complained to Keith, who replied, characteristically,
"Of the affairs of Malta I know nothing, they are in the Hands
of the General and I am glad of it. He had instructions of which
I was ignorant until after the Capitulation, I am glad we have
the Island, Naples could not have kept it and the other is quite
Mad."[62] As the English representative in Naples, Paget was
closest to the center of operations in the Mediterranean, and he
correctly assessed the repercussions that the change in policy
would have. He seriously considered resigning his post in protest,[63] and several months later in a letter to his father, the earl
of Uxbridge, he wrote, "I will tell you between ourselves, . . . that
had my advice been taken this rupture with Russia never could
have happened, at least on that ground."[64]

---

60. Paget to Pigot, 12 August 1800, in *Paget Papers*, 1: 265–66.
61. Paget to Pigot, 14 September 1800, ibid., pp. 269–70.
62. Keith to Paget, 18 December 1800, ibid., p. 289.
63. Paget to Minto, 29 August 1800, ibid., p. 269.
64. Paget to earl of Uxbridge, 3 March 1801, ibid., p. 321.

The strong reaction of the Russian tsar must have been expected. Was Malta considered worth the risk of a continental coalition against Britain? There was at least some justification for the British actions. Paul had already turned to the possibility of regaining the island through France because the British were uncooperative and unsuccessful in taking Malta. General Sprengporten was assigned to organize an expedition made up of former Russian prisoners in France and, in concert with Neapolitan troops, to assume defense of the island on behalf of the order.[65] Bonaparte had agreed to this arrangement after he had learned that the island was about to fall anyway. This French stratagem flattered Paul and widened the rift between Britain and Russia.

British military authorities, on the other hand, did not believe that the Russians should benefit from the costly British siege since they had not assisted in the capture. Grenville claimed that the clauses of the Convention of Saint Petersburg pertaining to the occupation of the island were only verbal and therefore not binding.[66] This excuse, which was given after the policy had been changed, does little credit to Grenville's leadership. The fact remains that the award of Malta to its generally acknowledged sovereign might have prevented the formation of an anti-British continental coalition at that time. The prejudices of a few influential men in London, such as Windham and Whit-

---

65. Italinsky to Paget, 6 January 1801, and Paget to Italinsky, 7 January 1801, ibid., pp. 300–2.

66. Rostopchin to Grenville, 3 November 1800, and Grenville to Rostopchin, 4 December 1800, in Sir Francis Piggott and G. W. T. Ormond, *Documentary History of the Armed Neutralities in 1780 and 1800* (London, 1919), pp. 420–25. Grenville may have been technically correct, but he possessed a copy of Paul's letter to Vorontsov detailing the agreement. Paul to Vorontsov, 30 December 1798, in *Dropmore*, 5: 419. A clause providing for joint allied occupation of Malta until the order could be re-established was included in the Russo-Neapolitan Treaty, which was a part of the general alliance that formed the coalition. See Piero Pieri, "La Questione di Malta e il governo napoletano (1798–1803)," *Archivio Storico Italiano*, 7th ser., vol. 7 (1927): 8–10, who argues that Malta should belong to Italy because of the general recognition of Neapolitan suzerainty over Malta in 1798.

worth, may have been enough to alter British policy and alienate Russia.

The reaction of Paul to the circumstances of the capture of Malta was quite predictable. He immediately reimposed the embargo on British shipping[67]; this action was taken in November and would have no serious effects until the next spring. It may have been intended only as a diplomatic ploy to force British compliance with the Convention of Saint Petersburg. Paul may have believed that the cutting off of supplies of Russian naval stores would be of great consequence to Britain.[68] Russia, of course, would suffer greatly by a permanent commercial break with England, but she had nothing to lose from a temporary, midwinter embargo. While the earlier Armed Neutrality of 1780 may have been a deliberate Russian policy to enforce the shipping rights of neutral nations, the one of 1800 was an opportune political move to gain British concessions in the Mediterranean.[69] Both were used by the smaller Baltic nations to support their genuine grievances against the British violations of maritime neutrality. These searches and seizures had little effect on Russian shipping, which was comparatively insignificant and generally in the best interests of Britain. The Russian embargo and the Armed Neutrality isolated Britain from its former continental allies, but they did not force her to grant concessions. Instead, the immediate results were Nelson's invasion of the Baltic, the destruction of the Danish fleet, and perhaps even the death of Paul.

---

67. Circular note of Rostopchin to the diplomatic corps, 6 November 1800, annex to no. 271 (Serracapriola to Acton—not found), ASN, 1681. Serracapriola replied on 7 November pointing out very diplomatically that the Maltese stipulations of the Convention of Saint Petersburg had not been formally ratified, despite his remonstrances. Rostopchin answered on 8 November: "The repeated assurances and offers of the Court of St. James had given to this project the authenticity necessary for basing our claims." Rostopchin to Serracapriola, 8 November 1800, ASN, 1681.

68. Whitworth had been warned by Grenville the year before for overemphasizing the importance of Russian masts, hemp, and sailcloth for the British navy.

69. For the first armed neutrality, see Isabel de Madariaga, *Britain, Russia, and the Armed Neutrality of 1780* (New Haven, 1962).

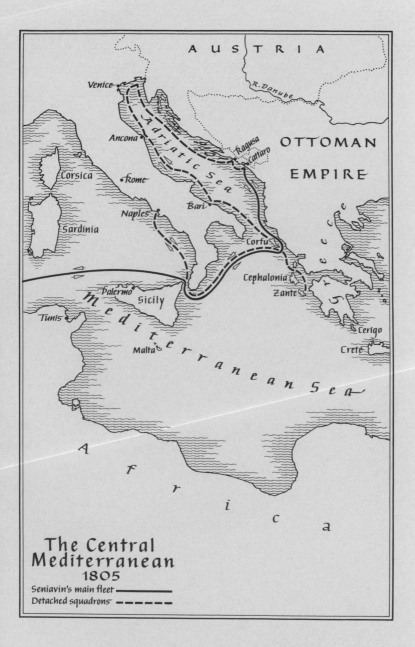

The Central
Mediterranean
1805

Seniavin's main fleet ————
Detached squadrons - - - - - -

AUSTRIA
TO 1806
FRANCE

Hvar

Vis

Korčula

Lastovo

OTTOMAN

RAGUSAN REP

Ragusa

MONTENEGRO

Cattaro
Cetinje

Bocche di Cattaro
Budva

Adriatic Sea

Bari

KINGDOM
OF ITALY

Brindisi

Otranto

EMPIRE

Corfu   Corfu

The Adriatic Campaign
1806

Seniavin's main fleet   Detached squadrons

THE CAMPAIGN TO INDIA

The Armed Neutrality and the embargo on British ships were interpreted in Britain as acts of war. Paul probably would not have disputed that view, for in another quarter Paul was preparing to launch a campaign that would have resulted in an attack on British territory. During the winter of 1800–1801 Paul made overtures to Bonaparte for a joint project against India that would involve 70,000 troops, half Russian, half French. Perhaps because of his recent experience in Egypt and the lack of adequate naval forces in the Mediterranean, Bonaparte was slow to join, but later at Saint Helena he observed that Paul's plan was far from impracticable.[70]

Paul's intelligence sources, as the English historian H. Sutherland Edwards suggested, may have been highly inaccurate regarding the type of terrain to be encountered in such a venture. But, although no detailed study has been made of the project, it appears that it was quite flexible and did not constitute a direct, massive blow at India as is usually depicted in the basic texts on Russian history, but was part of the long-run Russian expansion southward. The return of Platon and Valerian Zubov to official favor at the end of 1800, and the preparations for the formal annexation of Georgia, were related to the planning. After the Russians had secured bases, a French army of 35,000 would pass through Austria in the spring and proceed down the Danube to be transported by the Russian fleet across the Black Sea to the Caucasus.[71] Paul ordered that the autonomy and religious practices of the intervening areas were to be respected. The campaign was to proceed in stages and investigations were to be conducted in the territory to be covered to determine the practicality of various routes southward. Special provision was made for "scientists" and cartographers to accompany the troops. After at least two months preparations, in February 1801, 22,000

---

70. H. Sutherland Edwards, *Russian Projects against India from the Czar Peter to General Skobeleff* (London, 1885), pp. 32–35.

71. General Count de Björnstjerna, ed., *Mémoires posthumes du Feld-Maréchal Comte de Stedingk* (Paris, 1844–47), 2: 6–7.

Cossacks with 44,000 horses started into Central Asia.[72] More troops were to follow, but the advance army did not get far before Alexander recalled it, in March.

Paul's anti-British projects may have extended to the Mediterranean, although only partial, tentative plans have been uncovered. A squadron in the Black Sea was still under the flag of the Order of Malta, and General Sprengporten was gathering a small force in France to garrison Malta. Paul remained on good terms with Turkey and Naples and was apparently prepared to offer the kingdom of Naples a share of the Ionian Islands in return for its assistance in taking Malta. The vulnerability of a communications channel depending on the Straits and the superiority of the British navy would probably have prevented any Russian success in that area in 1801.

Could Russian resources adequately support the foreign projects of the Emperor Paul? This is a difficult question to answer, since the available material is subject to varying interpretations. As noted in chapter 2 above, Russia, compared with the rest of continental Europe, was industrially and commercially advanced. Her military capability had been proved at various times in the eighteenth century and finally in 1799. The war during Paul's reign was not as costly as might be supposed: less than 75,000 Russians were under arms abroad out of a standing army of over 400,000; in all three theaters supplies were furnished by England, Austria, or the Ottoman Empire (or, if supplies were not furnished, the Russians managed with what was available); and Russia received a sizable subsidy from England to defray the cost of initial equipping. War losses in men and material were small. With the rearmament and military reform programs of Paul bearing fruit by 1800, Russia was probably in a better relative military position in 1800 than in 1798. Russian prestige and national feeling had been increased by the 1799 campaigns.

Despite the worthy beginnings of administrative reform in Russia, waste, corruption, and inefficiency continued at all levels

---

72. Edwards, pp. 37–41.

throughout the country, and although Paul decried Catherine's lavish spending, he followed the same policy—rewarding favorites, requiring many new decorations and uniforms, refurbishing palaces, and building yet another imperial palace, the Michael "Castle." Paul's absorption in foreign affairs probably slowed the impetus for internal reforms; the groundwork was laid for the administrative reforms of Alexander I, but basic social backwardness remained. And the military successes of 1799, followed by withdrawal and isolation, minimized the effects of the international wave of the French Revolution in Russia.

THE MURDER OF PAUL

The murder of Paul has attracted the attention of many historians, dramatists, and others fascinated by assassinations; but, as is so often the case in political crimes, many aspects of it remain a mystery. The official version of Paul's death for over a hundred years was that he had a seizure of apoplexy.[73] It quickly became known in political circles, both at home and abroad, that the emperor's fatal illness was of a similar nature as his father's, that is, it was man-made. Two high-ranking court figures, Nikita Petrovich Panin and Peter Pahlen, were probably the most important leaders of the plot. Panin had been relieved of his post in November and left for his estates near Moscow in December 1800. He is credited, however, with securing the permission of Grand Duke Alexander for the removal (not the murder) of the tsar.[74] Pahlen's rise had been meteoric; he became governor-general of Saint Petersburg in November 1800, with control of the police in his hands, and after the fall of Rostopchin, he undertook the

---

73. René C. H. L. Prestre Chateaugiron, "Notice sur la mort de Paul Ier, Empereur de Russie" (n.p.,n.d.—copy in New York Public Library), pp. 5–6. For the details see Leo Loewenson, "The Death of Paul I (1801) and the Memoirs of Count Bennigsen," *Slavonic and East European Review* 29 (1950–51): 212–32, and Constantin de Grunwald, *L'Assassinat de Paul Ier Tsar de Russie* (Paris, 1960).

74. Shumigorskii, *Imperator Pavel I*, p. 818.

chancellor's duties. As the most powerful man in Saint Petersburg next to the emperor, he was chiefly responsible for bringing the conspirators together.[75]

Paul's foreign policy, as well as his domestic programs, had broken to some extent with the traditional pattern and had aroused the antipathy of a large proportion of the Saint Petersburg nobility. Moreover, much of the largess emanating from the crown, as in previous reigns, had gone to personal favorites; but under Paul several of these were non-Russians such as Kutaisov, a Turk, and Father Gruber, a German Jesuit.[76] And Paul's petty domestic regulations had antagonized Saint Petersburg society. This hostility created the psychological climate for the deed.

Most of the members of the plot bore grudges against the emperor for having dismissed them at one time or another from important positions. This is especially true of the Zubovs, General Bennigsen, and Admiral Ribas. Ironically, they returned to favor after October 1800, and this gave them the opportunity. Platon Zubov was recalled to head the Cadet Corps, and Nicholas Zubov was given command of a cavalry corps. Kutaisov, probably also involved, was instrumental in securing the removal of Rostopchin in early March. A new power clique formed around Kutaisov, Platon Zubov, Pahlen, Alexander Kurakin, and Father Gruber. These developments lead one to suspect

---

75. An Austrian agent reported in January 1801, that Paul intended to put an army of 160,000 in the field in the spring under Pahlen, and Kutuzov would become governor-general. Locatelli to Thugut, 4 January 1801, HHSA, 95 Russland II Berichte.

76. The plot apparently began in October or November, thus coinciding with the embargoes on English shipping. General Svechin was approached at this time by both Panin and Ribas, but declined to participate. Rouët de Journel, *Une Russe catholique: Madame Swetchine d'apprès de nombreux documents nouveaux* (Paris, 1929), pp. 30–32. News that something would be attempted even reached England. Shortly after talking to Whitworth, Novosiltsev wrote from London to Vorontsov that "something may happen yet" and advised him not to be discouraged. Vorontsov was not convinced, and compared the Russian state to a sinking ship. Novosiltsev to S. R. Vorontsov, 4 February 1801, in *Arkhiv Vorontsova*, 18: 438, and S. R. Vorontsov to Novosiltsev, 5 February 1801, in *Arkhiv Vorontsova*, 11: 380–81.

that the final decision to force Paul's removal was sudden and conditioned by the arrest of several officers of the Guard and vague disclosures of a cabal among ranking officials. Once complete details had become clear, repercussions would have been severe.[77]

The British involvement in Paul's murder cannot be adequately assessed. It is probable that Whitworth gave verbal encouragement and perhaps material support to the cause through his liaison with Madam Zherebtsova, who later appeared in London demanding large sums of money that had allegedly been promised.[78] The ambassador's "special" fund had always been large, and in his fit of anger at the emperor, Whitworth may have lent it for the purpose of bribing key officers of the Guard. But the British ambassador left Russia nine months before the event.

According to the reports, on the night of 23–24 March, Pahlen and the Zubovs assembled a number of disgruntled officers and divulged their objective. After fortifying themselves with champagne and vodka, the conspirators entered the heavily guarded new palace with amazing ease, found Paul in his bedroom hiding behind a fireplace screen (or draperies in another version), and strangled him.[79] The news of the tsar's death was received with joy in Saint Petersburg and London,[80] but with sorrow in some quarters. Bonaparte is reported to have uttered a rare cry of

---

77. Reports of Locatelli, 9 and 24 March 1801, HHSA, 95 Russland II Berichte. Locatelli noted that after the fall of Rostopchin, Pahlen and Alexander Kurakin were in charge of foreign affairs, and that Kutaisov and Gruber were very important. Rogerson, the imperial physician, and Maria Fedorovna, according to an Austrian report, were very unhappy with Pahlen for failing to acclaim Maria empress. Report of Schwartemberg, 9 July 1801, HHSA, 95 Russland II Berichte. See also Count L. L. Bennigsen, "Konchina Imperatora Pavel I," *Istoricheskii Vestnik* (April 1906), pp. 72–85.

78. S. R. Vorontsov to A. R. Vorontsov, 12 August 1801, in *Arkhiv Vorontsova*, 10: 113. Kutaisov had received large amounts from Whitworth.

79. The screen is now on display in Paul's restored library at Pavlovsk.

80. Whitworth remarked upon hearing the news, "I shall, so long as I live, celebrate as a festival the day on which I learned the death of that arch-fiend Paul." Whitworth to Grenville, 16 April 1801, in *Dropmore*, 7: 4.

despair and immediately to have blamed the British for the whole affair. One can guess that the knights of the Order of Malta, Roman Catholic officials, and the participants in the Armed Neutrality regretted Paul's passing.

PAUL AND THE MEDITERRANEAN

The Russian presence in the Mediterranean under Paul was an important feature of the international relations of the period. The original motivation was a desire to protect the Ottoman Empire from the direct threat posed by the Eastern ambitions of General Bonaparte and revolutionary France and to safeguard the economic and political life of new territories in south Russia and Poland. Paul's personal aim to save Europe through the Order of Malta added another dimension. The Ionian Islands passed under Russian control, but Russia had no intention of annexing them, because this would have jeopardized her alliance with Turkey and her position in the Mediterranean, depending largely as it did upon free passage through the Straits. Acutely interested in Malta and Italy, Paul reacted sharply to actions taken by his allies in these areas. And it was chiefly over the circumstances of the capture of Ancona and Malta that Paul broke relations with Austria and England and drew into an alliance with France. But once established, the Russian involvement in the Mediterranean could not be liquidated along with Paul.

7

Alexander and the Mediterranean, 1801-1803

In Saint Petersburg it was hoped that Paul's son and successor would be an "Augustan" ruler who would restore the grand age of the Russian nobility of Catherine's reign. He lived up to some of their expectations by initiating reforms that modernized Russian administration and by becoming "the savior of Europe" in the Napoleonic Wars. Russian historians of the nineteenth century sang his praises, and even Soviet scholars have glorified the military and diplomatic accomplishments of his reign, but some of his contemporaries and later critics were disappointed by Alexander's unfulfilled promises, vanished dreams, and deepening mysticism. In most of the Western biographies he is described rather unsatisfactorily as "the enigmatic tsar" or the last of the great philosopher-kings.[1]

---

1. There is no first-class biography of Alexander in any language. Two in English can be used with caution: Leonid I. Strakhovsky, *Alexander I of Russia, the Man Who Defeated Napoleon* (New York, 1947); and Georges Maurice Paleologue, *The Enigmatic Czar: The Life of Alexander I of Russia* (London, 1938). Perhaps the best short biographies are Constantin de Grunwald, *Alexandre Ier, le tsar mystique* (Paris, 1955), and A. E. Presniakov, *Aleksandr I* (Petrograd, 1924), while the most complete are M. I. Bogdanovich, *Istoriia tsarstvovaniia imperatora Aleksandra I i Rossii v ego vremia*, 6 vols. (Saint Petersburg, 1869–71), N. K. Shil'der, *Imperator Aleksandr Pervyi: ego zhizn' i tsarstvovanie*, 4 vols. (Saint Petersburg, 1904–6), and K. Waliszewski, *La Russie il y a cent ans: le règne d'Alexandre Ier*,

The accession came at an unfortunate time for the young Alexander; he had barely begun to realize the difficulties of implementing his vague, idealistic plans for constitutional government in the large socially backward country of Russia. Although he had apparently approved of his father's removal, he had counted on an orderly transition through abdication. Alexander's behavior then and throughout his twenty-five-year reign proved that he had inherited his father's sensitivity and dedication to service but that he lacked Paul's strongest qualities—courage and conviction.

Alexander was probably less prepared for the enormous task of governing the Russian Empire than Paul had been. His education had been supervised in a haphazard manner during Catherine's reign. La Harpe, his chief tutor, represented the liberal views associated with the French Enlightenment.[2] But during the most important years of his education, after 1790, La Harpe's role decreased, and much of Alexander's time was passed in frivolous social affairs and long conversations with friends of his own age. At this time he also learned to drill soldiers at his father's court at Gatchina.

It has been difficult for historians to appraise accurately the personality of Alexander. Most of them have concentrated on the development of his mystical and religious outlook, which was accompanied by a shift toward conservatism after the middle of his reign.[3] In 1801 the twenty-three-year-old successor to Paul was still in the process of gaining self-assurance and maturity. He had not yet resolved the conflict between the two great influences of his youth—the liberal education of the Enlightenment and the military atmosphere of Gatchina. It seems appar-

---

3 vols. (Paris, 1923–25). For a good factual survey and a more complete bibliography, see Hugh Seton-Watson, *The Russian Empire, 1801–1917* (Oxford, 1967), pp. 69–112 and 749–53.

2. A. V. Fadeev, *Doreformennaia Rossiia, 1800–1861* (Moscow, 1960), pp. 29–31; Presniakov, p. 14. For a traditional account of La Harpe's role in Alexander's education, see Waliszewski, *La Russie il y a cent ans*, 1: 5–9.

3. Many of the records and personal papers of the tsar were systematically destroyed by Nicholas I, his successor. Florinsky, *Russia: A History and an Interpretation*, 2: 629.

ent, however, that he did not have strong religious convictions at the beginning of his reign.

Since Alexander had been close to several young anglophiles—among whom were Kochubei, Stroganov, Novosiltsev, and Czartoryski (his future "young friends"), and Panin—the British had reason to expect a quick change of policy. The new tsar, however, was at first separated from most of his friends and temporarily under the influence of those in power. Pahlen exercised the office of chancellor and tried to serve as Alexander's mentor, but he did not possess the abilities of Bezborodko. The College of Foreign Affairs was immediately reorganized with the following members in order of rank: Alexander Kurakin, Pahlen, Panin, Tatishchev, and Muraviev.[4] Panin resumed his former post as vice-chancellor after his arrival from Moscow on 1 April, and the veteran ambassadors, Vorontsov and Razumovsky, were asked to reopen their vacated embassies in London and Vienna.[5]

Friendly intentions toward Britain were declared immediately, and the campaign against India was canceled, but the tsar and even the anglophile members of Saint Petersburg society began to resent the British naval threats that were being thrown on their doorstep in the Baltic. The Battle of Copenhagen, only a few days after the change of rulers in Saint Petersburg, was considered a grave challenge to Russian interests in the Baltic; Denmark was, after all, an ally of Russia. On 14 April, Tatishchev listed the foreign policy objectives of the new government: (1) peace with France, since "Bonaparte, wanting to consolidate power in his own lands, can no longer be an enemy of monarchical governments, because he obviously tends toward the same end himself"; (2) complete restoration of relations with Austria, although Prussia is preferred; (3) the convention with Sweden and Denmark (armed neutrality) to be upheld; (4) friendship with the Porte, (5) the emperor wants neither the title of grand master nor the island of Malta, but it should not go to the

---

4. Tatishchev to S. R. Vorontsov, 25 March 1801, in *Arkhiv Vorontsova*, 18: 352.
5. Pahlen to S. R. Vorontsov, 25 March 1801, in VPR 1: 11–12.

British, "and on this he will insist"; and (6) peace with Spain.[6]

Alexander's attitude stiffened toward Britain as Nelson continued to advance into the Baltic to force the abandonment of the Armed Neutrality, but at the same time the tsar wanted to do everything possible to avoid hostilities. It is interesting to speculate what would have resulted if the emperor's inclination for peace had not been so strong, or if Paul had still ruled. Would the British have been forced to retreat? Nelson's destructive and vengeful victory at Copenhagen had caused his military luster to tarnish in northern waters, and Russia was not as vulnerable as is often pictured. After learning of the British attack on Denmark, Alexander wrote to his ambassador in London that he sincerely wanted friendship with Britain, but "I have the right to employ all the resources and all the means that Providence has put in my hands for repulsing force by force."[7] In April a number of steps were taken to strengthen the coastal defenses, and though Nelson discounted Russian naval strength, a large, strongly armed fleet was in being and, even if incapable of sailing, presented a worthy anchored defense. If the great English admiral had chosen to sail into Riga, Revel, or Kronstadt with guns blazing, he might have ended his days much less gloriously than he did a few years later at Trafalgar.

Nelson received a cold reception at Revel on 12 May. Pahlen warned him in a note of 14 May that Russia would not negotiate until the fleet had withdrawn: "His Majesty orders me to declare to you, My Lord, that the only guarantee that He will accept of the loyalty of Your intentions is the prompt withdrawal of the fleet that you command and that any negotiation with your court cannot take place while a naval force can be seen from his ports."[8] Nelson realized that he should not aggravate the situation and wisely offered to withdraw. Russia then declared a readiness to negotiate its differences with Britain on 18 May and

---

6. Tatishchev to A. R. Vorontsov, 14 April 1801, in *Arkhiv Vorontsova*, 18: 353–54.

7. To S. R. Vorontsov, 18 April 1801, in *Arkhiv Vorontsova* 28: 417–18.

8. Pahlen to Nelson, 14 May 1801, Nelson Papers, XLVII, Add. MSS., BM, 34,948, f. 82.

Lord St. Helens, a special envoy from London, was escorted by Nelson to Saint Petersburg.[9] Panin moderated his anglophile tendencies and insisted on the recognition of neutral rights by Britain in accordance with the principles of the armed neutrality; he saw that Russia was in a strong diplomatic position.

The Anglo-Russian convention, signed in Saint Petersburg on 17 June 1801, was a fair and clear declaration of neutral shipping rights and restraints, and Russia agreed to negotiate a settlement for damages caused by the embargo, which was now lifted.[10] In a secret article, Britain was obliged to remove her fleet from the Baltic.[11] Vorontsov, the Russian ambassador in London, was surprised at the strong restrictions on traditional British naval practices in regard to neutral shipping and proceeded to alter the wording in London in order to secure easier acceptance and ratification by the British government. The Russian ambassador even complained bitterly of Panin's "anti-English" influence upon Alexander.[12]

Meanwhile, Russia maintained a strict neutrality. Negotiations begun with France by Kolychev in 1800 were continued by Morkov, an experienced but stubborn diplomat of Catherine's era.[13] On 8 October a simple treaty of friendship, based on Kolychev's work, was signed by Talleyrand and Morkov. This was followed on 10 October by a secret convention which provided for the withdrawal of all troops of both nations from Italy and guaranteed the independence of the Ionian Republic. The new

---

9. Pahlen to Nelson, 18 May 1801, ibid. The embargo continued; in fact, Alexander was insistent that the restrictions be maintained until the convention was ratified and the British fleet withdrawn from the Baltic.

10. "Anglo-Russkaia morskaia konventsiia," 17 June 1801, in VPR 1: 28–34.

11. "His Britannic Majesty, wishing to demonstrate unequivocally the confidence that He places in the magnanimous concerns of His Majesty the Emperor of all the Russies for the reestablishment of peace in the North, . . . pledges to give immediate orders to effect, as soon as possible, the return of His Squadron in the Baltic Sea to the North Sea." Ibid., p. 33.

12. S. R. Vorontsov to A. R. Vorontsov, 14 August 1801, in *Arkhiv Vorontsova*, 10: 117.

13. P. V. Bezobrazov, *O snosheniiakh Rossii s Frantsiei* (Moscow, 1892), p. 364.

Franco-Russian agreements, coinciding with negotiations for the preliminaries to the Treaty of Amiens between France and Britain, were part of the general peacemaking atmosphere of the last half of 1801. Weary of war, everyone seemed to be following Alexander's desire for peace.

Even so, a considerable amount of compromising took place. The Russian Empire recognized the French Republic on a basis of equality with other European states. By article 9 of the secret convention, France recognized the independence and constitution of the Ionian Republic, thereby acknowledging Russia's position in the islands, but Morkov failed to secure French agreement to the restoration of all the former territory of Sardinia. Russia also approved the Treaty of Florence of 28 March 1801 between France and the kingdom of Naples, which provided for the annexation by France of the territories of Elba and Piombino and for the temporary occupation by French troops of the strategic ports of Otranto, Taranto, and Brindisi in southern Italy. Russian diplomacy had been successful in forcing Talleyrand to commit France to a certain and limited position in Italy.[14]

Russia also renewed formal relations with Austria. Muraviev-Apostol was dispatched on a special mission in the spring of 1801 to reopen the embassy.[15] Razumovsky, who had returned to Russia in 1800, stopped off in Saint Petersburg in the summer of 1801 to confer with Panin and Alexander and arrived in Vienna on 1 October and Muraviev-Apostol continued on to Spain.[16] Diplomatic relations were thus restored with all countries of Europe.

ALEXANDER AND THE ORDER OF MALTA

The island of Malta played an important role in Alexander's

---

14. Ibid., pp. 368–69; V. G. Sirotkin, "Iz istorii vneshnei politiki Rossii v sredizemnomor'e v nachale XIX v., *Istoricheskie Zapiski* 67 (1960): 215; Articles 4, 5, 6, and 9, "Russko-frantsuzskaia sekretnaia konventsiia," 10 October 1801, in VPR 1: 98–99; Stanislavskaia, pp. 211–13.

15. Vasil'chikov, *Semeistvo Razumovskikh*, 3: 383.

16. Ibid., pp. 384–85. Austria was slow to reciprocate. Count Saurau was sent to Moscow in September 1801 for the coronation, but a regular Austrian ambassador did not arrive until the end of June 1803.

policy during the first year of his reign. On 28 March 1801, only a few days after Paul's death, Alexander announced his refusal to take the title of grand master. He regarded the Order of Saint John simply as a foreign state that should return to its former position in the Mediterranean; Russia should have no more involvement with it than absolutely necessary.[17] A sudden withdrawal of Russia from the order could not be expected since Pahlen and Kurakin, who directed Russia foreign policy during the first two months of Alexander's reign, both held high offices in the order. The center of the knights remained at Saint Petersburg under the "protection" of the emperor. Pahlen sat as grand chancellor at a meeting of the Council in March; Saltykov was confirmed as lieutenant of the grand master and temporary director of the knights.[18]

At another session of the Council, on 23 May the question of Hompesch's guilt was reconsidered. The Council approved the retraction of the original letter of accusation from the Bailli de Tigné, now admitted to be a forgery, but considered that Hompesch remained guilty and that his abdication was a matter of record.[19] But arrangements were not made until July for the election of a new grand master by a general chapter of the order. A protocol signed by Alexander provided that the new grand master was to be a Catholic. Yet after July a surprisingly large number of new Russian knights were named to positions within the order, and significantly most of these new knights came from the oldest and most aristocratic Russian families. By March 1802, the list of Russian knights included the following prominent names—Pahlen, Kurakin, Rostopchin, Arakcheev, Czartoryski, Nesselrode, Dolgoruky, Uvarov, Golitzin, Naryshkin, Sheremetev, Kutuzov, Iussupov, Volkonsky, Gagarin, Saltykov, Kushelev, Sievers, Rumiantsev, Musin-Pushkin, and Grand Duke Constantine.[20] The order was obviously still considered quite

---

17. Alexander I to Morkov, 16 November 1801, in VPR 1: 137; Antoshevskii, *Derzhavnyi Orden Sviatago Ioanna Ierusalimskago*, p. 49.
18. Minutes of Grand Council, 14th Session, 28 March 1801, in "Protocole du Sacré Conseil SMOM," no. 136, pp. 121–23.
19. Ibid., 15th Session, 23 May 1801, pp. 125–30.
20. Ibid., 17th Session, 1 August 1801, pp. 148–53 et passim.

fashionable in Russia, though the great increase in the number of Russian knights, reducing drastically the proportion of foreign knights in Saint Petersburg, was probably a measure of the anti-foreign reaction of the court. A few non-Russians like Pignatelli and Maisonneuve retained high posts, however.

The main problem of the order also turned out to be a major stumbling block on the road to the conclusion of a durable peace —the island of Malta itself. Although the diplomatic arrangements of 1801, and the Treaty of Amiens between Britain and France, stipulated that the island should return to the order, the question of its security remained. Britain and France both insisted on a strong and active guarantee of the island's neutrality by a third power, and only Russia could satisfy this requirement.[21]

In October 1801, St. Helens presented a request from Hawkesbury, the British secretary for foreign affairs, for a Russian guarantee of the island which would be incorporated into the peace treaty with France. Panin did not think that Alexander would approve and cited Catherine's refusal of protection to Minorca. But when St. Helens mentioned that Britain would pay at least part of the cost of a Russian garrison, Panin said that this might induce the emperor to approve.[22] The Malta question was then debated at length in the Imperial Council in Moscow (during the coronation), and immediately afterward Panin was forced to resign. St. Helens blamed Panin's insistence upon a guarantee for Malta as the reason for his dismissal. "Had Count Panin remained in office I have the strongest reason to believe that the proposal would have been adopted."[23] Kurakin announced, and Kochubei confirmed, that Russia's interest in the order did not extend beyond the two priories within Russian borders, and that the kingdom of Naples, the legal suzerain,

---

21. Hawkesbury to St. Helens, 12 September 1801, PRO, FO 181/1; Hedouville to A. R. Vorontsov, 3 November 1802, in *SIRIO* 70: 541–43.

22. St. Helens to Hawkesbury, 8 October 1801, PRO, FO 181/1.

23. St. Helens to Hawkesbury, 12 and 15 October 1801, PRO, FO 181/1. The quotation is from St. Helens' next dispatch, dated simply October 1801.

should be considered the logical guarantor.[24] This opinion derived from Alexander's resolve to refrain from involvements in the affairs of Europe. Russia did approve the principle of a guarantee of the island, but the guarantor was assumed to be Naples. When the wording of article 10 of the Treaty of Amiens became known in Russia, the emperor was disturbed on two counts: the treaty emphasized the role of Russia as the guarantor; and the provisions for the election of the grand master, which Alexander had drawn up, had been altered in minor details.[25]

Alexander's desire to get Maltese affairs out of his hands is understandable. The overinvolvement of Paul had been one of the reasons for his unpopularity. Alexander was probably embarrassed by the presence of a knightly institution so intimately associated with his father. In addition, Alexander was practicing very stringent economy in central government operations and wished to cut expenses abroad. Lord St. Helens listed this latter motive as the primary reason for Russian refusal to garrison the island, but that was probably an exaggeration.[26] Another factor that might have been significant in forming Russia's new policy toward the Order of Malta—the presence of an anti-Roman Catholic sentiment at the court—cannot be supported from available evidence. On the contrary, Alexander at first continued Paul's Catholic policy, and Father Gruber remained a most influential representative of the church until the arrival of a new papal nuncio, Arezzo, in April 1803. Alexander refused to receive

---

24. Kurakin to Kochubei, 3 November 1801, in VPR 1: 125–26; "Notes of the Conference to Count Kochubei with the English ambassador," 13 November 1801, in VPR 1: 132–34.

25. Alexander to Stackelberg, 28 May 1802, ibid., 210; St. Helens to Paget, 1 May 1802, in *Paget Papers*, 2: 52; Kurakin to St. Helens, 13 August 1802, in VPR 1: 272–74.

26. St. Helens to Paget, 1 August 1802, in *Paget Papers*, 2: 59. Hudelist, the Austrian chargé d'affaires, noted in a secret memoir that the experience of the last coalition inclined all power to act alone, but that in isolation they were weak and a prey to Bonaparte's maneuvers. He viewed the major obstacles to a reformation of the coalition "the feeble, apathetic, and variable character of Alexander I, the fear of his ministers to compromise, and the state of finances of this empire." Memoir of Hudelist, 6 February 1802, HHSA, 96 Russland II Berichte.

Arezzo formally because of the pope's rapprochement with France. The church and the order just did not suit Alexander's anglophile "young friends." The new tsar may have had more faith in Paul's ideal of the order as an aristocratic brotherhood than is generally supposed. His limited support for it probably saved the order from extinction.

The easiest way for Russia to disentangle herself from the order was to obtain the restoration of the knights to their former position on Malta. All powers agreed in principle to this, but Britain, correctly doubting the ability of the order or Naples to furnish an adequate defense, demanded that Russia guarantee the security of the island. Alexander, with the Ionians under his "protection," already had more security problems than he wanted in the Mediterranean. Though certain parties in France and Britain may have wished to compromise Russian neutrality, the main reason for the awkward Maltese arrangement was the desire of both countries for peace. But Malta was the main focus of the British opposition—now including Grenville and Dundas— to the Treaty of Amiens; now that Russia had "territory" in the Mediterranean and Italian harbors were denied to the British, a naval base in the central Mediterranean was needed more than ever. In December 1802, Russia was still insisting that article 10 be clarified to include the following provisions: restoration of the island to the Order of Malta, under the suzerainty of the king of the Two Sicilies; perpetual neutrality; natives of Malta to be received into the ranks of the order; a Neapolitan garrison to be furnished until the order could maintain its own; and the guarantors to include Russia, Austria, Spain, Naples, and Prussia. Yet Morkov reported from Paris in March 1803 that "everyone" believed that a compromise would put a Russian garrison on Malta.[27] This kind of revision would have been difficult to obtain even if circumstances had been more favorable. By refusing to act as the sole guarantor and to furnish a garrison, Russia shares the blame for the failure of the peace settlement.

---

27. Hudelist to Cobenzl, 7 December 1802, HHSA, 98 Russland II Berichte; Morkov to S. R. Vorontsov, 24 March 1803, in *Arkhiv Vorontsova* 20: 144–45.

IONIAN PROBLEMS

The withdrawal of Ushakov's fleet and the shifts in Russian policy in 1800 and 1801 produced chaos in the Adriatic. The British consul in Venice advised in March 1801 that French privateers operating out of Ancona controlled the seas and that British merchant vessels headed for the "currant islands" should turn back.[28] General Hutchinson at Malta was ordered to send a garrison to the Ionians, but he could not spare men immediately. The small Russian garrisons were withdrawn to Corfu to await transport to the Black Sea. In this situation central authority broke down completely. Colonel Callender, an advance scout from Malta, arrived at Zante in February to promise annexation by Great Britain, to the joy of the leading inhabitants. His reception and the raising of the British flag on Zante led him to assert, "The island of Zante is to be considered as actually annexed to the British Empire," but his action was refuted by the consul-general, Foresti.[29] Callender remained in control of Zante, with Albanian mercenaries, until September.

The Russians were hampered by conflicting orders. Captain Voinovich was relieved of command by Paul over his part in the Ancona affair in March, but was reinstated shortly before the remaining Russian forces returned to the Black Sea in August 1801. The arrival of a Turkish squadron only caused more trouble, since the islanders refused to allow any Turks to land. Foresti reported at this time:

> In general, the inhabitants of these Islands have been so much accustomed to being governed by Foreigners, and so few of the natural aristocracy enjoy the consideration of the people, that they unanimously regret that any of their own country should be their rulers. It has unfortunately happened too that the obvious evils occasioned by the French while they held these Islands, have been followed by a spirit of discord excited by the Russian officers; and it is but too true that the French at present avail themselves

28. John Watson to Grenville, 7 March 1801, PRO, FO 81/14.
29. Colonel Callender to Government of Zante, 27 February 1801, and Foresti to Grenville, 23 May 1801, PRO, FO 42/4.

of their position in the Neapolitan state to correspond with
the disaffected, for the purpose of increasing the ferment.[30]

But he succeeded, with the help of Captain Ricketts, in driving
Callender out of Zante in September. A British frigate, *El Corso*,
under Ricketts was the principal police force in the islands for
several months. Elgin and Foresti both pressed London for
military assistance. The latter wrote, on 17 January 1802, "And
the experience of every day adds to my conviction, that, unless
some foreign force (not Turkish) should be obtained, to maintain a proper Government at each Island, affairs cannot but
become progressively worse."[31] The Porte formally requested
English assistance, and Captain Martin, with the *Northumber-
land* and two other British vessels, arrived in March and landed
his marines on Corfu. A Turkish firman indicated that the British
forces were to be used to restore order only until the arrival of a
Russian garrison.[32]

In the middle of all of this turmoil, a national assembly managed to meet on 25 October 1801 to promulgate a new constitution, which had been drawn up by Tomara and the Ionian
delegation to the Ottoman court.[33] This "Byzantine" or "Constantinople" constitution replaced the provisional one that had
been issued by Ushakov. It favored the old aristocracy, and was
similar to Venetian rule. But since the republic had no effective
enforcement apparatus, the new constitution was put into practice initially only at Corfu.[34] The other islands were, in fact, independent. The lower nobility and the middle class, excluded from
government by the constitution, expressed their dissatisfaction
to Tomara over the disordered state of affairs of the islands.[35]

---

30. Foresti to Foreign Office, 29 August 1801, PRO, FO 42/4.
31. Foresti to Hawkesbury, 17 January 1802, PRO, O 42/4.
32. Foresti to Hawkesbury, 10 March 1802, PRO, FO 42/4.
33. E. Rodocanachi, *Bonaparte et les îles Ioniennes* (Paris, 1899), p. 182.
34. VPR 1: 706, n. 88. This constitution was approved by the Turks
on 2 November, but Russia delayed ratification. A constitution drafted
separately for the island of Corfu showed an amazing sophistication but was
also complex. "Piano Constituzionale formato della deputazione della città,
borghi, e villa dell isola di Corfu le XXI Ottobre MDCCCI" (Corfu, 1801).
35. Lefcochilo to Tomara, 24 November 1801, and Tomara to Kochubei,
28 November 1801, in VPR 1: 146, 703.

And the Russian ambassador was quite happy to forward their complaints and requests for Russian troops, since, in spite of his remonstrances, the senate had discharged his old friend Antonio Lefcochilo as envoy to Constantinople.[36]

On 30 December 1801, Victor Kochubei, who was then at the head of foreign affairs, handed the emperor a memorandum on the background to Russian activities in the Ionian Islands. In this report Kochubei stressed Russia's obligation to provide protection for the islands according to the convention of April 1800, and outlined a plan for the employment of the Russian forces in Naples to reestablish order.[37] This recommendation, drafted —ironically—by the man who had opposed the sending of the fleet by Paul in 1798, was the first positive foreign policy move to be adopted by Alexander.

Kochubei suggested that George Mocenigo, a native of the island of Zante who had been Paul's minister to Tuscany, direct the "reoccupation." Mocenigo had visited Vorontsov in London during the summer, and with his recommendation he went to Saint Petersburg to seek employment and to make representations on behalf of the Ionian Republic.[38] The remaining portion of Ushakov's force at Naples under Captain Sorokin, about 600 soldiers with two frigates, was ordered to accompany Mocenigo to the Ionians. At the same time, the rest of the "Neapolitan Guard" under Borozdin was withdrawn to the Black Sea.

Dispatches were soon sent to Morkov, the special Russian envoy to Paris, and to Tomara, to prepare the acquiescence of France and Turkey to actions contrary to recently signed conventions calling for the complete withdrawal of Russian forces.[39]

---

36. Tomara to Ionian Senate, 28 August 1801, SS, DAE, Box 22, no. 27.

37. "Zapiski o Respublike Semi Soedinennykh Ostrovov," n.d. [1802], in VPR 1: 367–70.

38. Kochubei to Alexander I, 30 December 1801, in VPR 1: 157–59; S. R. Vorontsov to A. R. Vorontsov, 24 September 1801, in *Arkhiv Vorontsova* 10: 129.

39. Alexander I to Mocenigo, 12 March 1802, in VPR 1: 182. Alexander even wrote to Bonaparte personally on the Russian restoration of order at Corfu, 11 June 1802, in *SIRIO* 70: 444; Morkov to Mocenigo, 28 June 1802, in VPR 1: 231–32. See also Alexander I to Morkov, 20 Feb-

In the peacemaking atmosphere of 1802, little difficulty was encountered. Mocenigo, appointed Russian plenipotentiary to the Ionians, spent the first six months of 1802 preparing for the movement of troops and corresponding with leaders on the islands and with Russian diplomats in the area. In Naples he conferred with a representative of the senate, Dmitri Naranzi, who was later to be the republic's minister to Russia, and with the Russian ambassador at Naples, Italinsky, who presented Mocenigo with a draft of another constitution, which, the special envoy advised in a letter to the tsar, would need to be adapted to conditions in the islands.[40]

Mocenigo arrived at Corfu on 16 August 1802. When the Russian soldiers on three transports and accompanied by the two frigates arrived on 29 August almost exactly a year after the previous garrison had left, Mocenigo published a manifesto in Greek, Italian, and French addressed to "The Inhabitants of All Classes and All Ranks of the Republic of the Seven United Islands: The Emperor of All the Russias, my August Master, informed of the troubles that have broken out in the Republic and very much concerned by the misfortunes which cause you to live in this state of anarchy, has taken the generous resolution to reestablish order and tranquility."[41] In his first letter to Saint Petersburg Mocenigo observed that the republic had been subject to four governments in four years amid the confusion of war.[42] In his initial attempts to restore order, Mocenigo solicited the assistance of two leading local officials, Spiridion Theotokis and Jean Capodistrias. Russian detachments were sent to the other islands accompanied by Capodistrias and reestablished central authority on each island under a governor appointed by the

---

ruary 1802, in *SIRIO* 70: 349–51; and Alexander to Tomara, 27 February 1802, in *VPR* 1: 175–76.

40. Mocenigo to Alexander I, 6 August 1802, in *VPR* 1: 255–58, 711, n. 151.

41. Proclamation of Mocenigo, 1 September 1802, enclosure in Foresti to Hawkesbury, 1 September 1802, PRO, FO 42/4.

42. Mocenigo to Alexander I, 20 September 1802, in *VPR* 1: 293–95; Mocenigo to Kochubei, 20 September 1802, in *VPR* 1: 297–98.

senate.[43] Theotokis retained his post as president of the senate, which now became little more than an advisory council to the Russian administration. Mocenigo removed the leading trouble-makers from the islands by appointing them to miscellaneous posts at Corfu and assigned one of the frigates to cruise regularly from island to island.[44] Upon the successful accomplishment of his mission of restoring central authority, Capodistrias was named secretary for foreign affairs, navy, and commerce of the republic, the beginning of an illustrious public career.[45]

An assembly met in 1803 to consider a new constitution. It had been composed mostly by Mocenigo, who used the basic outline drawn up by Italinsky. The complex document of 212 articles broadened the basic structure of the government and increased the powers of the central government at Corfu.[46] The senate was elected from the old nobility, which also controlled the executive organs, but the "second class," consisting of smaller landholders and merchants, could now participate in the elections and provide half the members of the assembly, which could review and veto the acts of the senate. Projects could be presented to the senate by this lower house, but formal initiative rested only with the senate and the executive.[47] The new constitutional arrangement was put into effect gradually in 1803

---

43. S. Th. Lascaris, *Capodistrias avant la révolution grecque* (Lausanne, 1918), pp. 13–15; Shapiro, *Istoricheskie Zapiski*, 55: 267. Foresti reported, "The engine that now moves the Machine is Count Mocenigo, as nothing is, or can be, done by the Senate without his consent or orders." He also claimed that the high-handed attitude of the Russians was resented: "It is certain that the wish of the Common Order of People (I mean that Class that has not got any thing to lose) is more in favor of the French than of any other Nation, France having been the first Nation which gave them a relish for what they call Liberty. . . . I still find these People intoxicated with the joyful memory of those who have liberated them, and they can only see France as the Nation which brought them happiness and their full rights. . . . With respect to the Russians it is their bayonets that are respected; from a combination of causes they have not one per cent in their favor in this Republic." Foresti to Hawkesbury, 2 July 1803, PRO, FO 42/5.
44. Foresti to Hawkesbury, 9 December 1802, PRO, FO 42/4.
45. Lascaris, p. 19.
46. Ibid., p. 21; Rodocanachi, pp. 187–88.
47. Lascaris, p. 22.

but did not become official until the end of the year. The delay was caused by waiting for the protecting powers to ratify the constitution; although approval by the Porte was secured through the diplomatic efforts of Italinsky, now Russian ambassador in Constantinople, the Russian government, surprisingly, refused at first to ratify the constitution because, according to Lascaris, the rights of the protecting powers were not sufficiently guaranteed.[48] The new constitution, however, was in operation during the slow process of solving the problem that prevented Russian approval.

International relations were little affected by the new Russian activities in the Ionians. In Constantinople, Tomara secured the acquiescence of the Ottoman government to the necessity of a peacetime Russian garrison in the Ionians.[49] The Porte was more concerned about the wording of the Treaty of Amiens, which recognized the Ionian Islands as an independent republic without mentioning the suzerainty of Turkey and the cession to the Porte of the continental enclaves of the former Venetian territory.[50] Both France and Britain came forth with assurances that the slight was unintentional.

Bonaparte's interest in the Ionians had not ended with the disaster of the Egyptian campaign or the Treaty of Amiens, however. A French agent of considerable prestige and diplomatic ability, Romieu, was sent to Corfu as consul-general. Arriving there in March, several months before Mocenigo, he was able to take advantage of the state of unrest to promote pro-French feelings among the populace.[51] Bonaparte soon thereafter

---

48. Ibid., pp. 22–24. In regard to the constitution of 1803, Foresti noted, "I am led to believe by information which I have received from Men of all Ranks, that it has met with but little approbation, and that a present, which we must suppose that His Imperial Majesty meant should be received with pleasure by all, has in fact been relished by few." He enclosed a seventy-one page copy of the constitution. Foresti to Hawkesbury, 16 December 1803, PRO, FO 42/5. Most sources agree that Mocenigo and the island authorities had difficulties from the beginning with this constitution because of its complexity.

49. Tomara to the Turkish government, 26 October 1802, in VPR 1: 315–16.

50. Ibid.; and Tomara to Alexander I, 28 April 1802, in VPR, 1: 194–95.

51. Douin, *La Mediterranée de 1803 à 1805: Pirates et corsaires aux îles*

approved the Russian military build-up, and in October Talleyrand sent instructions to Romieu to cooperate with Mocenigo.[52]
Although disagreements over the supression of village revolts at
first clouded relations between Romieu and Mocenigo, the two
men seem to have gotten along very well in 1803 and 1804. In
December 1802, another experienced French agent, Colonel
Horace Sebastiani, stopped at Zante on the way to Constantinople and received a warm reception, much to the annoyance
of the Russian garrison.[53]

An Ionian delegation sent to Paris by the preceding government caused Mocenigo some concern. In October 1802, Morkov
complained that Talleyrand was evading his requests, prompted
by Mocenigo, for the dismissal of these envoys.[54] Mocenigo then
had the senate cancel the authority of this delegation and agree
that the republic's foreign relations with France and Britain
were henceforth to be handled by the Russian representatives.
The Ionian Republic had again become a self-governing Russian
colony just in time to prevent a real contest between France and
Britain over the islands.

The nearby area of the Balkans remained in turmoil, however.
Ali Pasha continued his cruel repression of the Souliot con-
federacy, and Pasvan-oglu was again on the offensive in Wallachia. In Serbia, Bosnia, and Hercegovina local disturbances
were threatening to develop into a major revolt against Turkish
administration, while Austrian, French, and Russian agents
infiltrated with gifts and promises. Following Sebastiani's mission, there was a decided increase in French attempts to win
the Balkan peoples. French privateers distributed guns and supplies along the coast. The conviction was growing everywhere
that the Ottoman Empire was really on its deathbed. Russia was

---

Ioniennes (Paris, 1917), p. 125; Foresti to Hawkesbury, 2 January and 26
May 1803, PRO, FO 42/5. The senate had complained to Mocenigo in
September 1802 of the activities of Romieu, and he in turn had reported this
to Saint Petersburg. VPR 1: 718, n. 200.
  52. Morkov to A. R. Vorontsov, 20 October 1802, in VPR 1: 311–12.
  53. Foresti to Hawkesbury, 10 December 1802, PRO, FO 42/4.
  54. Morkov to A. R. Vorontsov, 20 October 1802, in VPR 1: 311–12.

in an especially awkward position, trying to maintain friendly relations and predominance at Constantinople for the sake of Black Sea trade and her need to defend the Ionian Islands, but also wanting to protect the Christian population against outrages by uncontrolled pashas.[55]

While Russian agents tangled with the French in the principalities and in Constantinople itself, Austria concentrated on Serbia, Bosnia, and Hercegovina. After the Treaty of Lunéville, Austria had shifted her attention eastward from Italy to the Balkans, where she already had attained important bases by the annexation of the Dalmatian territories of Venice. Montenegrin infiltration of the coastal towns of Budva and Cattaro created a thorny problem in Austro-Russian relations.[56]

POLICY FORMULATION IN SAINT PETERSBURG

Political leadership in Russia shifted as much in the first year of Alexander's reign as in the last year of Paul's. After the general purge of those responsible for the coup that brought Alexander to the throne, culminating in the sudden resignation of Panin in October 1801, Alexander's "young friends," or Secret Committee, were in dominant positions. Kochubei assumed the administration of foreign affairs in October and steered Russia along a neutral course during an important period of transition. He was probably influential in opposing the garrisoning of Malta by Russian troops and in favoring a reinforcement of the Ionian Islands. Kochubei also strengthened the policy of friendship with the Ottoman Empire, recalled Tomara—ostensibly over a slight religious offense—and silenced suggestions that Russia should prepare to partition Ottoman territories.[57] He was also

---

55. Foresti to Hawkesbury, 26 May 1803, PRO, FO 42/5; Douin, p. 146.
56. Saurau to Cobenzl, 17 August 1802, HHSA, 98 Russland II Berichte; Russia repeatedly reassured Austria that she had no designs on the Ottoman Empire, but suspicions grew. In the summer of 1803, Stadion reported that Tomara said, "All of Europe united cannot sustain for long the existence of the Ottoman Empire." Stadion to Cobenzl, 19 August 1803, HHSA, 102 Russland II Berichte.
57. Alexander I to Italinsky, 11 September 1802, in VPR 1: 283–87.

instrumental in arranging a visit by Alexander with the Prussian king, Frederick William III, to Memel in June 1802—a meeting that was of major significance because of the attachment that Alexander developed to the Prussian court, especially Queen Louisa. But when the ministerial reform was effected in September 1802, Kochubei became minister of interior and Alexander Vorontsov, the chancellor, administered foreign affairs.

In the years 1802 to 1804 most questions of policy were discussed by the Secret Committee or in regular meetings of the larger Committee of Ministers. Because of Vorontsov's ill health, Adam Czartoryski, the assistant minister of foreign affairs, attended these meetings and became the chief adviser to the tsar on foreign policy matters.[58] While Kochubei was a "neutralist," Czartoryski advocated a stronger policy vis-à-vis France, and he was supported by Vorontsov, Zavadovsky, the minister of education, and Novosiltsev and Stroganov, assistant ministers of justice and interior, respectively. Nicholas Rumiantsev, the minister of commerce, was the main exponent of accommodation with France. He promoted the diversification of Russian trade by a renewed concentration on the Black Sea and by sponsoring Rezanov's voyage to Japan, Alaska, and California. Mordvinov, the new naval minister, although an anglophile, tended to support Rumiantsev's position.[59]

Anti-French sentiments began to prevail from the end of 1801 when Caulaincourt, Bonaparte's special emissary to the coronation, was received very coldly by Alexander, and Hédouville, the French ambassador, was never made to feel very welcome. The recall of Tomara, the assignments of Italinsky to Constantinople, Tatishchev to Naples, and Mocenigo to Corfu, and the reappointment of Razumovsky to Vienna strengthened, especially in the Mediterranean, the Vorontsov-Czartoryski views

---

58. Hudelist to Cobenzl, 7 and 26 December 1802, HHSA, 98 Russland II Berichte.

59. V. G. Sirotkin, *Duel' dvukh diplomatii: Rossiia i Frantsiia v 1801–1812 gg.* (Moscow, 1966), pp. 12–15; Hudelist to Cobenzl, 21 September 1802, HHSA, 98 Russland II Berichte; P. V. Zavadovsky to S. R. Vorontsov, 11 April 1803, in *Arkhiv Vorontsova*, 12: 270–74.

on foreign policy. Though it would be tempting to credit these changes to one person, Czartoryski, they were the result of the new political atmosphere in Saint Petersburg. It so happened that the most likely candidates for diplomatic posts were protégés of the "young friends" or of the Vorontsovs. Their establishment by 1803 at Constantinople, Naples, Corfu, London, and Vienna, while an "out-of-touch" diplomat of the old school was negotiating in Paris, was certainly influential on the course of Russian foreign policy. The new foreign diplomats in Saint Petersburg were of limited ability. The short tenures of St. Helens, who had been ambassador to Russia in the 1780s, and of Warren handicapped their chances of establishing any influence. The French ambassador was completely isolated, and a fully empowered envoy did not arrive from Austria until the summer of 1803. Moreover, Alexander avoided contact with all members of the diplomatic corps and his friends followed suit.[60]

Attempting to disengage from European affairs and reacting against the policy of his father, Alexander refused to commit Russia to a guarantee of the security of Malta on behalf of the order, thereby leaving unsolved a volatile issue that was to be a major cause of the resumption of hostilities between Britain and France in May 1803. But where Russian presence had already been established—in the Ionian Islands—and Russian prestige and the practical interests of security were involved, Alexander agreed to reinforce the Russian position. The massing of French and Russian troops on opposite sides of the Adriatic was to be a chief reason for Russia's initial participation in the War of the Third Coalition.

---

60. Stadion to Cobenzl, 10 September 1803, HHSA, 102 Russland II Berichte.

8

The Third Coalition and the Mediterranean, 1803-1805

During the year following the conclusion of the Treaty of Amiens, the growing pro-British alignment of Russian diplomacy was watched with concern in Paris. This Russian shift toward Britain was especially noticeable in the Mediterranean area. Bonaparte, named First Consul for life in August 1802, still maintained a special interest in the Mediterranean. Bonaparte and his foreign minister, Talleyrand, using both aggressive threats and diplomatic bait, attempted to prevent a reencirclement of France by Britain and Russia. This only increased the hostility and closed the circle. At the famous meeting at Memel in June 1802 between the tsar and Frederick William III, Alexander had fallen under the spell of the young and beautiful Queen Louisa. His growing attachment to Prussia had a definite but hard-to-measure effect upon Russian foreign policy. This meeting "marked for Alexander an important step in the development of his anti-French feelings."[1]

Russian antagonism toward France increased after Morkov's audiences with Talleyrand and Bonaparte in late 1802 and early 1803, during which the fate of the Ottoman Empire was discussed and the possibility of its partition was suggested by the

---

1. A. A. Lobanov-Rostovsky, *Russia and Europe, 1789–1825* (Durham, N.C., 1947), p. 73.

French.[2] Though Morkov probably exaggerated these proposals in his dispatches to Saint Petersburg, there is little doubt that Bonaparte's thoughts were again turned toward the Near East. At the beginning of February 1803 Alexander declared to Simon Vorontsov, "The wisest system for Russia is to remain at peace and concern itself with internal prosperity." But he added,

> One of the circumstances about which I could not remain indifferent would be an invasion of the Ottoman Empire by the French. It appears that the First Consul is continually occupied with this project. . . . I am going to instruct Count Morkov to explain frankly to him that I would not in any case lend a hand to the dismemberment of the Ottoman Empire, which I believe to be an advantageous neighbor for Russia, and I desire to conserve it.[3]

Partition schemes conflicted with Alexander's conviction, bolstered by the influence of Kochubei and the Vorontsovs, that the Ottoman Empire should be preserved as a friendly buffer state against France.

Doubts about French sincerity grew stronger with the arrival of reports describing increased activities by French agents infiltrating across Austrian territory from Venice into the Balkans; these agents rendered moral and financial support to the pro-French hospodar of Moldavia, Murusi, and encouraged the rebellious pashas of Vidin and Janina. The new hospodar of Wallachia, however, appointed in 1802 through Russian pressure, was Konstantin Ypsilanti, a Phanariot Greek, who never wavered from his pro-Russian, pro-Greek sympathies.[4] While partition schemes were being tendered to Morkov in Paris and French agents in the Balkans were promising financial and military aid to the sultan's semi-independent pashas, Ali and Pasvan-oglu, France was pressing the Porte to allow French ships the same passage rights as Russian through the Straits. Russia favored the unrestricted sailing of merchant ships into the Black Sea but opposed the French demand for passage for military ships to de-

---

2. Morkov to A. R. Vorontsov, March 1803, in *SIRIO* 77: 67–71.
3. 1 February 1803, in *Arkhiv Voronstova* 28: 464–65.
4. A. R. Vorontsov to Mocenigo, 9 September 1803, in *VPR* 1: 513–15.

fend their commerce from piracy on those waters.[5] Russia wanted to maintain the Black Sea as a closed lake as far as outside naval forces were concerned. She was very conscious of the fact that the precedent of agreeing to allow Russian warships out of the Black Sea might be used to allow warships of other countries entrance into the Black Sea.

BLACK SEA TRADE AND RUSSIAN FOREIGN POLICY

Both Soviet and Western historians have emphasized the role of Russian trade in the formulation of foreign policies in Russia, Britain, and France.[6] Statistics have been amassed and published to illustrate the rapid increase of shipping from Russian Black Sea ports between 1800 and 1806. Marxist historians consider British and French interest in the exploitation of these new markets to be a major cause of the Anglo-French conflict in the Mediterranean. The opening of the Black Sea to international trade is considered one aspect of the commercial rivalry in the Mediterranean and the chief reason for Russia's involvement in Mediterranean affairs. The economic development of South Russia and the foundation of a regular trade across the Black Sea have already been examined as factors in the growth of Russian interest in the Mediterranean in the 1790s.

The first few years of the nineteenth century mark a decisive turning point in the commercial history of the Black Sea. According to statistics collected by Stanislavskaia, the proportion of the

---

5. Shapiro, p. 270; A. R. Vorontsov to Morkov, 24 August 1803, VPR, 1: 506–7.

6. For the Soviet views, with economic and national biases, see the works of Stanislavskaia, Sirotkin, Druzhinina, Shapiro, and Tarle, already cited, and S. B. Okun', *Istorii SSSR, 1796–1825: kurs lektsii* (Leningrad, 1947). Examples of Western scholarship, on the whole less satisfactory, are: Vernon J. Puryear, *Napoleon and the Dardanelles* (Berkeley, 1951); Alfred L. P. Denis, *Eastern Problems at the Close of the Eighteenth Century* (Cambridge, Mass., 1901); Captain A. T. Mahan, *The Influence of Sea Power upon the French Revolution and Empire, 1793–1812,* 2 vols. (Boston, 1893); and William Freeman Galpin, *The Grain Supply of England during the Napoleonic Period* (Philadelphia, 1925).

value of Russian Black Sea trade in the total value of the sea-borne commerce of Russia rose from 5.5 percent in 1802, to 8.4 percent in 1803, to 10.7 percent in 1804, to 12.9 percent in 1805.[7] This increase, when Baltic trade was also rising and Pacific trade was beginning, is quite remarkable. A number of factors can be cited as reasons for this "breakthrough": the durability of the Russo-Turkish Alliance after the war of 1799, the opening of the Black Sea to merchant vessels of all countries in 1802, a shortage of grain in France and two successive crop failures in Britain in 1799 and 1800,[8] the establishment of trade security by Mocenigo and the Russian squadron in the Adriatic, and the attempts of Nicholas Petrovich Rumiantsev, minister of commerce, to diversify Russian commerce.

Additional analysis is necessary to understand the true significance of the trade "boom" on the Black Sea. Of the 977 ships that arrived in Russian Black Sea ports in 1803, the great majority sailed under "local" flags: Turkish 353 (36.2 percent), Austrian 295 (30.2 percent), Russian 225 (23.1 percent), Ionian Republic 37, France 22, Britain 7, and others 38.[9] Was the trade then predominately Russo-Turkish? A sizable part of it was, perhaps one-third, but the flag under which a ship sails or the country from which it originates is not a good clue to the destination of its cargo. Most of the "Turkish," "Austrian," and "Russian" ships were really Greek and Italian ships. The orientation of

---

7. A. M. Stanislavskaia, Russko-angliiskie otnosheniia i problemy sredizemnomor'ia, 1798–1807 (Moscow, 1962), pp. 30–31.

8. Puryear, p. 10, mentions the grain shortage in France and claims that 25 percent of the Black Sea exports of grain went to Marseilles. Galpin, pp. 10–11, discusses the British crop failures. His statement, p. 126, that Britain received almost no grain from Odessa discounts the possibility of reshipment from Mediterranean ports. The figures presented by Vol'skii agree, however. Russia supplied only 8.4 percent of Britain's grain imports in 1801, only 1 per cent in 1802, 1.8 per cent in 1803, 0.5 per cent in 1804, and 11.6 per cent in 1805. Only in the last year Odessa may have supplied significant supplies of grain to Britain. Mikhail Vol'skii, *Ocherk istorii khbebnoi torgovli novorossiiskago kraia s drevneishikh vremen do 1852 goda* (Odessa, 1854).

9. Stanislavskaia, pp. 32–37. Sources vary considerably on the number of ships.

Black Sea exports and imports might be revealed more accurately by noting that the five commercial houses of Odessa in 1803 included one French, one British, one Italian, and two German (Austrian),[10] and that thirteen of the sixteen individual merchants listed there had Greek, Italian, or German names.[11]

Odessa, of course, was the most international of the Black Sea ports, but it was also the largest, receiving about 65 percent of the ships (and those vessels loading and unloading at Odessa were larger than the Black Sea average). Grain was the major export. A contemporary source reports that in 1802 the grain exports of Odessa were worth 1,329,776 rubles out of 1,525,671 rubles for the total exports. Imports of goods totalling 772,047 rubles in that year were, in order of value: incense, wool, dried raisins, olive oil, wines of Italy, Spain, and Greece, cotton, lemons, dried figs, and oranges.[12] Perhaps the most remarkable thing about this trade was that imports rose at a faster rate than exports. In 1805, 666 sea-going ships and 496 coastal vessels docked at Odessa, making it one of the largest ports in southern Europe. Exports of grain in that year were worth 5,700,000 rubles.[13]

Government measures facilitated the growth of Odessa. A free loan of 25,000 rubles to the city in 1800 spurred the development of the port. On 20 October 1802, the Novorossisk province was redivided into three: Nikolaevsk, Ekaterinoslavsk, and Tavricheskii, and a special investigation commission was appointed by Rumiantsev in 1802 for Odessa.[14] Also through the influence of the minister of commerce, the duc de Richelieu was named governor of Odessa on 8 February, 1803. His arrival in March marked the beginning of a phase of rapid development of the

---

10. J. Reuilly, *Voyage en Crimée et sur les bords de la mer noire pendant l'année 1803* (Paris, 1806), p. 264.

11. A. Skal'kovskii, *Pervoe tridsatiletie istorii goroda Odessy* (Odessa, 1837), p. 110.

12. Reuilly, pp. 270–73, tables I & II.

13. Stanislavskaia, p. 31; Skal'kovskii, p. 148. Vol'skii offers the following figures for grain exports from all of "New Russia:" 1802—519, 211 chetverts; 1803—950,141; 1804—1,004,108; 1805—1,645,229. Vol'skii, p. 78.

14. Skal'kovskii, pp. 107–8.

city.[15] In November 1803, the "Greek division" disbanded by Paul was revived as the "Greek battalion."[16] Richelieu resumed the policy of encouraging foreign settlement. According to a visitor, the population of Odessa was 4,500 in 1803 but had doubled to 9,000 in 1804.[17] A large scale movement of Bulgarians, escaping from Pasvan-oglu, and Moldavians into the Odessa area is reported.[18] And a significant number of Italians, especially from Genoa, Richelieu's birthplace, began to arrive. A new law of 1804 allowed goods to be stored in Odessa for six months, duty-free. Direct trade extended as far as Spain, as shown by the importation of a number of Merino sheep from Spain in 1804.[19]

The Russian presence in the Mediterranean safeguarded the transit of goods through the eastern Mediterranean, the Straits, and the Black Sea, and stimulated Mediterranean interest in Russian trade. Greek shippers, using Russian, Turkish, and Ionian flags, came to Russia in large numbers, established a network of communications throughout the eastern Mediterranean and Black Sea, and helped to found a Greek revolutionary center, the Hetaira, in Odessa in 1804.[20] Still, judging from the contents of ambassadors' reports and the correspondence of government leaders, political rather than economic factors determined the decisions that were made in Saint Petersburg respecting the Mediterranean.

ANTI-FRENCH ORIENTATION OF RUSSIAN POLICY

Relations between Britain and Russia were becoming more and

---

15. Ibid., pp. 115–17.

16. Ibid., pp. 66, 134.

17. Reuilly, pp. 263–65. Stanislavskaia, p. 39, reports the population in 1802 at 9,000.

18. Skal'kovskii, p. 137.

19. Ibid., pp. 146, 153; E. I. Druzhinina, *Severnoe prichernomor'e*, v 1775–1800 gg. (Moscow, 1959), p. 240.

20. O. B. Shparo, *Osvobozhdenie Gretsii i Rossiia, 1821–1829* (Moscow, 1965), p. 40; L. S. Stavrianos, "Antecedents to the Balkan Revolutions of the Nineteenth Century," *Journal of Modern History* 29 (1957): 342–43.

more harmonious. This was due not so much to English policy as to the proclivities of Russian leaders like the Vorontsovs, Czartoryski, and Novosiltsev, who were convinced that it was dangerous to be closely associated with France.[21] The prevailing anti-French mood of the capital was promoted by the complaints of Morkov, Italinsky, and other Russian agents about French military preparations and aggressive diplomatic activities.

Russia's continued involvement in the Mediterranean was mainly political in motivation, with four goals: (1) the territorial restitution of Sardinia and Naples, (2) the neutralization of Malta, (3) the maintenance of the Russian position on the Ionian Islands, and (4) the integrity of the Ottoman Empire. The overall aim of Russian policy was to block French expansionist aims and, at the same time, to prevent the dominance of other major powers in these areas.

Support of the independent kingdoms of Italy had been a policy of Emperor Paul and was continued by Alexander. Alexander's motivation was different, however. Whereas Paul's pro-Italian policy had been part of a general aim of strengthening legitimate rulers and the Roman Catholic Church against revolutionary France, Alexander, guided especially by Czartoryski, emphasized the rights of small nations and foresaw the possibility of substantial change toward more liberal, constitutional government in these areas. The church, though not entirely forgotten by Alexander and his advisers, played an insignificant role in Russia's Mediterranean policy after 1801. In Saint Petersburg the restoration or indemnification of the kingdoms of Naples and Sardinia was considered more important than the complex affairs of the Knights of Malta.[22] In the negotiations with France in October 1801, a complete withdrawal of all foreign forces from Italy was agreed upon, but the threat of French force and diplomatic pressure remained, and partly because the Maltese problem was still unresolved France left an army in Piedmont.[23]

---

21. Stanislavskaia, pp. 181–85.
22. Hedouville to Talleyrand, 11 November 1802, in SIRIO 70: 569–75.
23. Edouard Driault, *Napoléon et l'Europe: La Politique extérieure du Premier Consul, 1800–1803* (Paris, 1910), pp. 63, 208–10.

The French army of General Saint-Cyr moved down along the Adriatic coast into Apulia in the summer of 1803, following the rupture with Britain;[24] there it posed more of a threat to Russian interests in the Balkans and in the Ionians than to the British on Malta. Saint-Cyr's army was a direct violation of Neapolitan sovereignty, a point which could not escape the Neapolitan ambassador to Russia, Serracapriola. This veteran diplomat abetted Russia's pro-Italian policy during the reigns of Catherine, Paul, and Alexander. His polished diplomacy was soon aided by the recruitment by Russia of Pozzo di Borgo, an émigré agent from Corsica, and the arrival in Saint Petersburg of the famous Sardinian conservative, Joseph de Maistre, as ambassador from Sardinia.[25] With the rise of Adam Czartoryski, who had recently represented Russia at the Sardinian court, pro-Sardinian and pro-Neapolitan policies became keystones of Russian strategy.

The Russian Maltese policy from 1803 to 1805 was confused and contradictory. Russia consistently argued for the return of the island to the Order of Saint John, but this involved opposition to Britain rather than to France. The growing anglophile tendencies in Russia made ineffectual the proposals for securing neutralization that would satisfy both France and Britain.

When Bailli Buzi—a representative of the new grand master, Tommasi—arrived at Malta on 1 March 1803, Britain's excuse for refusing to leave the island to the Order of Saint John was the absence of a real guarantee of the neutrality of Malta.[26] As Bonaparte kept troops in northern Italy, both nations were thus violating the stipulations of the Treaty of Amiens. In June, Alexander, on the advice of Simon Vorontsov, made a belated effort to bring about a satisfactory Russian guarantee of the neutrality

---

24. Piers Mackesy, *The War in the Mediterranean, 1803–1810* (London, 1957), pp. 21–23.
25. Pierre Ordioni, *Pozzo di Borgo, diplomate de l'Europe française* (Paris, 1935), pp. 90–91.
26. L. F. de Villeneuve-Bargemont, Mounments des Grands-Maîtres de l'Ordre de Saint-Jean de Jerusalem (Paris, 1829), 2: 450.

of the island with a revision of Amiens.[27] But by that time Bonaparte and Talleyrand had concluded that Alexander was too much under British influence to provide suitable mediation.

Relations between France and Russia continued to stiffen, as expected. Bonaparte requested Morkov's recall in July 1803 after a series of disagreeable audiences relating to guarantees for Malta.[28] Although Alexander's personal inclination was still to mediate the differences between Britain and France, it was voiced with so little conviction and courage that Simon Vorontsov and Czartoryski were left to mold a stronger pro-British line. As Czartoryski gradually replaced Alexander Vorontsov as head of foreign affairs in 1803, Russia became firmly entrenched in the British camp.

It was at this time, in November 1803, that the decision was made to send additional reinforcements for the Russian garrison in the Ionians.[29] Mocenigo had been pressed to build up a local militia adequate to the defense of the republic but had encountered obstacles in training and supplying such a force from the islands' limited resources,[30] and though the project was not abandoned, it was deemed safer in Saint Petersburg to entrust the defense to an enlarged Russian garrison. Three frigates and a transport ship, commanded by Captain Leontovich, carrying 1100 soldiers under Colonel Papandopulo left Sevastopol in February 1804 for Corfu, to augment Captain Sorokin's small force; the ships arrived at Corfu on 26 March and became part of Sorokin's command.[31] This was followed by a series of additional

---

27. Alexander to Morkov, 5 June 1803, in *SIRIO* 77: 159–64; A. R. Vorontsov to Alexander, 1 June 1803, in *SIRIO* 77: 153–57.

28. P. Liupersol'skii, "Diplomaticheskiia snosheniia i bor'ba imperatora Aleksandra I s Napoleonom" (Kiev, 1878), pp. 6–7.

29. A. R. Vorontsov to Alexander, 24 November 1803, in *SIRIO* 77: 410–17.

30. Mocenigo to Ionian Senate, 11 January 1803, and 8 April 1803, SS, DAE, Box 23 (Mocenigo Papers), nos. 17 and 32.

31. Lt. K. Goloviznin, "Ocherki iz istorii russkago flota: Kapitan-Komandor Sorokin v Ionicheskoi Respublike," *Morskoi Sbornik* 192, no. 9 (1882): 33–34.

troop movements from the Black Sea. By July the total garrison had reached 4,700 (3,520 at Corfu), with 2,000 more ready to disembark and 4,000 on the way, according to a British eyewitness.[32] By the end of August 1804 the Russian force in the Ionian Republic had reached an impressive number of 11,000 soldiers with two ships of the line, three frigates, and twelve gunboats.[33] This force was more than sufficient for defending the Ionian Islands, since it actually included more men than did Saint-Cyr's landlocked army in Italy.

The potential of the Ionian Islands as an advance base in the Mediterranean to protect not only the Ionian Republic but also Naples and the whole Balkan coast of the Ottoman Empire was now being realized.[34] The supply of such an army in the Ionians, however, presented quite a problem to Mocenigo and the Russian consul-general and was a considerable burden to the Ionian economy.[35] The republic was still being forced to provide some of its own defense; in June, Alexander ordered Colonel Papandopulo to organize a recruitment effort among the inhabitants of the islands and the nearby coast to augment the Russian army.[36]

The command of the Russian forces was also confused at first. Units were collected as they arrived under Captain Sorokin, who was the senior ranking officer until the arrival of Major General Prince Viazemsky in July. Problems concerning jurisdiction and responsibility were complicated by the fact that Sorokin spoke no foreign language, Mocenigo did not know Russian, and

---

32. Morier to Nelson, 22 July 1804, Nelson Papers, BM, Add. MSS., 34,924, f. 308.

33. Goloviznin, p. 37; Sirotkin, "Iz istorii vneshnei politiki Rossii," *Istoricheskie Zapiski* 67: 224.

34. This is clear from the letters of Alexander I, of A. R. Vorontsov, and of Czartoryski to Mocenigo, and also from the secret instructions to General Anrep, dated 19 May 1804, reproduced in Goloviznin, pp. 40–44.

35. The Mocenigo Papers at Corfu contain numerous references to this problem. Russia tried to avoid the expense of maintaining a garrison there by requiring the islands, their Turkish suzerain, or even the British to pay for fortifications and supplies. The taxation levied on the inhabitants caused dissatisfaction and proved inadequate for Russian needs, and the Porte, as usual, procrastinated. SS, DAE, Box 23; Foresti to Hawkesbury, 30 April 1804, PRO, FO 42/5.

36. Mocenigo to the Ionian Senate, 1 July 1804, SS, DAE, Box 23, no. 106.

Viazemsky was a titled noble with little talent of any kind.[37] Fortunately, General Anrep, a senior officer with a knowledge of foreign languages, arrived at the end of August to head an Ionian defense committee and to command the combined forces.[38] Russia now possessed an offensive striking force on the shores of the Mediterranean that was as much a violation of the treaty arrangements as the British force at Malta; in fact, the size and position of the Ionians vis-à-vis Italy and the Balkans made them a much more advantageous base to Russia than Malta was to the British.

In Constantinople Italinsky tried to maintain Russia's influence over the Sultan, but in 1803 he was opposed by a very capable French diplomat, General Brune, who constantly endeavored to undermine the Anglo-Russian position. After limited success in 1803 in achieving recognition of French commercial rights in the Straits and the Black Sea, Brune turned to thornier problems in 1804—the recognition of Napoleon's imperial title and the closure of the Straits to Russian warships. On these matters Russia, with the support of Britain, prevailed; and, having threatened to leave Constantinople if the imperial title was not acknowledged, Brune set off for France in early 1805, leaving only low-ranking diplomatic personnel in the Ottoman capital.[39]

At the same time that Russia was winning a battle for her position at the Straits, other policies were being developed in Saint Petersburg that were eventually to play into French hands. As early as November 1804 Czartoryski was preparing for the possibility that the Ottoman Empire might not survive another major European conflict: "We support the Turkish Empire, but if the body is so rotten and gangrenous in its principal and vital parts, we will not allow [a partition] to be brought about in a manner contrary to the interests of Russia."[40] Czartoryski, following a pattern already set by Catherine II in 1780 and Rostop-

---

37. Goloviznin, p. 39.
38. Ibid., p. 40; Mocenigo to the Ionian Senate, 15 September 1804, SS, DAE, Box 23, no. 121.
39. Puryear, p. 36.
40. Czartoryski to S. R. Vorontsov, 6 November 1804, in *Arkhiv Vorontsova* 15: 278.

chin in 1800, proposed a partition of the Ottoman Empire that would take into account both Russian expansionist aims and his own interest in autonomy or independence for Poland. According to Czartoryski's plan, which was to be operative only in case of an Ottoman collapse, Austria would receive Croatia, part of Bosnia, Wallachia, Belgrade, and Ragusa; Russia would obtain Corfu, Cattaro, Moldavia, and Constantinople and the Dardanelles; Greece would be independent; and France and Britain would get Aegean islands and parts of Turkish Asia and Africa.[41] Support of the integrity of the Ottoman Empire remained the official Russian policy, but the plan could be of use in case the French succeeded in gaining control at Constantinople. This was one more partition scheme to give foundation to the many rumors about Russia's aim to annex more Turkish territory, and, in face of the Serbian revolts in 1804, revived old Turkish (and Austrian) fears about Russian intentions.

Besides responding to the movement of French troops into southern Italy with the rearmament of the Ionians, Russia also reacted to the growing French influence in the Balkans that was being established by French consular agents, led by Pouqueville, consul-general in Janina. In March 1804, a number of consuls were authorized in Saint Petersburg for the important Greek and Albanian towns. Though formally appointed by Italinsky, they were selected by Mocenigo and under his direct supervision. Their initial instructions, however, were drafted by Czartoryski, who called for them to divert the Greeks "from any ties with the French and to win their adherence to Russia."[42] The instructions also advised that French propaganda could be thwarted by having its inconsistencies pointed out, such as the suppression of liberty in Holland, Switzerland, and Italy. The compliance of Ali Pasha with an Ottoman directive, instigated by Italinsky, to withdraw his troops from the coastal towns facilitated the operations of the

---

41. Puryear, p. 27. For a discussion of Czartoryski's "grand design" for Europe, see M. Kukiel, *Czartoryski and European Unity, 1770–1861* (Princeton, 1955), pp. 41–60.

42. Stanislavskaia, pp. 283–85. The undated instructions ("not later than 19 April 1804") are cited from archival materials.

new Russian consuls.[43] Vlasopulo in Prevesa, Flori in Arta, and Sankovsky in Cattaro were the most active of the new consuls. A more practical achievement of Sankovsky and Fonton, the Russian consul-general at Ragusa, was the diversion of some Bosnian and Hercegovinian trade, which normally passed through Ragusa, to Ionian ships using Austrian and Turkish ports.[44]

THE FORMATION OF THE THIRD COALITION

Events in the Mediterranean were affecting the growth of anti-French sentiments in Russia. The Austrian ambassador's dispatches reveal that the inclination of the government in Saint Petersburg for participation in a coalition against France rose sharply between November 1803 and January 1804, well before the Enghien episode or the assumption of the imperial title by Bonaparte. The influence of Czartoryski, the Vorontsovs, and Razumovsky pushed Alexander into this more belligerent stance, but Stadion also noted the complementary rise of a "peace party" in February and March 1804, headed by the dowager empress Maria Fedorovna, the Zubovs, and Alexander Kurakin.[45] Alexander, also under pressure from the "peace party" and perhaps reacting to the rapid mobilization, hesitated to commit Russia to more definite offensive action. The shock of the execution of the duke d'Enghien (20 March 1804) strengthened the "war party," and Czartoryski's persuasion convinced Alexander of the value of defending the integrity of the small states of Europe against the ambitions of Napoleon.[46]

The formal coalition against France was achieved by the

43. Stanislavskaia, pp. 292–93.

44. Ibid., pp. 284–87; The Ragusan complaints were registered in Constantinople. "Lettere e Relazioni dei Nobili Paolo di Vladislavo de Gozze e Biazio di Manzo in Constantinopoli, 1804," letter dated 15 July 1804, Dubrovnik, Drzavni Arhiv.

45. Stadion to Cobenzl, 4 January 1804, and copy of memoir of A. R. Vorontsov, 1 January 1804, HHSA, 103 Russland II Berichte; Stadion to Cobenzl, 2 April 1804, HHSA, 104 Russland II Berichte.

46. Stanislavskaia, p. 347.

cooperative efforts of British and Russian diplomacy, led respectively by Pitt and Czartoryski. But Russia could effectively enter a major contest only on condition that Austria also join, since it was impracticable to participate in the war only through the Straits. Austrian territory would again have to provide the route for the main Russian armies. Despite differing aims and motives, Russian and British diplomats were able to coordinate their actions in Vienna, but Austria still hesitated. Alexander was upset in August by the news that Austria had recognized Bonaparte's imperial title. Special missions were immediately organized to impress on all European powers Russia's interest in an anti-French coalition.[47] Russia hurried to sign an alliance with Austria on 6 November 1804, but it was purely defensive in character.

In Naples there were both pro-British and pro-Russian adherents, but Alquier, the French ambassador, was able to exploit France's strong position in Italy.[48] The vulnerability of Naples on land left her more prone than Austria or the Ottoman Empire to French diplomatic and military threats. On the other flank, to the north of Austria, Prussia refused to be brought out of neutrality, in spite of her personal ties with Alexander.

The forming of the Third Coalition hinged upon Anglo-Russian cooperation, but negotiations in London and Saint Petersburg stalled several times during 1804 and 1805. Pitt, who had returned to power at the head of a coalition government in 1804, was reluctant to add more Russian subsidies to the mounting British war debt unless Austria and Prussia would also participate. The maintenance of a continental balance of power again played a role in British policy making. But deliberations continued between Britain and Russia on the respective share of the effort to be borne and on the tactics to be employed. Though

---

47. Stadion to Cobenzl, 28 August 1804, and 11 September 1804, HHSA, 105 Russland II Berichte.

48. Charles Auriol, *La France, l'Angleterre, et Naples de 1803 à 1806* (Paris, 1904), 1: 55; P. Coquelle, "L'Ambassade du Maréchal Brune à Constantinople (1803–1805)," *Revue d'historie diplomatique* 18 (January, 1904): 54–55.

the Russians wanted only 15,000 additional troops, the British, fearing a direct attack across the channel, were reluctant to send a large expeditionary army to the Mediterranean and believed that supply and transport of such a number of troops would be too difficult. The dramatic Novosiltsev mission to London in October and November 1804 failed to obtain the number of British troops that Russia wanted, but it did secure a more definite commitment to an alliance.[49] The details of the formal alliance were then worked out by Czartoryski and Leveson-Gower (Lord Granville), the British ambassador, and the treaty was finally signed in April 1805.

The allies were all more cautious in 1805 than they had been in the forming of the Second Coalition in 1798. Careful planning for the coordination of military campaigns resulted in costly delays. In the negotiations Russia finally settled for a smaller British contingent in exchange for overall Russian command, and naval transport and supply support for the expedition to Naples.[50] Although the size of the army was less than that originally proposed, the allies proceeded with plans to open an offensive in the Mediterranean on Neapolitan territory. This expedition proved to be one of the most worthless endeavors of the Napoleonic Wars.

Dmitri Tatishchev was sent to Naples in March 1805 to secure the adherence of the kingdom to the military plans of Britain and Russia.[51] He finally was able to overcome French influence and on 10 September concluded a secret convention with Luzzi and Circello representing the Neapolitan court.[52] Gallo, the ambassador to France, with the backing of the Neapolitan queen, signed a treaty with Talleyrand on 21 September that conflicted directly with the one signed with Russia.[53] The Russian

---

49. Kukiel, pp. 45–49; Alexander I to Novosiltsev, 23 September 1804, VPR 2: 138–46.
50. Mackesy, p. 57; Stanislavskaia, pp. 359–65.
51. Stanislavskaia, p. 377; Alexander to Tatishchev, 2 March 1805, in VPR 2: 329–30.
52. VPR 2: 570–74; Auriol, 2: 525–30.
53. Mackesy, pp. 80–81.

convention provided for allied armies to land in Naples, while the French treaty required strict Neapolitan neutrality in return for the evacuation of French troops from the territory. Alquier was ordered by Napoleon to ask for an immediate ratification, which the king granted on 8 October only four days after the treaty had been received;[54] but at the same time Ferdinand sent Tatishchev a secret note effectively annulling his open ratification of the neutrality treaty.[55]

Upon receipt of the ratification, the French fulfilled their part of the terms by ordering the withdrawal of Saint-Cyr's army from Neapolitan territory. They were happy to extricate this army without loss of prestige, since it might have been cut off by a Russian landing around Ancona. This action lessened the direct threat to Russian interests in the Adriatic, but the allies continued with their plans to defend Naples.

The details for the 1805 Mediterranean campaign were completed too late to allow a well-coordinated military assault to be planned. The elderly General Lacy was named by Russia to command the combined Anglo-Russian-Neapolitan army. He and his aide, Pozzo di Borgo, arrived in Naples during the summer of 1805 to draw up defensive plans, but no action could be taken until the British, who were detained at Gibraltar, had arrived at Malta, and the approval of Naples had been secured.[56] In October, after Saint-Cyr had withdrawn, orders were sent forward to General James Craig at Malta and Major General Anrep at Corfu to bring their respective commands to Naples, where they landed about 20 November.[57] The British force

54. Stanislavskaia, p. 378; G. Douin, *La Mediterranée de 1803 à 1805* (Paris, 1917), p. 240.

55. Auriol, 2: 603–04.

56. Stanislavskaia, p. 394; Mackesy, p. 83. Lacy was pessimistic about the campaign from the beginning. "Here I have found all the resources and means of the country quite inferior to the picture presented continually to our court. And because of the failure of zeal and good will of nearly all of those at the head of affairs, the expedition to Naples will not be easy and cannot promise much success unless the French are occupied in a very active war in the North of Italy." Lacy to S. R. Vorontsov, 4 August 1805 in *Arkhiv Vorontsova* 22: 211–12.

57. Auriol, 2: 745–748.

numbering only around 6,000, and the Russian army, 11,000 plus 1,600 Greek and Albanian militia, joined the Neapolitans. It was an unbalanced army very short of cavalry and artillery horses. Lacy considered it too small to employ for a spread-out defense of the whole kingdom, and planned instead a small perimeter defense around Naples.[58]

The French victories at Ulm, and then Austerlitz, left Lacy in a hopeless position. Massena's army of 35,000 in northern Italy was now free to move south. The British were anxious to embark while they had time to do so with ease, and as usual the Russians were short of supplies and lacked money and credit to buy them,[59] but Lacy was reluctant to order a retreat to safer and surer ground until he had received orders from Saint Petersburg. Alexander's order, written soon after Austerlitz and probably influenced by the experience of that battle, reached Naples on 7 January 1806; reminiscent of Paul's order to Ushakov six years earlier, it provided for a general withdrawal first to Corfu and then to the Black Sea. Despite the Neapolitan court's protests at being left alone after it had repudiated the agreement with France, the allied army was aboard ship and weighing anchor by 20 January 1806. Direct interference of Russia in the affairs of Naples had been brought to a dismal close. Alexander suggested only that Naples try to reinstate the neutrality agreement with France.

The Mediterranean, and particularly Italy, had been expected to become a major theater of operations in the campaigns of the Third Coalition. The plans for concerted action in Italy had degenerated into a miserable fiasco; allied military forces in Italy were too late to prevent a French concentration of military power against Austria and Russia in central Europe. After Napoleon's stand at Austerlitz on 2 December, the planned Russian sweep northward through Italy was impossible. Now a much larger allied force would have been necessary to prevent the occupation of southern Italy, but supply problems would have been tre-

---

58. Mackesy, pp. 86–89.
59. Ibid., pp. 90–91.

..dous; Russia did not possess the finances and Britain was ..willing to pay for such an adventure. A much smaller Russian corps could have preserved the Russian base in the Ionians and her interests in the Ottoman Empire. For the remainder of Russia's lukewarm participation in the War of the Third Coalition, Mediterranean activity was to be concentrated along the Adriatic and Aegean coasts of the Balkan peninsula.

During the organization of the Third Coalition, the acting naval minister, Paul Chichagov, was an important proponent of a more active Russian policy toward the Mediterranean. He was one of a number of young diplomats and naval officers who had come under the tutelage of Simon Vorontsov while serving or studying in England. Dedicated to the advancement of the Russian navy, he impressed Alexander with his efficient rebuilding of the Baltic fleet and his reforms of the corrupt naval administration between 1802 and 1805. Chichagov often complained, however, of the greater influence of the ministries of commerce and foreign affairs and actively opposed both Rumiantsev and Czartoryski in the Committee of Ministers. He supported the dispatch of the Baltic fleet to the Mediterranean and assigned his close friend, Alexis Greig, to command the first detachment in September 1804, but he resisted the subordination of the fleet to the army in the Mediterranean, for which he blamed Czartoryski, warned in vain against the use of his new Baltic fleet to transport the army of General Peter Tolstoy to Swedish Pomerania in 1805, and criticized the Caucasus campaign that was promoted by Rumiantsev.[60]

The naval ministry favored the Mediterranean campaign, because, as Chichagov explained to Simon Vorontsov,

The advantages that will result for us by this arrangement

---

60. Chichagov complained frequently of a poor division of responsibility between the new ministries: "All the ministries construct ports with the exception of the one of the navy. The ministers of war are the only ones who have nothing to do with military affairs. . . . They say that such is the custom in our country, but it was also the custom not to have any ministers at all." Chichagov to S. R. Vorontsov, 12 December 1804, in *Arkhiv Vorontsova*, 19: 121.

will be incalculable: the experience that will serve to train officers and crews, the pleasure of playing a role worthy of a power that has never appeared insignificant when it decides to act, the confidence that will be inspired in all peoples, which it is useful to attach to our principles, the facility and encouragement that will result for our commerce from the Black Sea, etc. etc. You know better than I all that will follow.

He added that Russians should play a larger role in Egypt than the British, because "we are closer to the gates of the Mediterranean."[61] And Greig was even more emphatic after his arrival at Corfu:

This island is without doubt of the greatest importance for Russia, as much for the political influence it gives her as for the excellent school it provides for the navy. Here the squadrons of the Baltic and of the Black Sea can be united and coordinated; here they appear so different that it is difficult to tell that they belong to the same sovereign. The port is excellent; one can nearly always be on cruise and learn more in one year than in ten in Russia.[62]

61. 14 September 1805, in ibid., pp. 146–147.
62. A. S. Greig to S. R. Vorontsov, undated (summer 1805), in ibid., p. 440.

9
The Adriatic Campaign

In preparation for the campaign in the Mediterranean in 1805, three Russian squadrons were sent from the Baltic Sea where better ships were available than in the Black Sea. Following the route of the 1769–70 expedition, the first squadron under Commodore Alexis Greig, the son of one of the leading commanders of the earlier adventure, arrived at Corfu in July 1805.[1] After two more squadrons appeared during the year, the Russian fleet had again approached considerable size—nine ships of the line, six frigates, seven brigs, one schooner, twelve gunboats, two transports, and one hospital ship.[2] During 1805 Russian operations were again handicapped by a divided command—Greig in command of the ships, Anrep commanding the army at Corfu, Mocenigo as special plenipotentiary, and Lacy as commander-in-chief

---

1. Not only was the Black Sea fleet in poor condition after Ushakov's expedition, but also relations with the Ottoman Empire deteriorated steadily during 1805, thus making the Straits a precarious supply and communications link for a large fleet. Chichagov, the acting naval minister, was instrumental in the decision to send ships from the Baltic, and some thought that a repetition of 1769 must have been in his mind when he appointed Greig to command the first squadron.

2. R. C. Anderson, *Naval Wars in the Levant, 1559–1853* (Princeton, 1952), pp. 430–31. Sources vary on the number and type of Russian ships; an up-to-date Soviet source lists 10 line-of-battle ships, 5 frigates, 11 brigs, brigantines and other small ships, and 12 gunboats. A. L. Shapiro, *Admiral D. N. Seniavin* (Moscow, 1958), p. 96.

of the Italian theater. After the arrival of the third squadron c
30 January 1806, overall Russian command was unified under
Vice Admiral Dmitri Seniavin, an able veteran of Ushakov's
campaign.[3]

Russia's naval position in the Mediterranean in 1806 was
considerably stronger than it had been in 1798–1800. Trafalgar
had not only crippled French naval power and weakened the
British, but it had also eliminated the primary Russian-hater in
the British navy. The Russian Mediterranean fleet consisted of
well-built ships now with more versatile and varied equipment
and crews than before; it was supported by sizable land forces
which Ushakov had sorely lacked. Seniavin had been trained in
England and had gained valuable experience with Ushakov; he
was also better provided with translators and diplomatic personnel than Ushakov had been.[4] Paul Svinin, a writer and artist
of later fame, was on the diplomatic staff.[5] Captain Henry Baillie,
who had been serving actively in the Mediterranean continuously
since 1798, was on hand to provide valuable assistance.[6] It was
certainly not the fault of these men that Russian activities in the

---

3. Stanislavskaia, (see chap. 8, n. 7), p. 408. See also E. V. Tarle,
Ekspeditsiia Admirala D. N. Seniavina v Sredizemnoe more (Moscow, 1954).

4. Ushakov himself was not considered for the command. Chichagov had
wanted at first to command the expedition but then decided to appoint a
veteran of Ushakov's campaign. Seniavin and Ushakov had not agreed during the first trip, but Ushakov nevertheless recommended him for the post:
"I do not like, cannot tolerate Seniavin, but if it were up to me, I would
appoint him." Shapiro, pp. 88–89.

5. Svinin, however, sailed aboard a later squadron of Captain Ignatiev,
which did not arrive in the Mediterranean until early 1807. His colorful
memoirs are filled with interesting anecdotes and descriptions. See his
Vospominaniia na flot Pavla Svin'ina (Saint Petersburg, 1819), which is
dedicated to Seniavin. For a biographical sketch of Svinin see D. Fedotoff
White, "A Russian Sketches Philadelphia, 1811–1813," *The Pennsylvania
Magazine of History & Biography* 75, no. 1 (1951): 3–24.
Two other memoirs should be noted: Vladimir Bronevskii, *Pis'ma morskago ofitsera* (Moscow, 1825), and B. L. Modzalevskii, ed., *Pis'ma morskogo ofitsera, 1806–1809, P. I. Panafidina* (Petrograd, 1916).

6. Baillie, an Englishman, had played a key part in Ushakov's activities
in Italy and had stayed behind at Naples in 1800. His importance in Russian affairs in the Mediterranean has been unduly deemphasized by Soviet
historians. Shapiro, pp. 101 ff.; Stanislavskaia, passim.

•diterranean did not seriously affect the outcome of the war.

About the same time that Ushakov's fleet arrived in the Ionians, Russia cultivated a special interest in the eastern coast of the Adriatic, but up to the beginning of 1806, Russian activities had been centered in the Ionian Islands, Malta, and Italy. Ushakov possessed too few ships and men and was too busy in these areas to be actively involved in areas farther north. Besides, almost the entire Adriatic coast was under the control of allies, Austria, and the Ottoman Empire. The hostility and independence of Ali Pasha, and the reluctance of Ushakov, Mocenigo, and Seniavin to deal with him, had eliminated Albania from the sphere of Russian interest. Russia's interest in the Balkan Slavs, which had been growing under Catherine, was limited after 1796 by Paul's policy of friendship with the Turks and Alexander's policy of noninvolvement.

The mountainous region to the north of Albania contained a tiny state that the Turks considered too poor to bother about, Montenegro. It was under the rule of an enterprising bishop-prince, Peter Negosh, who had traveled to Saint Petersburg twice, in 1778 and 1785, to seek financial and diplomatic support against the surrounding territories. Due to the opposition of Potemkin (who favored Ali Pasha), Negosh had failed to secure a subsidy —the eighteenth century equivalent of a grant to an underdeveloped country. But Paul was impressed by Peter's one-sided victory over an Albanian pasha in 1796 and agreed to recognize Montenegrin independence and award the new state an annual Russian subsidy of 3,000 rubles, beginning in 1799.[7] With the intention of continuing this arrangement, Negosh sent a special emissary, Vukotich, in 1801 with greetings and gifts for Alexander. In a complex Balkan intrigue, however, Vukotich turned against Peter and won from the inexperienced Alexander a ukaz condemning Peter. Colonel Marko Ivelich, a Serbian in Russian service, was ordered by Alexander to investigate, and conspired with Vukotich to remove Negosh, but Negosh's shrewdness and

---

7. Z. Dragovich, "Chernogoriia," *Russkaia Starina* 33: 419.

popularity saved him. By the end of 1803 additional emissaries and the intervention of the Russian consul in Cattaro succeeded in straightening out the affair, discrediting Vukotich, and restoring the subsidy to Peter.[8] Meanwhile France had also become interested in this territory and sent agents to flatter and influence its ruler. Negosh had secured the assistance of the pro-French Abbé Dolchi as secretary and administrative organizer, but the people and ruler alike, as Slavs and Orthodox Christians, were inclined more toward the Russians.[9] The Russian consuls in the commercial towns along the coast virtually conducted the limited foreign affairs of Montenegro.

The strategic trading centers along the coast and to the north of this country had been under Venetian control before Campoformio; after 1797 they became Austrian but were, in fact, virtually independent. These picturesque little towns like Budva, Castelnuovo, and Cattaro decayed slowly during and after the demise of Venice, only to revive as Yugoslav tourist resorts in the twentieth century.[10] By the Treaty of Pressburg, concluded on 26 December 1805, soon after the Battle of Austerlitz, Austria ceded these Adriatic enclaves to the French Empire.[11] But the Illyrian coastal terrain was as difficult to travel over then as now, and the French were faced with the problem of getting occupation forces to these territories. The strategic importance of these posts along the Adriatic did not escape the Russians, who, with command of the sea and adequate land forces, were in a position to arrive there before the French.

---

8. P. Coquelle, *Histoire du Monténégro et de la Bosnie depuis les origines* (Paris, 1895), pp. 254–60; Zhmakin, "Russiia i Chernogoriia," *Drevnaia i Novaia Rossiia* 19: 418–19, 437–42.

9. Zhmakin, pp. 414–17. Montenegrin affairs also continued to complicate Austro-Russian relations because of Austrian occupational control of neighboring areas. Stadion to Cobenzl, 8 November 1804, HHSA, 105 Russland II Berichte.

10. The summer palace of King Alexander was along this coast near Budva; Tito has also vacationed there. The area is rapidly being developed, unfortunately for those who like "unspoiled" terrain, as the Yugoslav Riviera.

11. Shapiro, p. 103.

BOCCHE DI CATTARO AND RAGUSA

Bocche di Cattaro (presently Kotor) was the most important to the Russians of all the former Venetian territories along the coast because of its proximity to Montenegro. Located along an enchanting gulf of blue water and at the foot of precipitous mountains, it contained several small towns that were the main commercial outlets for the Montenegrin and Hercegovinian hinterland. The Bocchesians and Montenegrins were unhappy at the prospect of French rule; a group of Bocchesian merchants claimed that Austria and France, by the terms of Campoformio, had no right to decide their sovereignty without their consent.[12] Invitations were sent to the nearby Russian ships to secure aid, which probably had already been offered. The Austrian commandant, Ghislieri, agreed to hand over the fortresses to Seniavin without a struggle. The Russians under Captain Baillie landed on 5 March gaining control of an important region on the Dalmatian mainland.[13] Contacts were established with neighboring Slavic areas, and contingents of armed men, mostly Montenegrin, were recruited to resist the anticipated French attempt to occupy the territory. This commitment was made by the local Russian commander, who did not have time to receive instructions from Corfu, let alone from Saint Petersburg.

Seniavin arrived at Cattaro on 25 March and conferred with the Russian consul, Sankovsky. In his letter to Alexander, the Russian admiral emphasized in justification for his actions that Cattaro was an important commercial station possessing 400 merchant ships, almost all of which were armed against corsairs, and 5,000 able seamen. In addition, he noted that 12,000 local citizens were under arms, probably an exaggeration.[14]

---

12. Memoir of Pozzo di Borgo to Czartoryski (received April 23, 1806), in Lujo Vojnović, *Pad Dubrovnika*, vol. 1: 1797–1806 (Zagreb, 1908), p. 396. See also Bronevskii, pp. 139–43.

13. Comte L. de Voinovitch (alias Vojnović), *Histoire de Dalmatie*; vol. 2: *Des griffes du lion ailé à la libération* (1409–1918), 2d ed. (Paris, 1934), p. 663; Stanislavskaia, p. 409.

14. Seniavin to Alexander I, 13 April 1806, in VPR 3: 116–17. With a population of about 10,000 the town of Cattaro had also become an im-

Austria was placed in a difficult position by the Russian occupation of Cattaro. France immediately demanded that Austria force Russia to leave and provide for passage of French troops over Austrian territory. These demands were accepted and embodied in a convention signed between Austria and France on 16 April.[15] By terms of the convention Austria made representations to Saint Petersburg claiming that the occupation of Cattaro jeopardized Austrian neutrality. Czartoryski replied for the tsar on 12 May with a refusal to withdraw, and insisted that terms of the Treaty of Pressburg were not applicable to Russia.[16] On 27 May the Russian minister protested the signing of the 16 April convention.[17]

The Republic of Ragusa was the most important commercial city along the Adriatic coast; its territory was separated from that of Bocche di Cattaro by only a narrow strip of Turkish soil, but the distance between the cities is difficult to traverse by land even today. Ragusa was an old trading republic, like Venice, which retained nominal independence though paying an annual tribute to the Ottoman Empire for naval protection from pirates and for commercial privileges. Like Venice, Ragusa had declined economically, and its aristocratic council was now racked by dissension and indecision.[18] Unfortunately for Ragusa, the French army was moving down from the north, the Russians were established on the border to the south, and the mountains to the rear were nearly impassable. Ragusa's hopes of exercising its traditional neutrality appeared dim.

Ragusa was militantly Catholic territory surrounded by predominantly Orthodox Slavs; the Franciscan and Dominican monasteries dominated the religious life of the community. Partly for religious reasons Ragusa's relations with neighbors and

---

portant Slavic cultural center; one of the first books in Serbian (Cyrillic) was published there in 1799. Miras Kicovic, "Jedan unikat neposnate cirilske stamparije u Kotoru" (Belgrade, 1955), p. 8.

15. VPR 3: 667–69, n. 76.
16. Czartoryski to Razumovsky, 12 May 1806, in VPR 3: 138–39.
17. Czartoryski to Razumovsky, 27 May 1806, in VPR 3: 174.
18. Luigi Villari, *The Republic of Ragusa, an Episode of the Turkish Conquest* (London, 1904), pp. 386–87.

with the Russian Empire had been anything but good. The formal practice of the Orthodox rite within the territory was forbidden by law until 1775, when a convention signed at Livorno by Alexis Orlov provided for the opening of a Russian consulate and an Orthodox chapel to serve it in exchange for Black Sea navigation rights for Ragusan ships.[19] According to the Serbian scholar Makushev, in 1807, out of a total population of 31,245 there were 108 Eastern Orthodox Christians and 227 Jews; the rest were Roman Catholic.[20] In December 1801, a new Russian consul-general, Charles Fonton, was appointed for the Dalmatian coast. Upon his arrival in Ragusa the following September a new era in Russo-Ragusan relations began.[21]

Although Fonton himself was Catholic, he employed Orthodox Slavs and entertained leading churchmen of the neighboring territories, for which he was also responsible. His vigorous representations on behalf of Russian and Ionian merchant ships apparently antagonized the senate of the Ragusan Republic.[22]

In January 1803, the chapel of the consulate was closed by the senate. Fonton immediately issued sharp protests over the violation of the 1775 Convention.[23] The religious problem was also connected with Fonton's personal quest for better quarters. The conflict was resolved by the senate's agreement to reopen the chapel if Fonton would move it and himself to more luxurious quarters outside the walls of the city.[24] In the meantime, Fon-

---

19. S. Dobranskii, *K istorii snoshenii Raguzskoi respubliki s Rossiei v XVIII i XIX vekakh* (Moscow, 1909), p. 34; Voinovitch, 2: 763. In 1790, "Greeks" were accorded the right to have a chapel two kilometers from the city. Voinovitch, 2: 764.

20. Vikentii Makushev, *Materialy dlia istorii diplomaticheskikh snoshenii Rossii s Raguzskoi respublikoi* in *Chteniia v Imperatorskom Obshchestve istoriia i drevnostei Rossiiskikh*, vol. 3, pt. 3, ed. O. M. Bodianskii (July-September, 1865), p. 50.

21. Dobranskii, p. 32; Fonton to the Rector of Ragusa (presentation of papers), 20 September 1802, Dubrovnik, Drzavni Arhiv, Prep 19 1.591, no. 1.

22. Fonton's letters to the Ragusan senate on behalf of Captain Mussuri in 1803, Dubrovnik, Drzavni Arhiv, Prep 19 1.591, nos. 10–28.

23. Fonton to the senate, 26 January, 1803, ibid., no. 31.

24. Fonton to Bonda, and Bonda to Fonton, several letters in May 1803, ibid., nos. 48–52, and Prep 19 1.592, nos. 16–17, 19–20. Ragusa decided

ton's initial complaint had reached Saint Petersburg and caused Alexander Vorontsov, in the name of the tsar, to issue a strong protest to Ragusa for discriminating against Orthodox subjects of Russia.[25] This episode was patched over, but relations between Russia and Ragusa remained uneasy, especially as the influence of Russia in the Adriatic increased in 1804 and 1805.

The Treaty of Pressburg made Ragusa a borderland between the armies of the two continental opponents. French pressure on the small republic had been growing rapidly, and forced loans had been made to the French government. In early 1806 a French army under General Molitor was marching down the coast, threatening the neutrality of the Ragusan Republic.[26] The Russians had landed and were gathering their forces on the border. On 15 March Captain Henry Baillie, commanding the Russian squadron off the coast, announced a strict blockade of the Adriatic coast, allowing only the trade of neutral or friendly ships with neutral or friendly ports.[27] Fonton assured the republic that the Montenegrin soldiers on the frontier were under Russian control and Ragusa had no alternative but to agree to the terms of the blockade. In order to implement this measure the fleet was divided into cruising squadrons. Some strategic positions along the coast, also formerly Austrian, were occupied. In April the important island of Curzola was captured, cutting the coastal sea route to the north of Ragusa.[28] In the middle of

---

at this time that it needed a representative in Saint Petersburg and picked Benvenuti, who was the papal envoy, but communications were slow through Rome. Benvenuti was able to improve Ragusan-Russian relations in conferences with A. R. Vorontsov and Czartoryski. Benvenuti to the senate, 3 January 1804, Dubrovnik, Drzavni Arhiv, Prep 19 2.201–391. See also Bogdan Krizman, *Diplomati i konzuli u starom Dubrovniku* (Zagreb, 1957), pp. 201–2.

25. Vorontsov to Ragusan Republic, 29 July 1803, in Makushev, pp. 173–74. Orsat Bonda, the Ragusan minister of foreign affairs replied in a long, detailed apology, dated 21 October 1803. Dubrovnik, Drzavni Arhiv, Prep 19 1.591, no. 26.

26. Paul Pisani, *La Dalmatie de 1797 à 1815* (Paris, 1893), pp. 155–59.

27. Makushev, pp. 47–48; Fonton to senate, 17 March 1806, Dubrovnik, Drzavni Arhiv, Prep 19 1.591, no. 85; copy of declaration, ibid., no. 86.

28. Fonton to senate, 11 March 1806, ibid., no. 84; Voinovitch, 2: 664.

May, Seniavin negotiated with representatives of Ragusa for an agreement to provide for the reception of Russian troops to defend Ragusa against the French if the latter crossed the frontier.[29] Molitor, the French commander in Dalmatia, sent General Lauriston ahead with about 1,000 soldiers. This corps reached Slan, near the Ragusan frontier, on 26 May,[30] marched on across the border, and requested 500 bottles of wine from Ragusa upon arrival at the gates of the city. By another ruse the French soldiers managed to get inside the gates and seized the principal forts without opposition.[31] A Russian squadron nearby could have supplied aid, but the senate decided that the French were the lesser of two evils. The Ragusans were motivated in part by the fear that a Russian occupation would lead to an influx of Orthodox Slavs, and they were impressed by the speed of the French. On 28 May the senate advised Fonton that Lauriston had ordered him to leave within twenty-four hours; and Fonton notified the senate in return that the independence of the Ragusan Republic could no longer be recognized.[32]

THE RUSSIAN SIEGE OF RAGUSA

Seniavin was ready to take the offensive. On 3 June, 160 Russian marines seized the town of Ragusa-Vecchia, strategically located on the coast below Ragusa and the first Ragusan territory to be occupied by the Russians. A larger force of 1,700 Russians under Major General Viazemsky and 2,500 Montenegrins and Bocchesians under Peter Negosh advanced across the narrow strip dividing Cattaro from Ragusa, and invaded the Republic.[33] These forces were joined by some disgruntled Slavic inhabitants, the Canalesi, in plundering the abandoned estates of Ragusan

---

29. Shapiro, pp. 137–38; Makushev, p. 51.
30. Shapiro, p. 137.
31. Ibid., pp. 138–39; Makushev, p. 54.
32. Senate to Fonton, 28 May 1806, Dubrovnik, Drzavni Arhiv, Prep 19 1.591, no. 98; Fonton to senate, 28 May 1806, ibid., no. 96; Emile Haumant, "Les Français à Raguse," *La Revue de Paris* 12 (1912): 158–59.
33. Makushev, pp. 57–58; Shapiro, p. 142; p. 349, n. 5.

aristocrats in the valley of Canali, causing much trouble for the Russian officers.[34] Lauriston had time to construct and man a formidable redoubt several miles south of the city. After a fierce battle on 17 June, this stronghold was captured by the Russo-Montenegrin army, and Lauriston withdrew behind the walls of the city.[35]

The allied army continued its advance with naval support and established batteries on the mountain directly behind Ragusa. Meanwhile, Sorokin's squadron was firing over the walls, and his marines captured the nearby island of Marka.[36] Despite offers of favorable terms from Seniavin and pressure from the inhabitants, who feared great damage to the city, Lauriston refused to give up. He was counting on relief from Molitor. The city as a consequence suffered a heavy bombardment from 18 June to 6 July, 1806. A number of merchant ships were seized by the Russian squadron in the Ragusan port of Kroche; a garrison was landed there, and the aqueduct supplying water to Ragusa was cut.[37] The city could not hold out much longer.

But on 5 July, General Molitor arrived with 3,000 reinforcements from the north, over Turkish territory. By this time a number of Montenegrin and Bocchesian irregular militia who were supporting the siege on the south had gone home, and the weakened besiegers were surrounded on three sides. An orderly evacuation was conducted onto the Russian ships at Kroche, and Ragusa was left firmly in French hands. Ragusa-Vecchia was retaken by the French on 8 July.[38]

RUSSIAN WITHDRAWAL FROM THE ADRIATIC

Part of the responsibility for the Russian failure to prevent the

---

34. Voinovitch, 2: 665; Shapiro, pp. 142–45.

35. Makushev, p. 58; Fr. M. Appendini, *Ratovane oko Dubrovnika godina 1806* (Dubrovnik, 1906), pp. 3–6; Pisani, p. 176.

36. Bronevskii, 2: 24.

37. Shapiro, p. 144; Appendini, pp. 11–15.

38. Appendini, p. 25; Makushev, p. 63.

fall of Ragusa to the French is due to the inconsistencies and peaceful inclinations manifested by Russian foreign policy.[39] Prompted by Oubril's arrival in Vienna on the way to open peace negotiations in Paris, Razumovsky sent an order on 5 June to Seniavin to hand Cattaro back to the Austrians; however, a letter sent a few days later advised the admiral to await confirmation from Saint Petersburg. Seniavin received the first order on 16 June, but he had experienced contradictions in orders before and decided to proceed with the planned attack.[40]

Alexander at first approved the siege of Ragusa, but then, perhaps counting on Oubril's mission to secure peace, decided against it and ordered the evacuation of Cattaro as well. Seniavin still held his ground, however, even though categorically ordered to surrender the territory by Oubril, who had promised to secure Russian withdrawal prior to the ratification of the peace treaty, which he, along with Talleyrand, signed on 20 July.[41] Upon rejection of the terms of this treaty in Saint Petersburg, Seniavin was again ordered to hold fast.

Alexander Lvovich Shapiro, the Soviet biographer of Seniavin, claims that this wavering disconcerted the local allies of Russia, increased their disaffection and desertion, and necessitated the withdrawal. The campaign's failure, according to this view, should be blamed on Alexander's confused state of mind rather than on Seniavin.[42] The plans and actions of the Russian admiral seem to have been appropriate to the situation; perhaps he could have employed a larger portion of the Russian troops at Corfu instead of counting so heavily on undependable local elements,

---

39. See the works by Stanislavskaia, Shapiro, and Tarle cited above.

40. Shapiro, pp. 148–49. Razumovsky also ordered Sankovsky, the Russian consul in Cattaro, to transfer the territory back to the Austrians as soon as detachments arrived from Trieste. Razumovsky to Sankovsky, 4 June 1806, in Vojnović, 1: 405–6. For a discussion of the confused and conflicting instructions under which Seniavin was operating, see his long letter to Alexander I, dated 30 August 1806, in VPR 3: 278–84.

41. Stanislavskaia, p. 428. For a copy of Oubril's "treaty" see VPR 3: 226–31. Much of this treaty pertained to Adriatic affairs, and it would appear that Russian commitments in that quarter prevented its ratification.

42. Shapiro, pp. 152–54.

but this would have required additional time for supply arrangements. The Montenegrin leaders considered the combined force too small to accomplish its mission without considerable cost; their own mission—plunder—had already been widely accomplished, and the campaign had lasted as long as the Montenegrins were accustomed to remain in the field without pay. When word of Molitor's approach was received, local support simply melted away.

Marshal Marmont, one of Napoleon's leading generals, had been placed in command of French Dalmatia and was ordered to clear the territory as rapidly as possible. He arrived in Ragusa with three infantry divisions on 2 August.[43] The French army now numbered well over 10,000.[44] Seniavin refused to surrender Cattaro to Marmont's emissary. Reliable reinforcements were brought up from Corfu under Papandopulo (now a general), and the Montenegrins and Bocchesians were more willing to fight now that their own territory was in danger of being attacked. A sudden assault on the allied defenses at the southern edge of the Ragusan territory on 30 September succeeded in driving them back to the vicinity of the town of Castelnuovo (in Hercegovina) in the territory of Cattaro.[45] There, on 1 October, a fierce, bloody battle was fought, but the French were unable to dislodge the defenders, chiefly because of Russian sea support.[46] At this point activities subsided for the winter.

A RUSSIAN COUNTEROFFENSIVE

In October 1806, more than half of the French army in Dalmatia was withdrawn to the north for action in central Europe. Seniavin took advantage of this partial retreat to recover some important islands along the coast that had been evacuated in the previous August and September and were now lightly defended.

---

43. A.-F.-L. Weisse de Marmont, *Mémoires du Maréchal Marmont Duc de Raguse de 1792 à 1841* (Paris, 1857), 2: 1–3.

44. Shapiro, p. 157.

45. Ibid., pp. 158–60; Marmont, 3: 11–13.

46. Shapiro, p. 158.

In November, Curzola was again brought under Russian control, and in December, Hvar (Lessina) and Brach surrendered to Russian squadrons dispatched by Seniavin.[47] These islands commanded the approaches to the most important ports of Dalmatia —Ragusa and Spalato (Split).

In a series of fleet maneuvers and land engagements the Russian and Montenegrin forces under Seniavin's command had managed to stop direct French penetration into the Balkans. Napoleon, on the other hand, had decided to concentrate his strength in central Europe while flooding the Balkans with agents. The Balkans simply were not suitable terrain for the massive armies that were a feature of the War of the Third Coalition. Ragusa was under French control, but it had been severely damaged by the siege, and the Russian domination of the waters around it prevented its use as a base of operations.

Russian relations with and influence upon the Slavs of the Dalmation coast had increased considerably as a result of the campaign. Montenegro now had free access to the sea in the ports of Cattaro and Budva, while the great rival port, Ragusa, had been permanently crippled. Of the 277 sailing ships belonging to Ragusan shippers in 1806, only 49 were in action four years later: three of them flew the French flag, 23 the British, 12 the Russian, and 11 ships were laid up in various Mediterranean ports without any registry.[48]

To support the military activity on the Adriatic coast, Russia proposed territorial settlements that would attempt the impossible: to satisfy the Great Powers, appease the aspirations of local allies, and maintain the alliance with the Ottoman Empire. In his instructions to Oubril in May 1806, Czartoryski presented two projects, both aimed toward an eventual accommodation with France: (1) to enlarge the Ionian Republic to include the coastal areas of Albania and Epirus and to create an autonomous Serbia within the Ottoman Empire; (2) to give the Ionians to

---

47. Bronevskii, 2: 224–27; Shapiro, pp. 163–64.
48. Stjepan Vekaric, "Podaci o Dubrovackim brodonima za vrijame í nakon francuske okupacije," *Annali Historijskoi Instituta Jugoslavenskoe Akademije Znanosti i Umjetnosti u Dubrovniku* 2 (1953): 359–68.

Sardinia in exchange for France's annexation of the mainland territory of Sardinia, to create an autonomous Serbia, and also to establish a new state centered on Montenegro which would receive the statutes of the Ionian Republic.[49]

The Montenegrin ruler, Peter Negosh, learned about the Russian plans from Seniavin and submitted, through Ivelich, his own proposal, which, as one would expect, placed more emphasis on an expansion of Montenegro—to include Cattaro (capital), Hercegovina, Ragusa, Dalmatia, and upper Albania—with the head of the administration to be a Russian "governor-general" like Mocenigo in the Ionians. Seniavin ordered Colonel Boissel to prepare a plan of attack on Ali Pasha, who was to be the chief victim of Russia's west Balkan projects.[50]

Russia's reluctance to abandon the position obtained over several years in the Mediterranean was a major factor in the failure of the peace attempt of 1806 and the continuation of Russia's participation in the war for another year. A military stalemate existed in the Adriatic theater, however, with neither side strong enough to dislodge the other, and probably the French could never have forcibly removed the Russians from mountainous Dalmatia or from the islands. The fate of Russian hegemony of the Adriatic was determined by activities in other areas.

---

49. V. G. Sirotkin, "Franco-russkaia diplomaticheskaia bor'ba na Balkanakh i plany sozdaniia slaviano–serbskogo gosudarstva v 1806–1807 gg.," *Uchenye Zapiski Instituta Slavianovedeniia* 25: 179. Czartoryski's plans, formulated as early as January and February 1806, were in part a response to a proposal sent by the head of the Serbian church in Austria, Stratomirović. Ibid., p. 178.

50. Ibid., pp. 181–82.

10

Russian Withdrawal
from the Mediterranean

While Seniavin was engaged in defending southern Dalmatia against French advances by direct military action, the Russian diplomatic and military position was being weakened by military reverses in central Europe. Czartoryski's vigorous anti-French foreign policy, supported by other members of the former Secret Committee that advised Alexander in the initial years of his reign, was losing the support of the emperor. The Russian foreign minister had hoped to use the rising national and religious feelings of the Balkan peoples, especially those along the Adriatic coast, to support the Russian opposition to France; at the same time Russia would help these peoples to gain greater autonomy within the Ottoman Empire. But pro-Russian Dalmatian enclaves along the Adriatic coast, supported militarily from Russia's Ionian base, posed a real threat to the aims of Napoleon in the Balkans and also, to a lesser degree, conflicted with British support of Ali Pasha. Indecision and vacillation at the highest levels of the Russian government also affected the success of these distant projects.

Alexander was inclined to pursue peace after his experience at Austerlitz; the preconditions for what resulted at Tilsit were already in the tsar's mind. A French émigré serving in the imperial foreign ministry, Oubril, was dispatched to Paris in May

1806 to undertake serious negotiations for peace.[1] Among the demands to be presented, according to his instructions, were a French withdrawal from Dalmatia, recognition of the Russian protectorate over the independent Ionian Republic, and the resurrection of the Bourbon and Savoy kingdoms in Italy.[2] After several months of conferences dominated by Talleyrand, Oubril signed a treaty which provided for a Russian withdrawal from the Ionians and the Adriatic—more than had been anticipated. Even Alexander was not prepared at that time to go so far, and the Oubril Treaty of 20 July 1806 went unratified; in fact, the tsar immediately dispatched another squadron to the Mediterranean to show his displeasure.[3] The French insisted on gains in the Mediterranean well beyond military achievement as the price for peace in central Europe. As Oubril informed Simon Vorontsov's agent in Paris, "Austria must be saved; if I did not sign some act of pacification the French would be in Vienna in fifteen days." He added that France would not make peace without Cattaro. "Bonaparte is furious about how his troops have been mistreated by the Montenegrins, aided by us."[4]

In an attempt to bolster Russia's position after the defeat of Austria, Paul Stroganov, a friend of the tsar and proponent of Czartoryski's plan for national client states in central and southern Europe, had been sent to London in December 1805 to secure a firm commitment for an 1806 campaign and British military support for preventing further French gains, but by the time Stroganov arrived in London, Alexander was reconsidering his participation in the Third Coalition. Because of Alexander's vague and contradictory instructions and the unsteadiness of the British government in the wake of Pitt's death (January

---

1. Paul F. Shupp, *The European Powers and the Near Eastern Question, 1806–1807* (New York, 1931), pp. 82–85.

2. Stanislavskaia, (see chap. 8, n. 7), pp. 421–22.

3. Puryear, *Napoleon and the Dardanelles*, pp. 96–97; Shapiro, *Admiral Seniavin*, p. 180.

4. N. M. Longinov to S. R. Vorontsov, 26 July 1806, in *Arkhiv Vorontsova* 23: 6–7.

1806), Stroganov was forced to return to Saint Petersburg empty-handed. Thus Anglo-Russian relations became strained after Austerlitz, despite the efforts of the "young friends" to maintain the close alliance.

This stiffening of the Russian attitude toward Britain was at least partly Britain's fault. In October 1804, a young, inexperienced ambassador, Leveson Gower (Lord Granville) had been appointed ambassador to Russia mainly on the strength of his family connections with the king and with Pitt.[5] Although in Saint Petersburg he demonstrated an enthusiastic interest in securing good relations, he was handicapped by the hostility of his incompetent predecessor, Warren, who remained for a while in Russia. Unfortunately, in the summer of 1805 Gower became more interested in a local romantic involvement than in the coalition. He left Russia in early 1806 to consult his family about marrying a Princess Galitzen.[6] Britain was therefore without an ambassador at Saint Petersburg during the critical period of the first half of 1806.

France, on the other hand, was making stronger efforts diplomatically. In January 1806, Czartoryski, who strove to maintain the coalition, was even forced by Alexander to hold conferences with a special French envoy, Consul-General de Lesseps.[7] Napoleon did not yet realize fully the extent of Alexander's readiness for peace, and failed at that time to capitalize on the tsar's vacillating moods and lack of enthusiasm for the coalition. The French emperor and his advisors paid more attention to the statements of Czartoryski, Stroganov, and others, and to the activities of Admiral Seniavin. An offer of better terms in July might have taken Russia out of the war. But French power in Europe was at its height, and Napoleon knew it. French diplo-

---

5. S. R. Vorontsov to A. R. Vorontsov, 22 October 1804, in *Arkhiv Vorontsova*, 10: 226; Puryear, p. 38.

6. Granville to Lady Bessborough, 16 February 1805, in Granville, *Private Correspondence, 1781 to 1821*, ed. Castalia Countess Granville (London, 1916), 2: 47, 234; see also an anonymous contemporary denunciation of British diplomats in Russia, *A Key to the Recent Conduct of the Emperor of Russia* (London, 1807).

7. Shupp, p. 31; Puryear, pp. 77–79; Stanislavskaia, p. 405.

macy concentrated instead on undermining Russian influence in Constantinople.

Alexander's vacillation between vigorous and passive foreign policies was thus relatively free from foreign intereference. Seniavin's initial successes in the face of a French Dalmatian offensive brought small consolation for Austerlitz. This achievement and Czartoryski's pressure produced a stronger Russian stand in the Mediterranean in April 1806; Alexander then decided to uphold Seniavin's offensive activities. But Czartoryski's long-standing criticism of Alexander's pro-Prussian inclinations and his insistence on promoting the war finally brought about his resignation at the end of June.[8] Baron Budberg, a Baltic German, became acting foreign minister in his place, setting the stage in Saint Petersburg for possible peace signing, but the terms of the Oubril "Treaty" allowed little room to salvage prestige. In September 1806, the "young friends" regained brief predominance, and Alexander again turned to active measures, belatedly attempting to stem the growth of French influence in the Turkish capital.

THE FRENCH IN THE BALKANS

After long and tedious negotiations, begun on Czartoryski's instructions, Italinsky succeeded in concluding a renewal of the 1798 alliance with the Porte on 23 September 1806.[9] The Straits' provisions remained essentially the same, with Russia receiving the right to send armed ships through as part of war operations against French threats to Russian and Ottoman interests in the Mediterranean (such as the Ionian Republic). Russian influence was strong in Constantinople, and although the Porte refused to participate actively in the coalition, it agreed to support the Russian armies which were to be used in its defense.

Before 1806 French diplomacy had been remarkably unsuc-

---

8. Stanislavskaia, p. 440.

9. S. M. Goriainov, "Dogovor 11 (23) sentiabria 1805 goda mezhdu Rossieiu i Turtsieiu," *Izvestiia Ministerstva Inostrannykh Del* 5 (1912): 233–35.

cessful in gaining influence in Constantinople. Selim III and his officials probably considered Napoleon's letters crude and vulgar. One, received in 1805, read:

> Are you blind to your own interests? If Russia has an army at Corfu, do you believe it is directed against me? Your dynasty is about to descend into the night of oblivion. Your Grand Vizier betrays you; half your Divan is sold to Russia. I have warned you twice; I warn you once more. Dismiss your Grand Vizier and your Divan, or you are lost. . . . Trust only your true friend, who is France, or you and your religion and your family will perish.[10]

Fortunately for Napoleon, there were people in French service more knowledgeable and adroit in Turkish affairs. Some of these were sent to infiltrate and propagandize at the Turkish administrative centers in the Balkans, in particular, near the Russian border in Jassy and Bucharest.

In these territories, Wallachia and Moldavia, the French found that the administration was under the control of two hospodars, Ypsilanti and Murusi, that had been appointed by the Porte with Russian approval in 1802. Ypsilanti, the hospodar of Wallachia, resisted French influence and remained inclined toward the Russians, but Murusi in Moldavia was won over in 1805 by French agents, and, with their aid, actively sought to build up an anti-Russian federation of Turkish administrators in the Balkans. Subsequent French pressure was concentrated at Vidin, Pasvan-oglu's headquarters, where Adjutant-Commander Meriage was appointed consul in 1806, despite Russian objections.[11] A full-fledged consular war was being waged in the Balkans.

French attention also turned to the Straits. Austerlitz provided a big opening by giving Russian prestige a tremendous setback. Soon afterward, in January 1806 the sultan recognized the imperial title of Napoleon, thereby reversing the policy that had been shaped by Russian pressure. The formal acceptance of

---

10. Frank Ives Scudamore, *France in the East: A Contribution towards the Consideration of the Eastern Question* (London, 1882), p. 91.

11. Stanislavskaia, p. 435; Shupp, pp. 51–52.

French consular agents in provincial centers followed despite Italinsky's objections.[12] The change in the attitude of the Turkish government toward the French brought a corresponding change in French policy. Instead of trying to weaken the Ottoman Empire within and to create pro-French pashadoms, Napoleon switched from partition plans to the Russian strategy of preserving the empire as a whole; the aim was now to replace Russian influence with French and to maintain Turkey as a French ally. This was only a change of emphasis, of course, and did not mean that the consular agents were recalled.

Evidence of this shift can be seen in the sending in July 1806 of a new French ambassador to the Ottoman Empire. Sebastiani was respected as a tireless and skilled general-diplomat both in France and in the Ottoman Empire. An outline of the new French policy is provided by Napoleon's instructions to Talleyrand regarding the new appointment.

> The unwavering aim of my policy is to form a triple alliance of Myself, the Porte, and Persia, aimed directly or implicitly against Russia.
>
> The continual endeavors of my ambassador must be to bring disfavor upon Russia. He must deprecate her military forces and the bravery of her troops by all means and constantly. . . . As the relations of France and Russia will be elsewhere, at Constantinople the French must always treat the Russian legation coldly. On the other hand, they should be on good terms with Austria, Prussia, and Britain, when peace is made.
>
> The goal of all negotiations must be the closure of the Bosporus to the Russians and the cessation of passage from the Mediterranean into the Black Sea of all of their ships, armed or unarmed; not to allow any Greek to navigate under the Russian flag; to fortify and to arm all strategic places against Russia; to support the Georgians; and to restore to the Porte absolute authority over Moldavia and Wallachia.
>
> I do not want to partition the empire of Constantinople; if they offered me three-quarters, I would not take it. I want

---

12. Eduard Driault, *La Politique orientale de Napoléon: Sebastiani et Gardane*, 1806–1808 (Paris, 1904), pp. 58–60.

to reaffirm and consolidate this great empire to serve as an opposition to Russia.[13]

1798 in reverse! Sebastiani arrived in Constantinople on 9 August after a difficult journey through Bucharest, where he tried unsuccessfully to win Ypsilanti to the French side.[14] Upon arrival he immediately began distributing bribes *à la Tomara* and within a short time was well along the way to accomplishing all the aims set forth by Napoleon.

While French influence in 1806 was rising in the eastern Balkans, especially just across the Russian frontier in Moldavia, Russia was gaining important positions in the western provinces. Because of the Russo-Montenegrin army in Dalmatia, the presence of a large fleet in the Adriatic, and the success in winning local Greek and Albanian populations through the activities of consular agents and by accepting their leaders into Russian service, French influence was sharply curtailed south of Ragusa. Sensing the approach of Russo-Turkish hostility, even Ali Pasha offered his alliance to Russia in 1806 in a war against the Porte.[15] The Serbian revolts that began in 1804 lost their Austrian support as a result of Austria's defeat and alliance with France (Napoleon promised Selim III to support the restoration of Turkish authority in Serbia). Russia began in 1806 the first significant aid to a Balkan Slav revolt by sending money and advisers to the Serbs.[16]

The fall of Russian prestige after Austerlitz had opened the way for Sebastiani at Constantinople, but the independent actions of Seniavin along the Adriatic coast were even more worrisome for the Ottoman court, for now Balkan Slavs owing their allegiance to the Sultan were being organized and encouraged in their national aims. Moreover, a large Russian naval force from the Baltic had now been assembled in the Mediter-

13. Napoleon to Talleyrand, 9 June 1806, in *Correspondance de Napoléon Ier* (Paris, 1863), 12: 449–50, no. 10339.

14. P. Coquelle, "Sebastiani ambassadeur à Constantinople, 1806–08," *Revue d'histoire diplomatique* 18 (1904): 579.

15. Stanislavskaia, pp. 436–38.

16. Ibid., pp. 447–48.

ranean, placing the Turkish navy at a considerable disadvantage. Ushakov's Black Sea fleet in the Mediterranean in 1799 was less of a threat to Turkey than it was in the Black Sea, but Seniavin's Baltic fleet in the Mediterranean, with the Black Sea fleet still intact in that sea, presented an unprecedented hazard to the Turks. With more skillful diplomacy this potential power position might have been used by Russia to maintain her position in Constantinople, but Czartoryski's Balkan Slav interests and Alexander's preoccupation with Prussia effectively tied Italinsky's hands.

It is not surprising that the French ambassador made gains in this situation, although it is not clear what role Sebastiani played in the important replacement of the pro-Russian hospodar of Wallachia in August 1806.[17] The change took place only about a week after his arrival but it was a clear indication of the changing sentiments of the Ottoman court toward Russia. Italinsky, backed by Arbuthnot, the British ambassador, made strong remonstrances over the removal of the hospodar, claiming that this was a violation of the agreement of 1802, which provided for consultation of Russia in the matter. Most of all, it meant a weakening of Russian influence in the principalities.[18]

The Russian ambassador soon had more to protest about. On 26 September the Porte, at the urging of Sebastiani, requested the cessation of Russian military transit through the Straits.[19] This would hinder the supply of the Russian forces in the Adriatic, effectively prevent the merging of the Baltic and Black Sea fleets, and cut off an important avenue of retreat for Seniavin's fleet, for even without French warnings the Porte had realized the potential danger of a concentration of all of Russia's naval forces in either the Black Sea or the Mediterranean.

Diplomatic manipulations at Constantinople were not easy to conduct at long range from London and Saint Petersburg. Napoleon had the advantage in the fall of 1806, with his com-

---

17. Puryear, pp. 101–2; Shupp, pp. 145–47.
18. Ibid.
19. Stanislavskaia, pp. 438–39.

.nand centered first in Berlin, then in Warsaw. Distant communications may in fact have been responsible for the outbreak
of war between Russia and Turkey, not so much because of the
overlapping of communications as because of the unreliability of
control of distant operations, which had already proved a serious
problem in Dalmatia.

After Italinsky's failures to prevent the rise of French influence
and the Turkish removal of the hospodars, Alexander I, frustrated diplomatically, on 27 October ordered the occupation of
the principalities of Moldavia and Wallachia by General Michelson's army of observation on the frontier. But on 4 November,
Italinsky's dispatch reporting the Turkish willingness to recon-
sider and to restore the old hospodars arrived in Saint Petersburg.[20] Although Michelson knew of this moderate Turkish step
and Alexander still had time to withdraw his order, the Russian
army, wanting to establish bases before winter, crossed the
Dniester River on 23 November. Ostensibly the reason was to
restore order in the principalities and to stop a French build-up in
the Balkan provinces; a demonstration of force might also help
to bring about a reduction of French influence in Constantinople.

But Sebastiani's role in Ottoman affairs grew as Napoleon
continued scoring victories in central Europe, occupying Berlin
after defeating the Prussian army at Jena. The details of this
last blow to the Third Coalition reached Constantinople in the
middle of November and strengthened the resolution of the
Ottoman Empire to oppose Russia. Arbuthnot's active mediation on behalf of Italinsky delayed the actual declaration of war
by the Ottoman government until 27 December, 1806.[21] On
that date Michelson occupied Bucharest deep within Ottoman
territory.

THE RUSSO-TURKISH WAR

Neither Russia nor Turkey wanted this war, and both were un-

---

20. Ibid., pp. 443–44; Driault, p. 74.
21. Stanislavskaia, p. 447; Puryear, p. 123. Diplomatic relations were
broken on 24 December, when Italinsky was given three days to leave the
country.

prepared for it. Although the Ottoman army was weakened and disorganized by reform attempts, it was still large, and Russia could spare only a small army of 40,000 in opposition.[22] Besides, campaigning in the Balkans became very difficult in winter. The naval situation at first favored Russia, however. Sebastiani had urged the repair of fortifications on the Bosporus and Dardanelles upon his arrival. Traditionally the Bosporus was well defended but the Dardanelles were weak. In Saint Petersburg, Chichagov, in charge of the naval ministry, conceived a master plan for enveloping the Balkan Peninsula by combined attacks of the Baltic and Black Sea fleets at the Straits. Orders were sent out to the respective commander—Seniavin and the Duke de Traverse—but it took some time for either to get into action. The Black Sea fleet as usual was unprepared logistically for a full campaign, and Seniavin's fleet was scattered along the Dalmatian coast.[23]

Ironically hostilities in this area were initiated by Britain. The London Foreign Office was dismayed by the rapid Russian reversals and the French successes. At Arbuthnot's urgings, orders were sent to Lord Collingwood, the British Mediterranean commander, in November to dispatch a squadron to the Straits to cooperate with the Russian fleet of Seniavin.[24] Two ships under Admiral Louis were sent ahead through the Dardenelles in December, and Arbuthnot used one of them in January to make his escape. Italinsky boarded the other British ship to exit with official permission secured in December by Sebastiani (since war had already been declared), thus breaking an established Ottoman tradition of throwing the Russian ambassador in the notorious Seven Towers prison at the outbreak of war.[25]

Admiral Duckworth arrived at the entrance to the Straits on 10 February 1807. Following the advice of Arbuthnot as ordered,

---

22. Stanislavskaia, p. 445.
23. Shapiro, pp. 177–83. This source stresses Russia's unpreparedness for the war and places Michelson's army at only 30,000. Most of the Russian army was in central Europe and had suffered severe losses, while Alexander's inclinations toward peace hindered recruitment and training.
24. Mackesy, pp. 161–63.
25. Ibid., pp. 167–68; Driault, pp. 76–89.

he advanced his fleet of seven ships of the line, two frigates, two sloops, and two bomb vessels through the Dardanelles on 19 February.[26] He made the passage without difficulty, since the fortifications were still weak. Handicapped by lack of troops, Duckworth decided to avoid hostilities if possible, but the rising tide of popular sentiment on shore and the arrival of French engineers to supervise the artillery emplacements made negotiations fruitless. After delays caused by bad weather and indecision, threatening moves by the Turks forced Duckworth to retreat through the Dardanelles, which were more heavily fortified by that time, and a number of ships were damaged on the return passage.[27] Duckworth's failure to accomplish anything only aggravated the situation, strengthened Turkish opposition, and fostered much criticism in London.

On 7 March, a few days after running the gauntlet, the British fleet met Seniavin's at the island of Tenedos. The Russian admiral tried to organize a combined counterattack on the Straits, but Duckworth argued that even with the addition of the eight Russian ships of the line, with 2,000 troops aboard, a passage would be more than hazardous.[28] By that time Turkish defenses were too strong to be dislodged by a small number of marines, and the naval artillery of fifteen to twenty ships would be ineffective against these shore defenses. Seniavin appeared satisfied with Duckworth's opinion and made no effort to proceed with a separate attack.

Russian historians have blamed the British for failure to cooperate, claiming that Duckworth should have waited until Seniavin's arrival, or at least combined with Seniavin for another attempt.[29] The British, however, maintain that it was Seniavin's

---

26. Stanislavskaia, p. 464; Mackesy, p. 163; Shapiro, p. 193; Puryear, p. 141, lists five ships of the line, four frigates, and two bomb vessels. A good account of the action can be found in Shupp, pp. 376–388, and in O. Shcherbachev, *Afonskoe Srazhenie* (Moscow-Leningrad, 1945), pp. 22–23.

27. Mackesy, *The War in the Mediterranean*, p. 178; Shapiro, p. 194. The Russian source lists the English loss considerably higher than other sources. See also Driault, pp. 99–108.

28. Puryear, p. 146.

29. Stanislavskaia, p. 466; Shapiro, pp. 195–97; O. Shcherbachev, Afonskoe srazhenie (Moscow and Leningrad, 1945), pp. 32–35.

tardy arrival that caused the failure; there was no way for the British commander to tell when the Russians might arrive, since they were usually so undependable and communications were chaotic. So the British decided to take advantage of the unprepared Turks while they could.[30] It seems probable that the combined squadron could have sailed through the Straits in March, but the possibility of accomplishing anything in the Sea of Marmora with only a small number of troops would have been remote. Seniavin's mistake in bringing only a small portion of the Russian troops at Corfu can be excused by lack of transports. The combined squadrons were thus too weak in ships and manpower to accomplish anything by attacking through the Straits; their vulnerability in the narrow waters would have resulted in unnecessary damage. The chance of a coordinated attack with the Black Sea fleet was ruled out by the slowness and unpreparedness of those ships in coming into action.

Even though the British fleet pulled back to concentrate its efforts on other areas of the empire, especially Alexandria, action against the Straits was still possible. Seniavin's fleet could effectively blockade the mouth of the Dardanelles and isolate Constantinople almost indefinitely. The island of Tenedos was occupied, and the Russians settled down for a long blockade.[31] This was probably as effective as bombarding the city itself, and on 22 May 1807, the blockade brought out the Turkish fleet in an effort to break through, but the Russians turned them back in a brief but furious conflict, known as the Battle of the Dardanelles.[32]

At the end of June the reorganized Turkish fleet made another excursion from the safety of the Dardanelles. On 1 July the largest Russian naval battle of the Napoleonic Wars was fought near the Straits.[33] Although Seniavin, reinforced by the squadrons of Greig and Pustoshkin, won a victory over the Turks, the cele-

30. Shupp, pp. 389–391; Mackesy, pp. 179–81.
31. Shapiro, pp. 198–206.
32. Ibid., pp. 212–23.
33. Ibid., pp. 235–59; Shcherbachev, pp. 35–57; Robert W. Daly, "Operations of the Russian Navy during the Reign of Napoleon I," *Mariner's Mirror* 34, no. 3 (1948): 175.

ration of that victory by Russian historians as "the Russian Trafalgar" is exaggerated. The Turkish fleet was crippled but not destroyed; the Russian blockade remained unbroken, but the Dardanelles were still well defended.

TILSIT

The Treaty of Tilsit was signed before news of the Russian victory had arrived, but it would not have made any difference. Even at the Straits, where negotiations were reopened by Pozzo di Borgo and Arthur Paget with the new sultan, the victory had little effect.[34] The British occupation of Alexandria probably carried more weight in the negotiations than the Russian naval victory. These pourparlers continued for several weeks after the battle, with little accomplished before the terms of the Treaty of Tilsit were received.

By the terms of this treaty Alexander agreed to abandon the Mediterranean, withdraw from the Third Coalition, accept French mediation on the Russo-Turkish conflict, and join the Napoleonic continental system. The Ionians and Dalmatia were to be delivered to the French; a strong naval position and base facilities in an important international body of water were thus lost by Russia and gained by France.

The reasons for Alexander's decision to conclude peace included military defeats in central Europe, culminating in the Battle of Friedland; growing court pressure for peace, especially within the imperial family; and the sentiments of the tsar himself, who had never been enthusiastic about the war. The extent of the Russian concessions, particularly in the Mediterranean, is harder to explain. The outbreak of the war with Turkey had changed Russia's position decidedly, but there would be reason to expect a favorable turn of events in that sphere through an alliance with France. One can only conclude that Alexander was less interested in the Mediterranean than in central and northern Europe, and sacrificed the Ionians and Cattaro for Prussia.

---

34. Shupp, pp. 548–49.

The expense of Russian activities in the Mediterranean and the difficulty of control were two possible reasons for this fading interest. Seniavin complained throughout 1806 of lack of funds to meet necessary supply and repair purchases, and financial support arrived haphazardly in rather small amounts.[35] Russian operations in the Mediterranean were severely limited because of the inability or unwillingness of the government to provide financial help.

The difficulties of controlling operations in the Mediterranean were another factor retarding the development of Russian interest. Lack of familiarity with the nature of problems in the distant seas, the awkwardness of long-range communications, and the consequent tendencies toward independent, localized authority added to the reluctance of the court to maintain its involvement in that area. French military successes in central Europe and the related diplomatic success in Constantinople jeopardized the Russian position in the Adriatic. The defense of the Ottoman Empire no longer made sense, and the creation of Slavic or Greek bases on the Adriatic coast was not considered worth the cost.

The abrupt halt in commerce between the Mediterranean and the Black Seas as a result of the Russo-Turkish War in 1807 was crippling Russia's Black Sea trade, and Russia's military situation did not promise a victory over the Turks that would reopen the Straits. Napoleon's agreement at Tilsit to mediate the conflict seemed more certain to obtain results. And, though the war continued, commerce was in fact resumed through the Straits thanks to French pressure on the Porte.[36]

35. Shapiro, pp. 180–81.
36. After a sharp decline in the number of ships arriving at Odessa in 1806 and 1807, in some measure due to the severe drought of 1805, the number rose again to 399 in 1808, and Black Sea trade actually flourished, in comparison with the Baltic, because of the Continental System. The increase in cotton imports for Russia and central Europe was especially striking; in 1810 the first American ship, the *Calumet* from Boston, was recorded at Odessa. Skal'kovskii, (see chap. 8, n. 11), pp. 153–71; Sicard, *Lettres sur Odessa*, pp. 87, 138.

11

Conclusion

As a result of Tilsit, Russia left an entire fleet in the Mediterranean without bases. The two possible routes home had become quiet dangerous. The Turks were unlikely, even during the period of armistice that followed Tilsit, to allow the Baltic fleet into the Black Sea; and Seniavin did not attempt to pursue that route. The chances of returning successfully through the English Channel and the North Sea were rather slight, due to English hostility. The only alternative was to seek neutral ports and to hope for the best. The army in Dalmatia and on Corfu was evacuated through Trieste and Austrian territory to Russia. Some of the ships remained in that port to be scuttled, surrendered to France, or sold to Austria in 1809–10;[1] but most of Seniavin's command set sail for the Atlantic, successfully making Lisbon before being blocked by the British fleet and eventually captured. In 1813 two haggard refugee ships, all that remained of one of Russia's finest fleets, sailed home to the Baltic.[2] Thus one result of the Treaty of Tilsit which is usually overlooked was one of Russia's worst naval disasters, a sorry conclusion to a generally successful military performance in the Mediterranean.

---

1. D. Fedotoff White, "The Russian Navy in Trieste during the Wars of the Revolution and the Empire," *American Slavic and East European Review* 6 (December 1947): 33–41.

2. Daly, "Operations of the Russian Navy," p. 178.

Conclusion

The Ionian Republic was incorporated into the sprawl French Empire, but the memory of its independence lived on in the hearts of many Greek leaders. Efforts were made by Capodistrias, who joined Russian service in 1809, and Mocenigo to secure the interest of the Great Powers in their behalf at the Congress of Vienna. Although they were employed as advisers of Alexander at the Congress, Russia gave their cause only half-hearted support. Alexander's primary concerns were Prussia and the Holy Alliance. The second Treaty of Paris, signed on 5 November 1815, did restore the independence of the republic but under the protection of a single power, Great Britain, which had occupied all but Corfu before the end of hostilities.[3] The local government was to retain the constitution in effect in 1807, but Britain chose instead to administer the islands under the Colonial Office as an ordinary part of her empire. Though the resurrection of an independent Greece may have been advanced by the Ionian Republic's brief existence, the island did not become a part of the Greek kingdom until 1864.

The island of Malta, of course, remained a British possession. The Order of Malta survived, though rather precariously for some time. Russian attachment to the order, especially among the imperial family after Alexander I, remained a somewhat embarrassing factor in the history of an order that became strictly Roman Catholic in the nineteenth century. A group of Russian émigrés in Paris still maintain that the Russian priory survives but has failed to gain recognition from the order,[4] which is now a modern Catholic charity organization with sovereign historical roots.

Experiences in the Mediterranean were not completely forgotten through the remainder of the Napoleonic wars. The major reason for the appointment of Admiral Chichagov to

---

3. For a detailed treatment of the negotiations on the Republic at the Congress of Vienna, see Nicolas Timoleon Bulgari, *Les Sept-Îles Ioniennes et les traités qui les concernent* (Leipzig, 1859), and Demetrius Valsamachi, "Note sur la République des Sept-Iles, présentée au Congrès de Vienne par Demetrius fils de Pierre Comte Valsamachi" (Vienna, 1815).

4. Taube, *L'Empereur Paul Ier*, pp. 42–45, 52–63.

mand the Danubian army in 1812 was to enable him to implement his plan of crossing the Balkans to create a diversion in southern Europe by linking up with British naval and land forces, cutting off a valuable French supply route through the Balkans, invading the French Empire in Croatia and northern Italy, and forcing Austria into the war. Vice Admiral Greig traveled incognito through Constantinople to Palermo in 1812 to arrange for coordination, but he found that the British commander was uninformed of the plan. Then Napoleon's penetration so far into Russian territory required the use of the Danubian army elsewhere.[5]

Although there have been a few other attempts to reconstruct a Russo-Turkish alliance on the pattern of the 1798 precedent, Balkan problems prevented anything from coming of them. Historically, the only means by which Russia has achieved her goal of free navigation of the Straits for all Russian ships, naval and commercial, have been either a policy of friendship toward the Turkish government and military cooperation against a common foe, or an international agreement. Absolute control over the Straits, an unrealistic objective when both alternatives were attainable, has never been possible, since it would have involved making a sizable portion of Asiatic and European Turkey a Russian satellite or part of Russia itself. The ideological and national involvements of Russia and the Soviet Union in the Balkans have effectively nullified this possibility by creating international opposition. The passage of warships through the Straits in peacetime has been recognized by international agreement, making it possible for Russia to maintain a sizable naval force in the Mediterranean. In 1798–1807 that force served as a visible demonstration of Russian presence that could influence Mediterranean peoples.

The annexation of the Black Sea coastal region by Catherine

---

5. Chichagov to S. R. Vorontsov, 9 October 1813, and A. S. Greig to S. R. Vorontsov, 30 August, 16 September, and 4 October 1812, *Arkhiv Vorontsova*, 19: 206–9, 450–61.

the Great was an important precondition for Russia's involvement in Mediterranean affairs. The rapid commercial development on the Black Sea in the 1790s provided an underlying support for a Russian policy of friendly relations with the Ottoman Empire and the Italian states.

The Emperor Paul maintained a much greater personal interest in the Mediterranean than did Alexander, for ideological reasons—mainly, Paul's conservative convictions and a desire to bolster and protect the interests of legitimate authority everywhere. A key element in the formulation of Russian policy during this period was Paul's interest in the Knights of Malta as a crusading order to revitalize the European aristocracy.

But even in Paul's reign, political considerations were the most important determinants of Russian policy. Russia entered the War of the Second Coalition in order to protect sensitive border areas from approaching French armies and to decrease the danger of revolts that might be inspired by French revolutionary agents. Paul's policy was to fulfill this objective by meeting the French at an advance line of defense, bolstering the anti-French fears of established governments and supporting their efforts with diplomatic and military assistance. After Bonaparte's Egyptian campaign was launched across the Mediterranean into the territory of the Ottoman Empire, the Mediterranean lands became the most immediate area of conflict. Russia tried to prevent the weaker states of the Mediterranean from falling under the influence of the French, the primary threat, or of any other power. Russia's quick and decisive entry into the Mediterranean in 1798 and 1799 may have saved the Ottoman Empire and the Italian states from complete disintegration and prevented the partition of them among Austria, Britain, and France.

The Russian campaigns were a surprising success considering the handicaps of unfamiliar territory and peoples. The effectiveness of Russian Mediterranean policy during Paul's reign was limited by the distances involved and Russia's technical insufficiencies. Diplomatic and military channels of communication were not organized for coordination of policy with military operations. The staffs of embassies and military commands were too small and too inexperienced for the responsibilities placed upon them. In addition, the military command lacked the financial resources and equipment necessary for carrying out its mission without considerable local support. Despite these inadequacies the Russians surprised both their allies and the French by major accomplishments such as the establishment of an Ionian Republic. Russian successes so far from her own borders were resented by Austria and Britain, so that these two nations refused to cooperate in the best interests of the coalition.

The chief reasons for Paul's sudden withdrawal from the Second Coalition were his frustrations over the Austrian behavior in northern Italy, especially at Ancona, and the circumstances of the British capture of "his" island, Malta. Bonaparte's offer of the island to Paul paved the way for the Franco-Russian alliance of 1800. But Russia's Mediterranean interests did not end with Paul's sudden departure from the Second Coalition. She continued to maintain the alliance with the Ottoman Empire, to protect the Ionian Islands, and to defend the interests of Sardinia and Naples in peace negotiations.

At the beginning of his reign, Alexander attempted to disengage from European affairs and refused to garrison Malta and act as a mediator between British and French interests in the Mediterranean. But where Russian interests were involved—in supporting the Ottoman Empire, protecting trade, and strengthening the fragile Ionian Republic—Russia increased her commitments. When war was resumed between Britain and France, the Russian positions in the Mediterranean, especially in the Ionians and Naples, were again threatened. Despite his inclinations toward Britain, Alexander was reluctant to enter the conflict, and even after the Third Coalition had been formed, he participated in it with less enthusiasm than Paul had shown for the Second Coalition.

Militarily, Russia's position in the Mediterranean was considerably stronger in 1805–7 than in 1798–1800. Bases were already established; Russia provided an army and navy, based at Corfu, to defend Naples and to prevent French advances into the Balkans. A greater degree of coordination was achieved through the selection of experienced commanders, supported by larger staffs. The diplomat and the naval commander of the old Russian school—Tomara and Ushakov, respectively—were replaced by younger men with experiences in the West—Italinsky and Seniavin. Beginning as an offensive flanking movement for the main attack in central Europe, Russia's military position in the Mediterranean quickly became defensive as a result of Austerlitz.

Under the influence of the "young friends," especially Czartoryski, Alexander sent agents into the Balkans to win friends for Russia and counter French propaganda. This activity conflicted with the goal of maintaining an influence at Constantinople to assure free transit of the Straits for Russian warships. French success in undermining the Russian dominance at Constantinople jeopardized the whole Mediterranean operation. Therefore, Russia's surprisingly complete withdrawal from the Mediterranean at Tilsit was a logical move.

The stalemate that was produced in the Mediterranean—with the land under French control and the sea under British, and with the question of the Ottoman Empire's future still unresolved by France and Russia—was a major reason for Napoleon's concentration on German affairs and the closure of the continent to British shipping and goods. And the ensuing "Baltic" problem was the chief cause of the resumption of war in 1812.

Bibliography

The bibliography has been divided into six sections: (1) background and reference, (2) manuscript sources, (3) published documents and correspondence, (4) memoirs and other original materials, (5) monographs, and (6) articles.

MANUSCRIPT SOURCES

The most valuable unpublished manuscripts were found in the Public Record Office in London, the Italian State Archives in Naples, the Haus-, Hof- und Staatsarchiv in Vienna, and the Royal Library at Corfu. The diplomatic correspondence between London and Saint Petersburg in the Public Record Office is well organized and easily accessible to the researcher. Russian foreign policy regarding the Mediterranean plays a leading role in these communications because of Britain's own interest in that area. The dispatches from the British consul-general in the Ionian Islands are particularly informative.

The correspondence of the Neapolitan ambassador to Russia, Serracapriola, in the archives in Naples is a valuable source of information for this period of Russian history because of the ambassador's long stay in Russia and his intimate contacts at court, his natural concern with Mediterranean affairs, and his meticulous care in keeping his own court informed. The reports of the Austrian ambassadors to Russia constitute a detailed guide to Russian court affairs and to Austrian policy.

The Royal Library at Corfu houses the archives of the Ionian Republic. Miraculously saved from destruction during World War II, these archives are important for understanding local conditions on the islands and Russo-Ionian relations. They include the Mocenigo papers and the communications of the British and the Russian consuls, Foresti and Benacky, with the Ionian Senate.

Surviving records of the Order of Saint John of Jerusalem, preserved in the Chancellery of the order in Rome, include the minutes of the Grand Council in Saint Petersburg. The State Archives in

Dubrovnik has a number of documents pertaining to the history of Ragusa during this period.

PUBLISHED DOCUMENTS AND CORRESPONDENCE

Among the published documents are the political, military, and private correspondence of many of the leading figures of the period from 1797 to 1807. The large quantity of Russian materials published in the nineteenth century may have suffered intentional or unintentional omissions or expurgations. Nevertheless, these works are extremely valuable for reconstructing diplomatic relations, military operations, and court affairs.

The important Russian documentary collections are the Vorontsov Archives for the letters to and from Alexander and Simon Vorontsov, Vasil'chikov's compilation of the Razumovsky papers, Brikner's edition of the papers of N. P. Panin, Trachevsky's collection of the diplomatic correspondence between France and Russia, Bychkov's analysis of the correspondence of the Littas, and the Kurakin and Mordvinov archives.

The nineteenth-century Russian archival publications are supplemented by the efforts of the Soviet Ministry of Foreign Affairs to publish the important documents of the Imperial Foreign Ministry in their original languages, Russian and French. The first three volumes of *Vneshniaia Politika Rossii* . . . , amply footnoted and indexed, cover the period from March 1801 to July 1807. These do not pretend to be complete, but the editing, as far as one can tell without access to the total archives, is fairly objective.

Little has been published of the diplomatic papers before 1801. Except for the publication of Alexander's correspondence with Naoleon by Trachevsky and Vandal, the public and private papers of both Paul and Alexander are largely unpublished. Many of these are presumably lost, but some undoubtedly still exist in Soviet and Western archives.

Concerning Anglo-Russian relations, published documents may be found in many sources. The most valuable are the Dropmore Papers preserved by Lord Grenville and later published by the Historical Manuscripts Commission. The correspondence of Sir Arthur Paget contains evidence of a pro-Russian sentiment rarely held by a British diplomat in the late eighteenth and early nineteenth centuries. The diaries and correspondence of Sir James Harris are mainly important for the reign of Catherine the Great, but some observations of his are to be found on the later period. The published letters of another British ambassador to Russia, Lord Granville (Leveson-Gower), contain few useful items since they pertain chiefly to family matters.

On military affairs the Ushakov documents, edited by Mordvinov, and the Nelson Papers provide an interesting contrast in culture and personality as well as material on naval operations. A useful source on Russian naval history of the eighteenth century is the seventeen volumes of documents, *Materialy dlia istorii russkogo flota,* published by the Imperial Naval Ministry. On the British side, the Nelson letters are supplemented by the excellent editions of the Navy Records Society of the dispatches of St. Vincent, Spencer, and Keith.

The only "Russian" political memoirs worth special mention in a scholarly bibliography are the famous ones of Czartoryski and Chichagov; these were written many years after the events and cannot be relied upon for details. The naval memoirs of Svin'in, Bronevskii, and Panafiden are more picturesque than informative. The French military anecdotalists, Mangourit, Bellaire, and Marmont, glorify their own and Napoleon's accomplishments.

Russian relations with the Order of Malta and with Rome are documented by the memoirs of Georgel and the collections of Vatican papers edited by Rouet de Journel. Copies of the pertinent conventions and treaties concerning the Mediterranean can be found in the publications of Martens, Hurewitz, and Xenos.

MONOGRAPHS

For the general political background to the period the books by Brunn, Deutsch, M. S. Anderson, and Albret Sorel are most useful. The English have excelled in military history with notable contributions by R. C. Anderson and Piers Mackesy.

A. M. Stanislavskaia is the leading Soviet historian of Russian interest in the Mediterranean during this period. Her work stresses the economic role in Anglo-Russian relations, the influence of court "parties," and Russian military and diplomatic successes in the Mediterranean, utilizing archives in Moscow as well as many of the works listed in this bibliography.

A good book on Russo-Turkish relations for the 1797–1807 period is needed, although Puryear and Shupp deal with it in part. On the Ionian Republic the works of Lunzi and Rodocanachi are the most complete but are not readily available. The best book in English on Ionian problems is probably the old one by Jervis.

Biographies of the Russian naval heroes Ushakov and Seniavin are available only in Russian. The older, rare biography of Ushakov by Skalovskii is the most useful, and Shapiro's recent work on Seniavin can be recommended. Tarle's accounts of the expeditions, though deficient in footnotes, are excellent glorifications of Russian military exploits in the Mediterranean.

There are a variety of sources on Malta. Antoshevskii has written a rarely found classic in Russian. Other important books dealing with the Maltese problems are by Miège, Pierredon, and Taube. The only book in English specifically concerned with this area, by Hardman, is unsatisfactory. Regarding Russian relations with the Vatican, besides the excellent introductions to the documentary collections of Rouët de Journel, there is the interesting work by Moroshkin on the Jesuits in Russia and the excellent series by the Jesuit scholar Pierling.

Russo-Italian relations have fared better in historical study than have other aspects of Mediterranean affairs during this period. The recent works by Giuseppi Berti, in both Italian and Russian editions, and by Acton on Naples, and the earlier efforts by Auriol, Greppi, and Polievktov on Sardinia are relatively valuable, though they should be used with care.

The best general discussion of Adriatic affairs is by Vojnovic. Pisani is also useful. Villari's book on Ragusa, in English, is poor. On Franco-Russian relations the old works by Driault, Sorel, Scudamore, and Auriol are still valuable. Bezobrazov, Voenskii, and Balabanov are important for the Russian side.

ARTICLES

Some of the most important material on Russian participation in Mediterranean affairs is found in periodical sources. The nineteenth-century Russian articles are well worth the effort to find them in a wide variety of sources; the articles by Al'bovskii, Arkas, Aleksandrenko, Dragovich, Il'inskii, Tatishchev, and Zhamkin were particularly valuable. In the nineteenth century, French historians—Pinguad, Haumant, Coquelle, and Broglie—were also concerned with Russian activities in the Mediterranean during the Napoleonic era.

Bibliography

The pioneer efforts in Soviet historical writing by Kleinman, Shteinberg, and Lanin illustrate the early Soviet historical interest in the Mediterranean. In the past ten years Soviet historians have focused on Russian military successes, emphasizing the range of Russian interests in the Mediterranean. The articles of Sirotkin and Shapiro are noteworthy contributions to the Soviet interpretation of Russian imperial history.

BACKGROUND AND REFERENCE

Anderson, M. S. *The Eastern Question, 1774–1923: A Study in International Relations.* London: Macmillan, 1966.

Anderson, R. C. *Naval Wars in the Levant, 1559–1853.* Princeton: Princeton University Press, 1952.

Beskrovnyi, L. G. *Ocherki voennoi istoriografii Rossii.* Moscow: Akademiia Nauk, 1962.

Bolshaia Sovetskaia Entsiklopediia. 50 vols. Moscow, 1949–57.

Brunn, Goeffrey. *Europe and the French Imperium, 1799–1814.* New York: Harper's, 1938.

Columbia Encyclopedia. 3d ed. New York, 1963.

Entsiklopedicheskii Slovar'. 86 vols. Saint Petersburg: Brockhaus-Efron, 1890–1907.

Fadeev, Anatolii Vsevolodovich. *Doreformennaia Rossiia (1800–1861).* Moscow: MGU, 1960.

Florinsky, Michael T. *Russia: A History and an Interpretation.* 2 vols. New York: Macmillan, 1955.

Grey, Ian. *Catherine the Great: Autocrat and Empress of all Russia.* Philadelphia and New York: J. B. Lippincott Company, 1962.

Grunwald, Constantin de. *Trois siècles de diplomatie russe.* Paris: Calman-Lévy, 1945.

Horn, D. B. *Great Britain and Europe in the Eighteenth Century.* London: Oxford University Press, 1967.

Istoriia diplomatii. Edited by V. A. Zorin and others. 3 vols. Moscow: Akademiia Nauk, 1959–65.

Lederer, Ivo J., ed. *Russian Foreign Policy: Essays in Historical Perspective.* New Haven and London: Yale University Press, 1962.

Lefebvre, Georges. *Napoleon: from 18 Brumaire to Tilsit.* Translated by Henry F. Stockhold. London: Routledge & Kegan Paul, 1969.

Bibliography

Lobanov-Rostovsky, Andrei A. *Russia and Europe, 1789–1825.* Durham, N.C.: Duke University Press, 1947.

Mahan, Alfred Thomas. *The Influence of Sea Power upon the French Revolution and Empire, 1793–1812.* 2 vols. Boston: Little, Brown, and Co., 1893.

———. *The Life of Nelson.* 2 vols. Boston: Little, Brown, and Co., 1900.

———. *Naval Strategy, Compared and Contrasted with the Principles of Military Operations on Land.* London: Sampson Low, Marston & Co., Ltd., 1911.

Marriott, J. A. R. *The Eastern Question: An Historical Study in European Diplomacy.* 4th ed. Oxford: University Press, 1947.

Miazgovskii, E. A. *Istoriia chernomorskago flota, 1696–1912: udostoeno premii imeni grafa S. A. Stroganova.* Saint Petersburg: A. S. Suvorin, 1914.

Mohrenschildt, Dimitri S. von. *Russia in the Intellectual Life of Eighteenth Century France.* New York: Columbia University Press, 1936.

Okun', Semen B. *Istoriia SSSR, 1796–1825: Kurs lektsii.* Leningrad: LGU, 1947.

Rose, J. Holland. *The Revolutionary and Napoleonic Era, 1789–1815.* Cambridge: Cambridge University Press, 1935.

Rude, George. *Revolutionary Europe, 1783–1815.* New York: Harper Torchbooks, 1966.

Russkii Biograficheskii Slovar'. 25 vols. Saint Petersburg, 1896–1913.

Seton-Watson, Hugh. *The Russian Empire, 1801–1917.* London: Oxford University Press, 1967.

Thomson, Gladys Scott. *Catherine the Great and the Expansion of Russia.* New York: Colliers, 1962.

Ulianitskii, V. A. *Dardanelly, Bosfor i Chernoe more v XVIII veke: ocherki diplomaticheskoi istorii vostochnago voprosa.* Moscow: A. Gatpuk, 1883.

Voennaia Entsiklopediia. 18 vols. Saint Petersburg, 1911–15.

Voprosy voennoi istorii Rossii: XVIII i pervaia polovina XIX vekov. Edited by V. I. Shunkov, et al. Moscow: Akademiia Nauk, 1969.

Watson, J. Steven. *The Reign of George III, 1760–1815.* Oxford History of England, vol. 12. London: Oxford University Press, 1960.

Bibliography

Zatvornitskii, N. M. *Napoleonskaia Epokha: Bibliograficheskii ukaza-tel'*. 2 vols. Saint Petersburg: Trenke i Fiusno, 1914–15.

MANUSCRIPT SOURCES

Corfu, Royal Library
    Senate of the Ionian Republic
    Department of Foreign Affairs
        Box 1   Letters of deputies to Saint Petersburg
        Box 8   Letters of Felice Zambelli, Commissioner to Constantinople
        Box 9   Letters of Capodistrias from Santa Maura
        Box 12 Papers regarding Andrea Metaxa
        Box 22 f. 1 Notes of Russian ambassador at Constantinople, Tomara, 27 September 1799, to 23 January 1802
        f. 2 Notes of ambassador at Constantinople, Italinsky, August 2, 1802, to September 24, 1806
        Box 23 Mocenigo Papers
        Box 24 Miscellaneous
        Box 25 Foresti Papers
        Box 30 Benacky Papers
        Box 32 Letters of Consul-General Romieu
        Box 40 Letters from envoy to Constantinople, Lefcochilo
Dubrovnik, Drzavni Arhiv
      1.1–200 Letters from Tomara and Italinsky to Ragusa
      591 Letters from Fonton to the Ragusan Senate, 1801–5
      4.586–587 Letters of Ayala, Ragusan consul in Vienna, to the Ragusan Senate, 1803–6
      2.201–391 Letters from Maroti, Ragusan consul in Rome, 1800–1807
London, British Museum
    Add. MSS. 12096 Paul to Whitworth
    Add. MSS. 33110 Pelham Papers
    Add. MSS. 33544 Bentham Papers
    Add. MSS. 34908, 34909, 34916, 34924, 34948 Nelson Papers
    Add. MSS. 37050 Affairs in the Mediterranean, 1806–14
    Add. MSS. 37852 Windham Papers
    Add. MSS. 38355 Liverpool Papers
London, Public Record Office
    Foreign Office
        FO 42/3–6 Ionian Islands
        FO 65/40–46 Russia

FO 94–206 Anglo-Russian Treaty of 29 December 1799
FO 84/14 Venice
FO 181/1–6 Russia
Naples, State Archives
Folios 2699–2702 Serracapriola Papers
Folios 1681–83 Russia diversi
Folio 322 Letters of Queen Maria Carolina
Rome, Sovereign Military Order of Malta
No. 136, Ar 16 Protocole du Sacré Conseil de l'Ordre Souverain de St. Jean de Jérusalem, St. Petersbourg
Registre des délibérations de la Vénérable Langue Bavaro-Russe, 1804–10
Conciliorum Liber, Anni 1803, 1804, 1804, 1806 (Vols. I–IV)
Vienna, Haus-, Hof-, und Staatsarchiv
82–92 Russland II Berichte (Reports of Cobenzl and Ferdinand de Wurttemburg)
93–95 Russland II Berichte (Reports of Cobenzl, Dietrichstein, Viazzoli, and Locatelli)
96–107 Russland II Berichte (Reports of Saurau, Hudelist, and Stadion)
180–186 Russland II Weisinger (Letters of Thugut and Cobenzl)
217 Russland II Corresp.
224–226 Russland II Noten
2 Ragusa Berichte (Reports of Timoli, Austrian consul-general)
127 Turkei II Berichte (Reports of Herbert and Testa)

PUBLISHED DOCUMENTS AND CORRESPONDENCE

Admiral Ushakov. Edited by R. N. Mordvinov. Vols. 2–3. Moscow: Voenizdat, 1952–56.

Alexander I. "Iz perepiski Aleksandra I s V. P. Kochubem." Edited by T. Bogdanovich. *Russkoe Proshloe* 1, no. 5 (1923): 100–11.

Arkhiv Grafov Mordvinovykh. Edited by V. A. Bilbasov. Vols. 1–4. Moscow, 1901–2.

Arkhiv Kniazia F. A. Kurakina. Edited by V. N. Smol'ianov. Vols. 5–10. Saratov, 1898–1904.

Arkhiv Kniazia Vorontsova. 40 vols. Edited by Peter Bartenev. Moscow: Universitetskaia tipografiia, 1870–95.

Bibliography

Correspondance de Napoléon Ier. Vols. 5–15. Paris: Henri Plon, 1863.

Correspondance inédite de Marie-Caroline reine de Naples et de Sicile avec le Marquis de Gallo. 2 vols. Paris: Émile-Paul, 1911. Edited by Commander M. H. Weil and Marquis C. di Somma Circello.

Czartoryski, Prince Adam. *Memoirs of Prince Adam Czartoryski and His Correspondence with Alexander I.* Edited by Adam Gielgud. 2 vols. 2d ed. London: Remington & Co., 1888.

Diplomacy in the Near and Middle East: A Documentary Record. Vol. 1, 1535–1914. Edited by Jacob Colman Hurewitz. Princeton: D. Van Nostrand Company, 1956.

Diplomaticheskie snosheniia Rossii s Frantsiei v epokhu Napoleona I. Vol. 1, 1800–1802; vol. 2, 1803–1804; vol. 3, 1805–1806. Sbornik Imperatorskago Russkago Istoricheskago Obshchestva, vols. 70, 77, 82. Saint Petersburg, 1890–92.

The Dispatches and Letters of Vice Admiral Lord Viscount Nelson. Edited by Sir Nicholas Harris Nicholas. Vols. 3–5. London: Henry Coburn, 1845.

Granville, Leveson Gower, Lord. *Private Correspondence, 1781 to 1821.* Edited by Castalia Countess Granville. 2 vols. London: John Murray, 1916.

Harris, James Howard, 1st Earl of Malmesbury. *Diaries and Correspondence of James Harris.* Vol. 4. London: Richard Bentley, 1844.

———. *A Series of Letters of the First Earl of Malmesbury, His Family and Friends from 1745 to 1820.* Edited by his grandson the Earl of Malmesbury. Vol. 2. London: Richard Bentley, 1870.

Kantsler Kniaz' Aleksandr Andreevich Bezborodko v sviazi s sobytiiami ego vremeni. Pt. 2. Edited by Nikolai Gregorovich. Sbornik Imperatorskago Russkago Istoricheskago Obshchestva, vol. 19 (1881).

"Imperator Pavel Petrovich, 1800–1801: Vysochaishiia poveleniia i ukazy s-peterburgskim voennym gubernatoram." Edited by Mikhail Dmitrievich. *Russkaia Starina* 33 (1882): 191–205.

"Imperator Pavel v ego deianiakh i prikazakh." *Russkaia Starina* 28 (1877): 279–305.

The Keith Papers. Edited by Christopher Lloyd. Vol. 2. London: Navy Records Society, 1950.

Konventsiia mezhdu imperieiu Vserossiiskoiu i Portoiu Ottomanskoiu o respublike sed'me soedinennykh ostrovov zakliu-

Bibliography

chennaia v Konstantinopole 21 marta 1800 goda. Saint Petersburg: Imperatorskaia tipografiia, 1801.

Konventsiia zakliuchennaia mezhdu Ego Velichestvom Imperatorom Vserossiiskim i Derzhavnym Ordenom Mal'tiiskim i Ego Preimushchestvom Gros-Meisterom. Saint Petersburg: Imperatorskaia tipografiia, 1798.

Letters of Admiral of the Fleet the Earl of St. Vincent whilst First Lord of the Admiralty, 1801–1804. Edited by David Bonner Smith. Vol. 1. London: Navy Records Society, 1922.

Litta, Giulio. "Depeshi Grafa Litty poslannika Mal'tiiskago Ordena v Peterburge pisanniia v kontse 1796 i nachale 1797 goda." Edited by A. F. Bychkov. In *Sbornik Imperatorskago Russkago Istoricheskago Obshchestva* 2 (1868): 164–274.

Martens, Fedor. *Sobranie traktatov i konventsii, zakliuchennykh Rossieiu s inostrannymi derzhavami.* 15 vols. Saint Petersburg: A. Benke, 1874–1909.

Materialy dlia istorii diplomaticheskikh snoshenii Rossii s Raguzskoi Respublikoi, iz istorii vneshnikh snoshenii Raguzskoi Respubliki. Edited by Vikentii Vasil'evich Makushev. Obshchestvo Istorii i Drevnostei Rossiiskikh, Chteniia, vol. 3. Moscow, 1865.

Materialy dlia istorii russkago flota. Vols. 15–17. Edited by S. Ogorodnikov. Saint Petersburg: Morskoe Ministerstvo, 1901–2.

Materialy dlia zhizneopisaniia grafa Nikity Petrovicha Panina. (1770–1837). 7 vols. Edited by A. Brikner. Saint Petersburg: Tipografiia Imperatorskoi Akademii Nauk, 1892.

Mémoires posthumes du Feld-Maréchal Comte de Stedingk. Edited by General Comte de Björnstjerna. 3 vols. Paris: Arthus-Bertrand, 1844–47.

Nonciatures de Russie d'après les documents authentiques. Vol. 1, *Nonciature de Litta,* 1797–1799; vols. 2–3, *Nonciature d'Arezzo,* 1802–1806; vol. 5, *Interim de Benvenuti,* 1799–1803. Edited by Marie Joseph Rouët de Journel, S.J. Studi e Testi, nos. 167, 168, 169, 194. Vatican City, 1943–1957.

Private Papers of George, Second Earl of Spencer, First Lord of the Admiralty, 1794–1801. Edited by Julian S. Corbett and Rear-Admiral H. W. Richmond. Vols. 2–4. London: Navy Records Society, 1914–24.

Report on the Manuscripts of J. B. Fortescue, Esq., preserved at Dropmore. Historical Manuscripts Commission. Vols. 4–8. London: H. M. Stationary Office, 1905.

Select Despatches from the British Foreign Office Archives Relating to the Formation of the Third Coalition against France, 1804–1805. Edited by John Holland Rose. London: Royal Historical Society, 1904.

Un Ambassadeur de Suède a la cour de Catherine II: Feld-Maréchal Comte de Stedingk, choix de dépêches diplomatiques, rapports secrets et lettres particulières de 1790 à 1796. Edited by Comtesse Anna Brevern de la Gardie. Stockholm: P. A. Norstedt & Sons, 1919.

Vasil'chikov, Aleksandr Alekseevich, ed. *Semeistvo Razumovskikh.* Vols. 3–4. Saint Petersburg: M. M. Stasiulevich, 1882–94.

Vneshniaia Politika Rossii XIX i nachala XX veka: dokumenty rossiiskogo ministerstva inostrannykh del. Seriia pervaia, 1801–1815 gg. Vol. 1, *Mart 1801 g.–aprel' 1804 g.*; vol. 2, *Aprel' 1804 g.–dekabr' 1805 g.*; vol. 3, *Ianvar' 1806 g.–iiul' 1807 g.* Edited by A. L. Narochnitskii, and others. Moscow: Ministerstvo Inostrannykh Del SSSR, 1960–3.

The Windham Papers. Edited by the Earl of Rosebury. Vol. 2. London: Herbert Jenkins, 1913.

MEMOIRS AND OTHER ORIGINAL MATERIALS

Anonymous. *A Key to the Recent Conduct of the Emperor of Russia.* London: Jordan and Maxwell, 1807.

————. *Coalition against France!!* London: Barnard and Sultzer, 1805.

————. *Coup-d'œil sur les relations politiques de la Russie avec la France.* London: W. Spilsbury, 1804.

————. *Observations d'un partisan de la liberté et de l'indépendance de toutes les nations sur l'intérêt que trouve la Russie dans la guerre.* Cologne: Pierre Hammer, 1807.

————. *Ragguaglio Istorico sulla vita, regno, ed azioni di Paolo I Imperatore di tutte le Russie.* Warsaw, 1801.

————. *Remarks on the Probable Conduct of Russia and France towards this Country, also on the Necessity of Great Britain becoming Independent of the Northern Powers . . . .* London: Jordan and Maxwell, 1805.

Anthoine, Baron de Saint-Joseph. *Essai historique sur le commerce et la navigation de la Mer-Noire.* 2d ed. Paris: V. Agasse, 1820.

Bellaire, J. P. *Précis des opérations générales de la division française du Levant chargée, pendant les années V, VI, et VII, de la défense des îles et possessions ex-vénitiennes de la mer Ionienne, formant aujourd'hui la république des Sept-Iles*. Paris: Magimel, 1805.

Bronevskii, Vladimir. *Pis'ma morskago ofitsera*. 4 vols. Moscow: Semen Selevanovskii, 1825.

Chateaugiron, René C. H. Le Prestre. *Notice sur la mort de Paul Ier, Empereur de Russie*. Paris, n.d. Copy in the New York Public Library.

Chichagov, Admiral Pavel V. *Mémoires de l'amiral Paul Tchitchagoff*. Edited by Charles Gr. Lahovary. Paris: Plon, 1909.

Dodwell, Edward. *A Classical and Topographical Tour through Greece during the Years 1801, 1805, and 1806*. 2 vols. London: Rodwell & Martin, 1819.

Doublet, Pierre-Jean-Louis-Ovide. *Mémoires historiques sur l'invasion et l'occupation de Malte par une armée française, en 1798*. Edited by le comte de Panisse-Passis. Paris: Firmin-Didot et Cie., 1883.

Eton, William. *A Letter to the Right Honorable the Earl of D . . . on the Political Relations of Russia in Regard to Turkey, Greece, and France; and on the Means of the French Establishing a Permanent Control over Russia*. London: T. Cadell and W. Davies, 1807.

Georgel, Fr. M. l'Abbé Jean François. *Mémoires pour servir à l'histoire des événements de la fin du dix-huitième siècle depuis 1760 jusqu'en 1806–1810, par un contemporain impartial*. Vol. 6. Paris: Alexis Eymery, 1820.

Hobhouse, John Cam, Baron Broughton. *A Journey through Albania and Other Provinces of Turkey in Europe and Asia to Constantinople during the Years 1809 & 1810*. 2 vols. Philadelphia: M. Carey and Son, 1817.

Holland, Henry. *Travels in the Ionian Isles, Albania, Thessaly, Macedonia, etc. during the Years 1812 and 1813*. London: Longman, Hurst, Rees, Orme, and Brown, 1815.

Hunter, William. *A Short View of the Political Situation of the Northern Powers: Founded on Observations Made during a Tour through Russia, Sweden, and Denmark, in 1800: with Conjectures on the Probable Issue of the Present Contest*. London: John Stockdale, 1801.

Maisonneuve. *Annales historiques de l'Ordre Souverain de St. Jean de Jérusalem depuis l'année 1725 jusqu'au moment présent*. Saint Petersburg: Imperatorskaia tipografiia, 1799.

Mangourit, Michel Ange Bernard de. *Défense d'Ancone, et des dé-*

partements romains, le Tronto, le Musone, et le Metauro, par le General Monnier aux années VII et VIII. . . . Vol. 1. Paris: Charles Pougens, 1802.

Marmont, A.-F.-L. Weisse de. *Mémoires du Maréchal Marmont Duc de Raguse de 1792 à 1841.* Vol. II. Paris: Halle, 1857.

Panafidin, P. I. *Pis'ma morskogo ofitsera (1806–1809).* Edited by B. V. Modzalevskii. Petrograd: Morskoe Ministerstvo, 1916.

Paulini, Giorgio. *Memorie storiche sulla fonazione della repubblica Jonica ossia della sette isole unite.* Italie, 1802.

"Petersburgskaia Starina," *Russkaia Starina* 41 (1884): 363–70, 619–26.

Pleschtjeief, Serge de. *Tableau abrégé de l'empire de la Russie d'après son état actuel.* Rev. ed. Moscow, 1796.

Pouqueville, F. C. H. L. *Travels through the Morea, Albania, and Several Other Parts of the Ottoman Empire to Constantinople during the Years 1798, 1799, 1800, and 1801.* London: Richard Phillips, 1806.

Reuilly, J. *Voyage en Crimée et sur les bords de la mer Noire pendant l'année 1803.* . . . Paris: Bossange, Masson et Besson, 1806.

Sicard, aîné. *Lettres sur Odessa.* St. Petersburg: Pluchart, 1812.

Stephanopouli, Dino and Nicolo. *Voyage de Dino et Nicolo Stephanopouli en Grèce, pendant les années 1797 et 1798 d'après deux missions, dont l'une du gouvernement français, et l'autre du général en chef Buonaparte.* 2 vols. Paris: Guilleminet, 1800.

Storch, Henri. *Tableau historique et statistique de l'empire de Russie à la fin du dix-huitième siècle.* Vol. 1. Basle and Leipsig, 1802.

Svin'in, Pavel. *Vospominaniia na flot Pavla Svin'ina.* Saint Petersburg: V. Plavil'shchikov, 1819.

Thornton, Thomas. *The Present State of Turkey, or Description of the Ottoman Empire.* 2 vols. London: Joseph Mawman, 1809.

Vaudoncourt, General Guillaume de. *Memoirs of the Ionian Islands . . . including the Life and Character of Ali Pacha.* Translated by William Walton. London: Baldwin, Cradock, and Jay, 1816.

Volney, C.-F. *Voyage en Égypte et en Syrie, pendant les années 1783, 1784 et 1785.* . . . 2 vols. 5th ed. Paris: Bossange, 1820.

Wood, Mark. *The Importance of Malta Considered in the Years 1796 and 1798, etc.* London: John Stockdale, 1803.

Bibliography

MONOGRAPHS

Acton, Harold. *The Bourbons of Naples, 1734–1825.* London: Methuen and Co., 1957.

Adams, Ephraim Douglass. *The Influence of Grenville on Pitt's Foreign Policy, 1787–1798.* Papers of the Bureau of Historical Research, no. 13. Washington: Carnegie Institute, 1904.

Andrushchenko, A. I. *Admiral Ushakov.* Moscow: Uchpedgiz, 1951.

Antoshevskii, Ivan Kazimirovich. *Derzhavnyi Orden Sviatago Ioanna Ierusalimskago imenuemyi Malt'iiskim v Rossii.* Saint Petersburg, 1914. Limited edition of 450 copies; copy that belonged to Tsarevich Alexis in the New York Public Library.

Appendini, Fr. M. *Ratovane oko Dubrovnika godine 1806.* Dubrovnik: Kolendić i Nagy, 1906.

Arsh, G. L. *Albaniia i Epir v kontse XVIII-nachale XIX v.* Moscow: Akademiia Nauk, 1963.

Auriol, Charles. *La France, l'Angleterre, et Naples de 1803 à 1806.* 2 vols. Paris: Plon, Nourrit et cie., 1904.

Badham, F. P. *Nelson at Naples: A Journal for June 10–30, 1799, Refuting Recent Misstatements of Captain Mahan and Professor J. K. Laughton.* London: David Nutt, 1900. Mahan's personal copy with annotations in the British Museum.

Bagally, John W. *Ali Pasha and Great Britain.* Oxford: Basil Blackwell, 1938.

Balabanov, M. *Rossii i velikaia frantsuzskaia revoliutsiia.* Rossiia i evropeiskie revoliutsii v proshlom, pt. 1. Kiev: Gosudarstvennoe Izdatel'stvo Ukrainy, 1923.

Beauchamp, Alphonse de. *The Life of Ali Pacha of Jannina, late Vizier of Epirus surnamed Aslan, or the Lion.* 2d ed. London: Lupton Relfe, 1823.

Berti, Giuseppe. *Russia e stati italiani nel Risorgimento.* Turin: Giulio Einaudi, 1957.

Bezobrazov, P. V. *O snosheniiakh Rossii s Frantsiei.* Moscow: Universitetskaia tipografiia, 1892.

Bjelovučić, Harriet Towers. "The Ragusan Republic: Victim of Napoleon and Its Own Conservatism." Ph.D. dissertation, Columbia University, 1964.

Bogisić, Valtazar. *Razbor sochineniia N. A. Popova "Rossiia i Serbiia" s prilozheniem nekotorykh dokumentov.* Saint Petersburg: Imperatorskaia Akademiia Nauk, 1872.

Bibliography

Boppe, Auguste. *L'Albanie et Napoléon (1797–1814)*. Paris: Hachette, 1914.

Boudou, Adrien, S.J. *Le Saint-Siège et la Russie; leurs relations diplomatiques au XIXe siècle*. Vol. 1, *1814–1847*. 2d ed. Paris: Plon, 1922.

Bowman, Hervey Meyer. *Preliminary Stages of the Peace of Amiens: The Diplomatic Relations of Great Britain and France from the Fall of the Directory to the Death of the Emperor Paul of Russia, November 1799–March 1801*. Toronto: University of Toronto Press, 1901.

Bulgari, Nicholas Timoleon. *Les Sept-Iles Ioniennes et les traités qui les concernent*. Leipzig, 1859.

Butenko, V. A. *Kratkii ocherk istorii russkoi torgovli v sviazi istoriei promyshlennosti*. Moscow: Sytin, 1911.

Castelnau, le marquis Gabriel de. *Essai sur l'histoire ancienne et moderne de la Nouvelle Russie: statistique des provinces qui la composent, fondation d'Odessa, voyage en Crimée*. 3 vols. Paris: Rey et Gravier, 1820.

Charles-Roux, François. *Les origines de l'expédition d'Égypte*. Paris: Plon, 1910.

Chechulin, N. D. *Vneshniaia politika Rossii v nachale tsarstvovaniia Ekateriny II, 1762–1774*. Vol. 20. Saint Petersburg: Glavnoe Upravlenie Udelov, 1896.

Coquelle, P. *Histoire du Monténégro et de la Bosnie depuis les origines*. Paris: Ernest Leroux, 1895.

Damerini, Gino. *Le Isole Jonie nel sistema adriatica dal dominio Veneziano a Buonaparte*. Varese-Milan: Instituto per gli Studi di Politica Internazionale, 1943.

Dearborn, Henry S. *A Memoir on the Commerce and Navigation of the Black Sea and the Trade and Maritime Geography of Turkey and Egypt*. Vol. 2. Boston: Wells and Lilly, 1819.

De Bosset, Lt. Col. C. P. *Parga and the Ionian Islands Comprehending a Refutation of the Mis-Statements of the Quarterly Review and of Lt. Gen. Sir Thomas Maitland, etc*. London: John Warren, 1821.

Dennis, Alfred L. P. *Eastern Problems at the Close of the Eighteenth Century*. Cambridge, Mass.: Harvard University Press, 1901.

Deutsch, Harold C. *The Genesis of Napoleonic Imperialism*. Cambridge, Mass.: Harvard University Press, 1938.

Djuvara, Trandifir G. *Cent projets de partage de la Turquie (1291–1913)*. Paris: Felix Alcan, 1914.

Bibliography

Dobranskii, S. *K istorii snoshenii raguzskoi respubliki s Rossiei v XVIII i XIX vekakh.* Moscow: A. I. Snegirev, 1909.

Douin, Georges. *La Mediterranée de 1803 à 1805: Pirates et corsaires aux îles Ioniennes.* Paris: Plon, 1917.

Dranov, B. A. *Chernomorskie prolivy mezhdunarodno-pravovoi rezhim.* Moscow, 1948.

Driault, Edouard. *Napoléon et l'Europe: La politique extérieure du Premier Consul, 1800–1803.* Paris: Felix Alcan, 1910.

————. *La politique orientale de Napoléon: Sebastiani et Gardane, 1806–1808.* Paris: Bermer Baillière et Cie., 1904.

Druzhinina, E. I. *Kuchuk-Kainardzhiiskii mir 1774 goda: ego podgotovka i zakliuchenie.* Moscow: Akademiia Nauk, 1953.

————. *Severnoe prichernomor'e v 1775–1800 gg.* Moscow: Akademiia Nauk, 1959.

Edwards, H. Sutherland. *Russian Projects against India from the Czar Peter to General Skobeleff.* London: Remington & Co., 1885.

Fasanari, Raffaele. *L'Armata Russa del Generale Suvarov attraverso Verona (1799–1800).* Verona: Vita Veronese, 1952.

Ferrero, Guglielmo. *The Gamble: Bonaparte in Italy, 1796–1797.* Translated by Bertha Pritchard and Lily C. Freeman. London: G. Bell and Sons, 1961.

————. *The Reconstruction of Europe: Talleyrand and the Congress of Vienna, 1814–1815.* Translated by Theodore R. Jaeckel. New York: W. W. Norton & Company, 1963.

Firsov, N. N. *Pravitel'stvo i obshchestvo v ikh otnosheniiakh k vneshnei torgovle Rossii v tsarstvovanie imperatritsy Ekateriny II: ocherki iz istorii torgovoi politiki.* Kazan: Imperatorskii Universitet, 1902.

Galpin, William Freeman. *The Grain Supply of England during the Napoleonic Period.* Philadelphia: University of Pennsylvania, 1925.

Gerhard, Dietrich. *England und der Aufstieg Russlands: Zur Frage des Zusammenhanges der europäischen Staaten und ihres Ausgreifens in die aussereuropäische Welt in Politik und Wirtschaft des 18. Jahrhunderts.* Munich and Berlin, 1933.

Gill, Conrad. *The Naval Mutinies of 1797.* Manchester: University Press, 1913.

Goriainov, S. *Bosfor i Dardanelly—issledovanie voprosa o prolivakh po diplomaticheskoi perepiska khraniashcheisia v gosudarst-*

vennom i s-peterburgskom glavnom arkhivakh. Saint Petersburg: I. N. Skorokhodov, 1907.

Greppi, Giuseppe. *Sardaigne, Autriche, Russie pendant la premiére
et la deuxième coalition (1796–1802): Études diplomatiques
tirées de la correspondance officielle des envoyés de Sardaigne
à Saint Petersbourg.* 2d ed. Rome: Editione Romana, 1910.

———. *Un Gentiluomo milanese guerriero-diplomatico 1763–1839,
appunti biografici sul Bali Conte Giulio Litta Visconti Arese.*
Milan: Lombardi, 1896.

Grimstead, Patricia Kennedy. "Diplomatic Spokesmen and the
Tsar-Diplomat: The Russian Foreign Ministers during the
Reign of Alexander I, 1801–1825. Ph.D. dissertation, Univer-
sity of California, 1964.

Grunwald, Constantin de. *Alexander Ier, le tsar mystique.* Paris:
Amiot-Dumont, 1955.

———. *L'assassinat de Paul Ier, tsar de Russie.* Paris: Hatchette,
1960.

Guyot, Raymond. *Le Directoire et la paix de l'Europe des traités
de Bale à la deuxième coalition (1795–1799).* Paris: Felix
Alcan, 1911.

Halm, Hans. *Habsburgischer Osthandel im 18. Jahrhundert: Österreich und Neurussland (II): Donauhandel und- schiffahrt
1781–1787.* Veröffentlichungen des Osteuropas-Institutes
München, vol. 7. Munich, 1954

Hardman, William. *A History of Malta during the Period of the
French and British Occupations, 1798–1815.* Edited by J.
Holland Rose. London: Longmans, Green & Co., 1909.

Helleiner, Karl. *The Imperial Loans: A Study in Financial and Diplomatic History.* London: Oxford University Press, 1965.

Herold, J. Christopher. *Bonaparte in Egypt.* New York: Harper &
Row, 1962.

Il'inskii, V. P. *Admiral F. F. Ushakov v Sredizemnom More (1799
g.).* Saint Petersburg: Morskoi Sbornik, 1914.

James, William. *The Naval History of Great Britain from the Declaration of War by France in 1793 to the Accession of George
IV.* 6 vols. London: Richard Beally, 1847.

Jervis, Henry Jervis-White. *History of the Island of Corfu and the
Republic of the Ionian Islands.* London: Colburn & Co.,
1852.

Juchereau de St. Denys, baron. *Histoire de l'Empire Ottoman depuis
1792 jusqu'en 1844.* Vol. 2. Paris: Giusaudet et Jouaust, 1844.

Bibliography

Kallistov, N. D. *Korvet "Flora."* Moscow-Leningrad: Voenizdat, 1944.

Karnovich, Evgenii. *Mal'tiiskie rytsari v Rossii: istoricheskaia povest' iz vremen Imperatora Pavla Pervago.* 2d ed. Saint Petersburg: V. I. Bubinskii, 1897.

Kićivić, M. *Jedan unikat nepoznate cirilske stamparije u Kotoru.* Belgrade: Narodna biblioteka, 1955.

Klochkov, Mikhail V. *Ocherki pravitel'stvennoi deiatel'nosti vremeni Pavla I.* Petrograd: Senatskaia tipografiia, 1916.

Kobeko, Dmitrii Fomasovich. *Tsesarevich Pavel Petrovich (1754–1796).* Saint Petersburg: K. Rikker, 1882.

Kovalevskii, Egor P. *Graf Bludov i ego vremia (tsarstvovanie Imperatora Aleksandra I).* Saint Petersburg: Vtoroe otdel, E. I. V. Kantseliarii, 1866.

Krizman, Bogdan. *Diplomati i konsuli u starom Dubrovniku.* Zagreb, 1957.

Kroviakov, N. *Russkie v Korfu.* Moscow: Voenmorsizdat, 1943.

Kukiel, Maryan W. *Czartoryski and European Unity, 1770–1861.* Princeton, N. J.: Princeton University Press, 1955.

Lascaris, S. Th. *Capodistrias avant la révolution grecque: Sa carrière politique jusqu'en 1822.* Lausanne: Imprimerie centrale, 1918.

Lashkov, F. *Istoricheskii ocherk krymsko-tatarskago zemlevladeniia: sbornik dokumentov po istorii krymsko-tatarskago zemlevladeniia.* Simferopol: Tavricheskaia Gubernskaia tipografiia, 1897.

Liupersol'skii, P. *Diplomaticheskiia snosheniia i bor'ba Imperatora Aleksandra I s Napoleonom.* Kiev: M. P. Frits, 1878.

Lunzi, Ermano. *Storia della Isole Jonie sotto il reggimento dei repubblicani francesi.* Venice: Tipografia del Commercia, 1860.

———. *Della Repubblica Settinsulare.* Vol. 2. Bologna: Fava e Garagnani, 1863.

Mackesy, Piers. *The War in the Mediterranean, 1803–1810.* London: Longmans, Green and Co., 1857.

McKnight, James L. "Admiral Ushakov and the Ionian Republic: The Genesis of Russia's First Balkan Satellite." Ph.D. dissertation, University of Wisconsin, 1965.

Madariaga, Isabel de. *Britain, Russia, and the Armed Neutrality of 1780: Sir James Harris's Mission to St. Petersburg during the American Revolution.* New Haven: Yale University Press, 1962.

Bibliography

Mahan, Alfred Thomas. *The Influence of Sea Power upon the French Revolution and Empire, 1793–1812.* 2 vols. Boston: Little, Brown, and Co., 1893.

————. *Naval Strategy, Compared and Contrasted with the Principles of Military Operations on Land.* London: Sampson Low, Marston & Co., Ltd., 1911.

————. *Nelson at Naples.* London: Spottiswood & Co., 1900.

Marcere, Emile L. G. H. de. *Une ambassade à Constantinople: La politique orientale de la révolution française.* 2 vols. Paris: Felix Alcan, 1927.

Maresca, Benedetto. *Il cavaliere Antonio Micheroux nella reazione Napoletana del 1799.* Naples: Francesco Giannini & figli, 1895.

Markova, O. P. *Rossiia, Zakavkaz'e i mezhdunarodnye otnosheniia v XVIII veke.* Moscow: Akademiia Nauk, 1966.

Melvin, Frank Edgar. *Napoleon's Navigation Stystem: A Study of Trade Control during the Continental Blockade.* New York: D. Appleton & Co., 1919.

Miège, M. *Histoire de Malte.* 3 vols. Paris: Paulin, 1840.

Miliutin, Dmitri Alekseevich. *Istoriia voiny mezhdu Rossiei i Frantsiei v tsarstvovanie Imperatora Pavla I v 1799 g.* 5 vols. Saint Petersburg, 1852–53.

Miller, K. *Frantsuzskaia emigratsiia i Rossiia v tsarstvovanie Ekateriny II.* Paris, 1931.

Moroshkin, Mikhail Iakovlevich. *Iezuity v Rossii s tsarstvovaniia Ekateriny II i do nashego vremeni.* 2 vols. Saint Petersburg, 1867–70.

Mouravieff, Boris. *L'alliance russo-turque au milieu des guerres napoléoniennes.* Neuchâtel: Editions de la Baconnière, 1954.

Naff, Thomas. "Ottoman Diplomacy and the Great European Powers, 1797–1802." Ph.D. dissertation, University of London, 1960.

Narochnitskii, Aleksei Leont'evich. *Mezhdunarodnye otnosheniia evropeiskikh gosudarstv s 1794 do 1830 g.* Moscow, 1946.

Nebolsin, G. *Statisticheskiia zapiski o vneshnei torgovle Rossii.* Saint Petersburg, 1835.

Nolhac, Stanislas de. *La Dalmatie, les îles Ioniennes, Athènes et le mont Athos.* Paris: Plon, 1882.

Notman, K. V. *Vneshniaia politika tsarskoi Rossii kontsa XVIII i nachala XIX vekov.* Leningrad: Voenna-Politicheskaia akademiia RKKA imeni Tolmancheva, 1933.

Bibliography

Ordioni, Pierre. *Pozzo di Borgo, diplomate de l'Europe française.* Paris: Plon, 1935.

Osipov, K. *Alexander Suvorov.* Translated by Edith Bone. London: Hutchinson & Co., 1941.

Pauthier, G. *Les îles Ioniennes pendant l'occupation française et le protectorat anglais.* Paris: Benjamin Dupret, 1863.

Pierling, Pierre, S.J. *La Russie et le Saint-Siège: Etudes diplomatiques.* vol. 5: *Catherine II—Paul Ier—Alexandre Ier.* Paris: Plon, 1912.

Pierredon, Le Bailli Comte Michel de. *Exposition de l'histoire de l'Ordre Souverain de Malte au bénéfice du pavillon des lépreux.* Paris: Bibliothèque Nationale, 1929.

Piggott, Sir Francis, and G. W. T. Ormond. *Documentary History of the Armed Neutralities of 1780 and 1800* . . . . London: University of London, 1919.

Pingaud, Léonce. *Les Français en Russie et les Russes en France.* Paris: Librairie académique Didier, 1886.

Pisani, Paul. *La Dalmatie de 1797 à 1815: Épisode des conquêtes napoléoniennes.* Paris: Alphonse Picard et fils, 1893.

Platonov, Sergei Fedorovich, ed. *Rossiia i Italiia: sbornik istoricheskikh materialov i issledovanii, kasaiushchikhsia snoshenii Rossii s Italiei.* Vol. 4. Moscow: Akademiia Nauk, 1927.

Polievktov, Mikhail Aleksandrovich. *Proekt soiuza Rossii s Sardinskim korolevstvom v tsarstvovanie Imperatora Pavla I.* Saint Petersburg: Tipografiia Imperatorskoi Akademii Nauk, 1902.

Polivanov, M. *M. M. Borozdin, nachalnik okhrany neapolitanskago korolia, 1800–1802 gg.* Saint Petersburg: Pechatnyi Stanok, 1912.

Pratt, Fletcher. *The Empire and the Glory: Napoleon Bonaparte, 1800–1806.* New York: William Sloane Associates, 1949.

Presnaikov, Aleksandr Evgen'evich. *Aleksandr I.* Petrograd: Brokgauz-Efron, 1924.

Puryear, Vernon J. *Napoleon and the Dardanelles.* Berkeley and Los Angeles: University of California Press, 1951.

Ragsdale, Hugh A., Jr. "Russian Diplomacy in the Age of Napoleon: the Franco-Russian Rapprochement of 1800–1801." Ph.D. dissertation, University of Virginia, 1965.

Rodger, A. B. *The War of the Second Coalition, 1798–1801: A Strategic Commentary.* London: Oxford University Press, 1964.

Rodocanachi, Emmanuel. *Bonaparte et les îles Ioniennes: Un épisode*

Bibliography

des conquêtes de la République et du Premier Empire (1797–1816). Paris: Felix Alcan, 1899.

Ryan, Frederick W. *The House of the Temple: A Study of Malta and Its Knights in the French Revolution*. London: Burns, Oates & Washburn, 1930.

Saint-Vincent, Bory de, J. Baptiste G. Marie. *Histoire et description des îles Ioniennes depuis les temps fabuleux et héroïques jusqu'à ce jour avec un nouvel atlas*. Paris: Dondey-Dupré, 1823.

Samić, Midhat. *Les voyageurs français en Bosnie à la fin du XVIIIe siècle et au début du XIXe et les pays tel qu'ils l'ont vu*. Université de Paris, études de littérature étrangère et comparée, no. 38. Paris: Didier, 1960.

Samoilov, V. I. *Vnutrenniaia i vneshniaia politika Pavla I (1796–1801)*. Khlebnikogo: Voennyi Pedagogicheskii Institut Sovetskoi Armii, 1946.

Savvaitov, P. *Vziatie Anapy eskadroiu chernomorskago flota pod komandoiu kontr-admirala B. A. Pustoshkina v 1807 godu*. Saint Petersburg: Voenno-Uchebnykh Zavendenii, 1851.

Scott, James Brown. *The Armed Neutralities of 1780 and 1800: A Collection of Official Documents Preceded by the Views of Representative Publicists*. New York: Oxford University Press, 1918.

Scudamore, Frank Ives. *France in the East: A Contribution towards the Consideration of the Eastern Question*. London: Wm. H. Allen & Co., 1882.

Shapiro, Aleksandr L'vovich. *Admiral D. N. Seniavin*. Moscow: Ministerstvo Oborony SSSR, 1958.

Shcherbachev, O. *Afonskoe srazhenie*. Moscow and Leningrad: Voenmorsizdat, 1945.

Shil'der, Nikolai Karlovich. *Imperator Aleksandr Pervyi: ego zhizn' i tsarstvovanie*. 3 vols. Saint Petersburg: A. S. Suvorin, 1897.

———. *Imperator Pavel I: istoriko-biograficheskii ocherk*. Saint Petersburg: A. S. Suvorin, 1901.

Shiman, F. F. (Theodore Schiemann), and A. G. Brikner (Bruckner). *Smert' Pavla Pervago*. Moscow: Obrazovanie, 1909.

Shparo, Ol'ga Borisovna. *Osvobozhdenie Gretsii i Rossiia, 1821–1829*. Moscow: Mysl', 1965.

Shumigorskii, Evgenii Sevast'ianovich. *Ekaterina Ivanovna Nelidova (1758–1839)*. Saint Petersburg: Tip. "Obshchestvenaia pol'za," 1898.

Bibliography

————. *Imperator Pavel I—zhizn' i tsarstvovanie*. Saint Petersburg: V. D. Smirnov, 1907.

————. *Imperatritsa Mariia Fedorovna*. Vol. 1. Saint Petersburg: I. N. Skorokhodov, 1892.

Shupp, Paul F. *The European Powers and the Near Eastern Question, 1806–1807*. New York: Columbia University Press, 1931.

Sirotkin, Vladlen Georgievich. *Duel' dvukh diplomatii: Rossiia i Frantsiia v 1801–1812 gg*. Moscow: Nauka, 1966.

Skalovskii, R. *Zhizn' Admirala Feodora Feodorovicha Ushakova*. Saint Petersburg, 1856.

Skal'kovskii, A. *Pervoe tridtsatiletie istorii goroda Odessy, 1793–1823*. Odessa, 1837.

Somma, Carlo di, marquis de Circello. *Une mission diplomatique du marquis de Gallo à Saint-Pétersbourg en 1799*. Naples: Luigi Pierro e figlio, 1910.

Sorel, Albert. *Bonaparte et Hoche en 1797*. Paris: Plon, 1896.

————. *L'Europe et la Révolution Française*. Vol. 5, *Bonaparte et le Directoire, 1795–1799*. Paris: Plon, 1903.

————. *La question d'Orient au XVIIIe siècle: le partage de la Pologne et le traité de Kainardji*. 2d ed. Paris: Plon, 1889.

Sorgo, le comte duc de. *Fragments sur l'histoire de Raguse*. Paris, 1839.

Stanislavskaia, Avgusta Mikhailovna. *Russko-angliiskie otnosheniia i problemy sredizemnomor'ia, 1798–1807*. Moscow: Akademiia Nauk, 1962.

Suvorovskii sbornik; stat'i i issledovaniia. Edited by A. V. Sukhomlin, Moscow: Akademiia Nauk, 1961.

Tarle, Evgenii Viktorovich. *Admiral Ushakov na sredizemnon more (1798–1800)*. Moscow: Ministerstvo Oborony SSSR, 1948.

————. *Tri ekspeditsii russkogo flota*. Moscow: Ministerstvo Oborony SSSR, 1956.

————. *Zapad i Rossiia: Stat'i i dokumenty iz istorii XVIII–XX vv*. Petrograd: Byloe, 1918.

Taube, Michel de. *L'Empereur Paul Ier de Russie, Grand Maître de l'Ordre de Malte et son "Grand Prieuré Russe" de l'Ordre de Saint-Jean-de-Jérusalem*. Paris, 1955.

————. *Vostochnyi vopros i avstro-russkaia politika v pervoi polovine XIX stoletiia*. Petrograd, 1916.

Teplov, V. *Russkie predstaviteli v Tsar'grade, 1496–1891*. Saint Petersburg: A. S. Suvorin, 1891.

Bibliography

Terrinoni, Fr. Giuseppe. *Memorie storiche della resa di Malta ai francesi nel 1798 e del S. M. Ordine Gerosolimitano dal detto anno ai nostri giorni.* Rome: Belle arti, 1867.

Tucker, Clara Jean. "The Foreign Policy of Tsar Paul I." Ph.D. dissertation, Syracuse University, 1966.

Verbitskii, Sh. D. *Russko-frantsuzskie otnosheniia v 1800–1803 gg.: avtoreferat dissertatsii na soiskanie uchenoi stepeni kandidata istoricheskikh nauk.* Kherson: "Naddnipriians'ka Pravda," 1950.

Villari, Luigi. *The Republic of Ragusa, an Episode of the Turkish Conquest.* London: J. M. Dent & Co., 1904.

Villeneuve-Bargemont, vicomte L. F. de. *Monuments des Grands-Maîtres de l'Ordre de Saint-Jean de Jérusalem.* Vol. 2. Paris: J. J Blaise, 1829.

Voenskii, K. *Bonapart i russkie plennye vo Frantsii (1799–1801): epizod iz istorii franko-russkikh otnoshenii v kontse XVIII i nachale XIX veka.* Saint Petersburg: Ministerstvo Vnutrennykh Del, 1906.

Vojnović, Lujo Knez. *Pad Dubrovnika.* Vol. 1, 1797–1806. Zagreb: Tisak Dionicke, 1908.

———. (Voinovitch). *Histoire de Dalmatie.* 2d ed. Vol. 2, *Des griffes du lion ailé à la libération (1409–1918).* Paris: Hachette, 1934.

Vol'skii, Mikhail. *Ocherk istorii khlebnoi torgovli novorossiiskago kraia s drevneishikh vremen do 1852 goda.* Odessa: Frantsov i Nitche, 1854.

Waliszewski, Kazimiers. *Paul the First of Russia, the Son of Catherine the Great.* London: William Heinemann, 1913.

———. *La Russie il y a cent ans: le règne d'Alexandre Ier.* Vol. 1, *La Bastille russe et la révolution en marche (1801–1812).* Paris: Plon, 1923.

Weiner, Margery. *The French Exiles, 1789–1815.* New York: William Morrow & Co., 1961.

Xenos, Stefanos. *East and West, A Diplomatic History of the Annexations of the Ionian Islands to the Kingdom of Greece . . . and a Collection of the Principal Treaties, Conventions, and Protocols, concerning the Ionian Islands and Greece, Concluded between 1797 and 1864.* London: Trubner & Co., 1865.

Bibliography

Zaghi, Carlo. *Bonaparte e il Direttorio dopo Campoformio.* Naples: Edizione Scientifiche Italiane, 1956.

Zubow, Valentin. *Zar Paul I: Mensch und Schicksal.* Stuttgart: K. F. Koehler Verlag, 1963.

ARTICLES

Al'bovskii, Evgenii. "Imperator Pavel I i mitropolit Sestrentsevich-Bogush." *Russkaia Starina* 90 (1897): 179–282.

Aleksandrenko, V. N. "Imperator Pavel I i anglichane (izvlechenie iz donesenii Vitvorta)." *Russkaia Starina* 96 (1898): 93–106.

Aliab'ev, A. A. "Snosheniia Rossii s Mal'tiiskom Ordenom." *Sbornik Moskovskago Glavnago Arkhiva Ministerstva Inostrannykh Del.* Vol. 5 (Moscow: Lisner i Roman, 1893), 173–218.

Anderson, M. S. "Great Britain and the Russian Fleet, 1769–70." *Slavonic and East European Review* 21 (December 1952): 148–64.

————. "Russia in the Mediterranean, 1788–1791: A Little-Known Chapter in the History of Naval Warfare and Privateering." *Mariner's Mirror* 45 (February 1959). 25–35.

Antonopoulos, S. "Bonaparte et la Grèce." *La Nouvelle Revue* 60 (1889): 253–61.

Arkas, Z. "Deistviia Chernomorskago flota s 1798 po 1806 g.." *Zapiski Odesskago Obshchestva Istorii i Drevnostei* 5 (1863): 846–905.

Arsen'ev, S. V. Instruktsiia Imperatora Pavla I poslanniku v Konstantinopole V. Tomare." *Russkii Arkhiv* 55 (1917): 89–94.

————. "Raguzskaia respublika v XVIII veke (iz donesenii Rossiiskago general'nago konsula Grafa Dzhiki)." *Russkii Arkhiv* 55 (1917): 124–28.

Beeley, H. "A Project of Alliance with Russia in 1802." *English Historical Review* 195 (July 1934): 497–502.

Belokurovyi, S. A. "Spiski diplomaticheskikh lits russkikh za granitsei i inostrannykh pri russkom dvore." *Sbornik Moskovskago Glavnago Arkhiva Ministerstva Inostranykh Del* 5 (1893): 219–314.

Bourgeois, Emile. "L'Alliance de Bonaparte et de Paul Ier (1800–1801)." *Séances et travaux de l'académie des sciences morales et politiques* 82 (1922): 273–90.

Bray, François-Gabriel. "La Russie sous Paul Ier." *Revue d'histoire diplomatique* 23 (1909): 580–607; and 25 (1911): 559–90.

Bibliography

Brockman, Capt. Eric. "Background to Betrayal (June 1798)." *Annales de l'Ordre Souverain Militaire de Malte* 8, no. 3 (1960): 9–24.

Broglie, duc de. "Politique de la Russie en 1800 d'après un document inédit." *Revue d'histoire diplomatique* 3 (1889): 1–12.

Cart, J. "L'Empereur de Russie, Paul Ier et la révolution helvétique." *Revue historique vaudoise* 7 (1899): 384–87.

Coquelle, Paul. "L'ambassade du Maréchal Brune à Constantinople (1803–1805)." *Revue d'histoire diplomatique* 18 (1904): 53–73.

———. "La mission de Sebastiani à Constantinople." *Revue d'histoire diplomatique* 17 (1903): 438–55.

———. "Sebastiani ambassadeur à Constantinople, 1806–08." *Revue d'historire diplomatique* 18 (1904): 574–614.

Daly, Robert W. "Operations of the Russian Navy during the Reign of Napoleon I." *Mariner's Mirror* 34, no. 3 (1948): 169–83.

D'Istria, Countess Dora. "Les îles-Ioniennes sous la domination de Venise et sous le protectorat britannique." *Revue des deaux mondes* 16 (1858): 381–422.

Dragovich, Zhivko. "Chernogoriia i eia otnosheniia k Rossii v tsarstvovanie Imperatora Pavla," 1797–1801 gg." *Russkaia Starina* 33 (1882): 419–42; and 35 (1882): 362–73.

Dubrovin, N. "Serbskii vopros v tsarstvovanie imperatora Aleksan dra I." *Russkii Vestnik* 46 (1863).

Evstigneev, I. V. "K voprosu o tseliakh vneshnei politiki Rossii v 1804–1805 godakh" *Voprosy Istorii*, May 1962: 204–10.

Falk, Minna R. "Stadion, adversaire de Napoléon (1806–1809)" *Annales historiques de la Révolution Française*, no. 169 (1962): 288–305.

Glover, Richard. "Arms and the British Diplomat in the French Revolutionary Era." *Journal of Modern History* 24, no. 3 (1957): 199–212.

Golitsyn, N. S. "Rasskazy ob Imperatorakh Pavle I i Aleksandre I." *Russkaia Starina* 29 (1880): 738–40.

Goloviznin, Lt. K. "Ocherki iz istorii russkago flota: Kapitan-Komandor Sorokin v Ionicheskoi Respublike." *Morskoi Sbornik* 192, no. 9 (1882): 33–54.

Goriainov, Sergei Mikhailovich. "Dogovor 11 (23) sentiabria 1805 goda mezhdu Rossieiu i Turtsieiu." *Izvestiia Ministerstva Inostrannykh Del* 5 (1912): 233–49.

Bibliography

Haumant, Emile. "Les Français à Raguse." *La Revue de Paris* 12 (1912): 150–74.

Hurewitz, Jacob Colman. "Russia and the Turkish Straits: A Reevaluation of the Origins of the Problem." *World Politics* 14, no. 4 (1962): 605–32.

Il'inskii, V. P. "Admiral F. F. Ushakov, k 100-letiiu so dnia smerti." *Morskoi Sbornik* 408 (April 1919): 65–90; 409 (May–June 1919): 83–103; 410 (July–August 1919): 147–66.

Kleinman, G. A. "Russko-turetskii soiuz 1799 g.." *Doklady i Soobshcheniia istoricheskogo fakul'teta Moskovskogo Gosudarstvennogo Universiteta*, 3 (1945): 17–24.

Klochkov, Mikhail V. "Pavel i Frantsiia." In *Otechestvennaia voina i russkoe obshchestvo*, edited by A. K. Dzhevelov, et al., vol. 1. Moscow: I. D. Sytin, 1911.

Korf, Sergei Aleksandrovich. "Pavel I i dvorianstvo." *Golos Minuvshago* 1, no. 7 (1913): 5–18.

Kroviakov, N. "Russkii flotovodets F. F. Ushakov v sredizemnom mor'e." *Istoricheskii Zhurnal*, nos. 3–4 (1943): 31–37.

Lanin, R. S. "Vneshniaia politika Pavla I v 1796–1798 gg." *Uchenye Zapiski, Leningradskogo Gosudarstvennogo Universiteta, seriia istoricheskikh nauk* 10 (1941): 3–42.

Loewenson, Leo. "The Death of Paul I (1801) and the Memoirs of Count Bennigsen." *Slavonic and East European Review* 29 (1950–51): 212–32.

Markova, O. P. "O proiskhozhdenii tak nazyvaemogo grecheskogo proekta (80-e gody XVIII v.)" *Istoriia SSSR*, 1958 (no. 4): 75–81.

Metaks, Egor. "Ali Pasha." *Syn Otechestva*, no. 42 (1820), pp. 60–71; no. 43 (1820), pp. 97–112.

Meynadier, Robert. "Un plan de l'Empereur Paul de Russie." *La Revue de Paris* 27 (1920): 185–97.

Pieri, Piero. "La Questione di Malta e il governo napoletano (1798–1803)." *Archivio Storico Italiano*, 7th ser., vol. 7 (1927): 3–12.

Pingaud, Léonce. "L'Empereur Paul Ier de Russie d'après les documents nouveaux." *Le Correspondant* 269, no. 5 (1912): 926–46.

Pisani, Paul. "L'expédition russo-turque aux îles ioniennes en 1798–1799." *Revue d'histoire diplomatique* 2 (1888): 190–222.

Ragsdale, Hugh. "The Origins of Bonaparte's Russian Policy." *Slavic Review* 27, no. 1 (1968): 86–90.

Bibliography

Rangoni-Machiavelli, Luigi. "LXX—Fra Ferdinando von Hompesch (1797–1799)." *Revista del Sovrano Militare Ordine di Malta* 14, no. 3 (1950): 8–14.

———. "LXXI—Fra Giovanni Battista Tommasi (1803–1805)." *Revista del Sovrano Militare Ordine di Malta* 14, no. 4 (1950): 5–7.

"Razgovor Vitse-Admirala D. N. Seniavina s ministrom vnutrennykh del grafom Kochubeem." *Russkii Arkhiv* 3 (1875): 431–34.

Rose, John Holland. "Bonaparte's Eastern Expedition." *English Historical Review* 44 (January 1929): 48–58.

Rouët de Journel, M. Giuseppe, S.J. "L'Imperatore Paolo I e la riunione della chiese." *La Civiltà Cattolica* 110, no. 3 (September 1960): 604–14.

Sablukov, General Nikolai Aleksandrovich. "Reminiscences of the Court and Times of the Emperor Paul I of Russia, up to the Period of his Death: From the Papers of a Deceased Russian General Officer." *Fraser's Magazine* 72 (1865): 222–42.

Sadikov, P. "Neskol'ko materialov dlia istorii mer pravitel'stva Imperatora Pavla I protiv proniknoveniia v Rossiiu idei velikoi frantsuzskoi revoliutsii." *Dela i Dni: Istoricheskii Zhurnal* 3 (1920): 391–97.

Savant, Jean. "Napoléon et la libération de la Grèce." *L'Hellénisme contemporain*, July–October 1950, pp. 321 41; and November–December, 1950, pp. 474–85.

Semevskii, M. "Materialy k russkoi istorii." *Vestnik Evropy* 2, no. 1 (1867): 297–330.

Shapiro, Aleksandr L'vovich. "Sredizemnomorskie problemy vneshnei politiki Rossii v nachale XIX v." *Istoricheskie Zapiski* 55 (1955): 253–88.

Shiman (Schiemann), F. F. "Imperator Aleksandr Pavlovich i ego dvor." *Russkaia Starina* 29 (1880): 793–822.

Shteinberg, E. "S. R. Vorontsov i anglo-russkie otnosheniia na rubezhe XVIII i XIX vekov." *Istoricheskii Zhurnal*, nos. 3–4 (1943), pp. 34–40.

Sirotkin, V. G. "Franko-russkaia diplomaticheskaia bor'ba no Balkanakh i plany sozdaniia slaviano-Serbskogo gosudarstva v 1806–1807 gg.," *Uchenye Zapiski Instituta Slavianovedeniia* 25 (1962): 171–92.

———. "Iz istorii vneshnei politiki Rossii v sredizemnomor'e v nachale XIX v." *Istoricheskie Zapiski* 67 (1960): 213–33.

Bibliography

Sokol, A. E. "Nelson and the Russian Navy." *Military Affairs* 13 (1949): 129–37.

Sorokin, Al. "Morskiia kampanii 1798 i 1799 gg." *Zapiski Gidrograficheskago Departamenta Morskago Ministerstva* 8 (1850): 278–366.

Stavrianos, L. S. "Antecedents to the Balkan Revolutions of the Nineteenth Century." *Journal of Modern History* 29, no. 4 (1957): 335–48.

Stepanov, M. "Zhozef de Mestr v Rossii." *Literaturnoe Nasledstvo,* nos. 29–30 (1937), pp. 577–726.

Taube, Michel de. "Le tsar Paul Ier et l'Ordre de Malte en Russie." *Revue d'histoire moderne* 5 (1930): 161–77.

Trachevsky, A. "L'Empereur Paul et Bonaparte, Premier Consul." *Revue d'histoire diplomatique* 3, no. 2 (1889): 281–86.

Vekarić, Stjepan. "Podaci o Dubrovackim brodomina za vrijame i nakon francuzke okupacije." *Annali Historijskoy Instituta Jugoslavenskoe Akademije Znanosti i Umjetnosti u Dubrovniku* 2 (1953): 359–68.

White, D. Fedotoff. "A Russian Sketches Philadelphia, 1811–1813." *The Pennsylvania Magazine of History & Biography* 75, no. 1 (1951): 3–24.

—————. "The Russian Navy in Trieste during the Wars of the Revolution and the Empire." *American Slavic and East European Review* 6, nos. 18–19 (1947): 25–52.

Zelenin, V. V. "Pervoe Serbskoe vosstanie i Avstriia, 1804–1807 gg." In *Iz istorii obshchestvennykh dvizhenii i mezhdunarodnykh otnoshenii: sbornik statei v pamiat' akademika Evgeniia Viktorovicha Tarle.* Moscow: Akademii Nauk, 1956.

Zhmakin, V. Rossiia i Chernogoriia v nachale XIX veka. *Drevniaia i Novaia Rossiia* 19 (March 1881): 407–54.

Index

Index

Index

Index

Mahan, Arthur Thomas, 89, 110
Maisonneuve (historian-knight of Malta), 77, 162
Maistre, Joseph de (Sardinian envoy to Russia, 1803–17), 48n, 182
Makarov, Michael (admiral), 62
Malta, island of: Anglo-Russian agreement on, 73; as British base, 190, 223; British capture of, 130, 142–48; British siege of, 118–22; French capture of, 39–42, 62; guarantee for, 160–64, 181–83; and Russia, 65–67, 71, 128. See also Malta, Order of
Malta, Order of: Black Sea squadron under flag of, 150; and France, 39–40; possession of island by, 33, 139–41, 145–46; and Russia, 32–38, 44–46, 50–52, 71, 74–76, 161–63, 181–82, 223, 225. See also Hompesch, Ferdinand von; Paul; Tommasi, Jean
Manzaro, Calichiopoulo, 102
Marengo, Battle of (1801), 131
Maria Carolina (queen of Naples), 94, 107
Maria Fedorovna (empress of Russia), 27, 72, 153n, 187
Maria Theresa (empress of Austria), 11
Marmont, Auguste-Frédéric-Louis de, 205
Massena, Andre, 191
Messer, Thomas (captain), 78, 90
Messina, 115, 125
Metaxa, Egor (captain), 19, 78, 86
Michael Castle, 151, 153

Michelson, John (general), 216–17
Micheroux, Antoine (Neapolitan minister of war), 89, 114
Minorca, 116, 122, 124, 162
Mocenigo, George (Russian plenipotentiary in Ionian Islands, 1802–7), 19, 167–71, 178, 183–84, 186, 194, 196, 207, 223
Moldavia and Wallachia, 8, 58, 96, 100, 171, 176, 186, 212–14
Molitor, Gabriel (general), 201–3, 205
Montenegro, 95, 132n, 172, 187, 196–98, 202–3, 206–7
Mordvinov, Nicholas (admiral, naval minister), 13, 18, 58, 61–62, 173
Morkov, Count Arkady (Russian ambassador to France, 1801–3), 159, 164, 167, 171, 176, 181
Mouravieff, Boris (émigré historian), 69n
Muraviev-Apostol, Ivan (Russian ambassador to Spain, 1802–5), 160
Murusi, Alexander (hospodar of Moldavia, 1802–6, and of Wallachia, 1806–7), 176, 212
Musin-Pushkin-Bruce, Vasily (Russian ambassador to kingdom of Naples, 1799–1800), 115, 118

Naples, city of, 20, 27, 89; Russian forces in, 109–10, , 121, 131, 167
Naples, kingdom of: and Great Powers, 188–89; premature attack of, 73–75, 107–8;

Index

Index

Index

Uniate Church, 47
Ushakov, Fedor (admiral), 18, 58, 78, 196, 227; Black Sea preparations of, 60–63; in Constantinople, 65–67; at Corfu, 84, 88–91, 97–98, 132; diplomatic talents of, 87, 92–93; in Italy, 108, 113, 115–19; and Nelson, 120–25; recall of, 126–30, 139, 191; and Seniavin, 195n; and Tomara, 103–4
Ushakov Constitution, 97, 100, 132

Valetta. See Malta
Vatican. See Roman Catholic Church; Rome
Venice, 9, 13, 27, 40, 56–60, 81–82, 85, 106, 128
Viazemsky (major general), 184–85, 202
Vido, 90–91
Vienna, Congress of, 223
Villettes (general), 94
Viomesnil, 137, 141n
Volkonsky, Dmitri (major general), 123, 125, 132
Voinovich, Nicholas (captain), 115, 131–32, 138, 165
Vorontsov, Alexander (chancellor, 1802–5), 134, 173–74, 176, 181, 183, 187–88, 201
Vorontsov, Simon (Russian ambassador to Britain, 1784–1800, 1801–6), 31, 53–54, 58–59, 69–72, 112, 134, 136, 140, 152n, 157–59, 167, 173–74, 176, 182–83, 187, 192, 209

Vukotich (Russian envoy to Montenegro, 1799), 196–97

Wallachia. See Moldavia and Wallachia
War party, 54, 187
Warren, John (British ambassador to Russia, 1802–4), 174, 210
Whitworth, Charles (British ambassador to Russia, 1788–1800), 44n, 53, 62, 69n, 71, 74, 128, 133, 137–40, 148n, 152–53
Wilhelmina (princess of Hesse-Darmstadt), 26
Windham, William, 147
Wood, Sir Mark, 59, 64
Woodhouse (lieutenant), 87

Ypsilanti, Konstantin (hospodar of Wallachia, 1802–6), 96, 176, 212, 214–15
"Young friends," 157, 172–74, 208, 210, 227

Zagorskii (Russian consul at Zante), 57
Zante, 55–57, 81, 84, 101, 165, 171. See also Ionian Islands
Zherebtsova, Madam Olga, 139, 153
Zubov, Nicholas, 152–53
Zubov, Platon, 15, 18–19, 30–32, 34–35, 149, 152–53, 187
Zubov, Valerian, 15, 31, 149, 152–53, 187

Имнераторъ Александръ I   L'Empereur Alexandre I